Warcraft
and the Fragility of Virtue

Warcraft
and the Fragility of Virtue
An Essay in Aristotelian Ethics

Grady Scott Davis

University of Idaho Press
Moscow, Idaho

Published 1992 by the University of Idaho Press, Moscow, Idaho
83843
© 1992 Grady Scott Davis
Printed in the United States of America
96 95 94 93 92   5 4 3 2 1

Library of Congress Cataloging-in-Publication Data
Davis, Grady Scott.
    Warcraft and the fragility of virtue : an essay in Aristotelian
ethics / Grady Scott Davis.
        p.   cm.
    Includes bibliographical references and index.
    ISBN 0-89301-154-1
    1. War.   2. Just war doctrine.   3. Aristotle--Ethics.   4. Justics.
5. Pacifism.   I. Title.
B105.W3D38   1992
172'.42--dc20   91-20166
                                                          CIP

Contents

Preface

Michael Dummett remarks—I think it's in the preface to his Frege book—that authors owe their readers a preface, and since reading that as an undergraduate I've thought he was right. Human beings make books and other ones read them, and it is natural to want to know something about an author's relation to his book. I, at least, end up projecting myself as a friend of the authors I admire, and have caught myself more than once, perfectly sober (if that's not an oxymoron), carrying on animated conversations with Aristotle and Wittgenstein, Chaucer and Basho and Jane Austen. My own public reticence makes it easier to talk to the dead. This book is a record of those conversations and many more besides. I'd like it to be devastatingly compelling and the harbinger of some new era of moral seriousness, but I'll settle for a few people getting the point and maybe doing it better.

The origins of the book make a chronicle of the unexpected. In the spring of 1985, if memory serves, I was invited by Jeffrey Stout to teach a course at Princeton focusing on war and traditions of moral reasoning. Although I had not previously explored the just war tradition, it dovetailed nicely with my interest in Aristotle and his place in contemporary moral theory. Out of this came further versions of the course and the title essay, which was first drafted in October of 1985 and read to colleagues at Columbia University. Another version was delivered at the annual meeting of the American Academy of Religion in Atlanta in November of 1986 and subsequently published in *Soundings* (G. S. Davis, 1987). The performance in Atlanta marked the first time I delivered a paper at a professional meeting, and it was my great good fortune to have Stanley Hauerwas as respondent. Early versions of chapters 2 and 3 were given as papers to diverse groups in Syracuse, Princeton, and New York. Thanks are due everybody who helped me out on these occasions, particularly Reverend Letitia Smith of Brown Memorial Methodist Church in Syracuse, who invited me to give what became chapter 2, and whose concerns for peace and justice shaped much of my early thinking about these topics.

In the spring of 1987, James Heaney of the University of Idaho Press asked if "Warcraft" were likely to become a book, and the rest, as they say, is wordprocessing. He has been a most gracious and patient editor, tolerating with equanimity the delays brought about by relocation, marriage, and babies. Those delays, however, have brought their own blessings. My move to the University of Southern California in the fall of 1988 put me in contact with Charles Curran, who not only contributed his time and insight to the content of several chapters but also with great tact led me to moderate some of the more tendentious and blustery qualities of my prose.

The style, I'm afraid, remains less than inviting, and I apologize for those parts I should have made better. The literary examples I've used to recall an image or instant of recognition I thought might make a point clearer or its significance more apparent. But I'm afraid that for some readers they will look rather like the tourist's strategy of repeating himself louder when he's not understood. Much the same might be said for the anthropological and historical examples, but one of the great pleasures of writing this book has been immersing myself in the literature of war. Michael Howard and John Keegan are a joy to read, and encountering Clausewitz's *On War* was a revelation. It was also a surprise to sit down and read great chunks of Jefferson. At the outset I never would have imagined that Aristotle and Wittgenstein would be joined by Clausewitz and our third president as this essay's heroes.

A note about pronouns. The venerable Strunk and White come down unashamedly in favor of "he" when the antecedent is a distributive expression "unless the antecedent is or must be feminine" (*Elements of Style*, 2d ed., p. 54). The more diplomatic but no less venerable Gowers advises the cautious author to "take evasive action where possible," though finally Sir Ernest grants that it may sometimes be "least clumsy to follow the traditional use of *he*, *him* and *his* to include both sexes, but you should then make it unmistakably clear that you are using these pronouns in this way" (*The Complete Plain Words*, p. 118). I should have followed their advice. My attempts at random variation I now find jarring and the feeling that it was necessary at all an expression of misplaced delicacy. Sexism is evil because it is a species of injustice, and this is not a matter of pronouns but of wicked habits and oppressive institutions.

Finally, something by way of dedication. My debt to family and friends, in particular my wife, Karen, far exceeds my ability to return. I have tried to record my intellectual debts in the notes and bibliography, but no doubt I have failed to accord someone his due. I am particularly aware of having read, very early on, material of Jeff Stout's that is only now finding its way into print. For his abiding generosity I stand happily in his debt. Special thanks are also due Stan Hauerwas and Charles Curran, friends of seemingly infinite patience. When I began this project I fully expected to enjoy the comments and criticisms of my great teacher and friend Paul Ramsey. Now I can only hope he would approve the effort; I miss him. For all the things I haven't done or done poorly, I await due and proper criticism. But for now,

> ter frustra comprensa manus effugit imago,
> par leuibus uentis uolucrique simillima somno.
> sic demum socios consumpta nocte reuiso.

Aeneid 2, 793–95

1.
Justice without Theory:
An Aristotelian Prologue

This is an essay in the just war tradition, but it is also an attempt to spell out the practical implications of adopting a self-consciously "Aristotelian" stance in moral theory. Much of the motivation for this will come out in the following chapters, as they examine alternative approaches to ethics and war. But it also reflects a broader dissatisfaction with the ability of the prevailing secular traditions to give a coherent account of our moral vocabulary. A habit of concentrating on duties, obligations, and those aspects of ethics in general that lend themselves to systematization and "theory" has led to the relative neglect of those facets of our vocabulary reflected in our day-to-day deliberations about action. This neglect is only "relative" because there has been a continuous minority presence critical of the mainstream. Thus, David Wiggins notes:

Aristotle still demands our attention in this subject because he perceived more clearly than have subsequent theorists of rationality, morality and the practical the openness, indefiniteness and unforeseeability of the subject-matter of *praxis*. . . . Aristotle's description of practical reasoning and the process of deliberative specification (for this or that context of acting) of a man's standing ends or concerns, excels anything to be found in present day studies of the canons of public and private rationality. (Raz 1978:150. The complete essay, lacking the note, is reprinted in Rorty 1980.)

"Rationality," "morality," "*praxis*," "deliberation," and "ends," Wiggins emphasizes, are central to an older understanding of what goes into a commendable human life, but have been displaced from too much of our recent ethical reflection. The implied contrast is with the approaches to rational action associated with Hume, on the one hand, and Kant, on the other, those twin peaks that have come to represent the seemingly irreconcilable demands of individual emotion and desire and impersonal duty and rational obligation.[1] In recent years the

1

most visible, and perhaps notorious critic of these traditions has been Alasdair MacIntyre; but well before MacIntyre, Aristotle found a powerful and consistent advocate in Stuart Hampshire, whose "Fallacies in Moral Philosophy" early called attention to the limits of moral theory in midcentury Oxford. Nonetheless, the trickle of methodological criticism has become a torrent since the appearance of MacIntyre's first edition of *After Virtue* in 1981. Unfortunately, the result has too often been polarization, even confrontation, among consequentialists, communitarians, deontologists, and other camps. Rather than rehearse familiar criticisms and counterarguments, I've thought it more useful to approach an issue, ethics and war, as it might present itself to Aristotle. This will not mean avoiding methodological disputes, but will at least have the benefit of testing rival positions in application.

On the few occasions Aristotle speaks of war, he treats it as a uniquely human activity as opposed to a conflict between beasts. As such it is a reasoned and purposive enterprise, directed toward achieving goods which can be recognized as such by mature persons. War is not some Hobbesian manifestation of the state of nature, but an activity which can only be undertaken by groups outfitted with a rich sense of what makes a human life worthwhile. Otherwise we could not distinguish war from random and unintelligible violence. From this, Aristotle draws the conclusion that war "must therefore be regarded as only a means to peace; action as a means to leisure; and acts which are merely necessary, or merely and simply useful, as a means to acts which are good in themselves" (*Pol.* 7:1333a). As a human act, war becomes intelligible through being related to the pursuit of the good. But this brings us up against a central problem, both in the ethics of war and in moral thought generally: how do we determine the good?

This was, of course, not a problem for the early development of the just war tradition, since its proponents wholeheartedly embraced belief in God. Most interpretations trace the development of the just war theory backwards from the early modern law of nations, through Thomas Aquinas to St. Augustine, who laid the foundations for thinking about justice in war, working with the comparatively meagre suggestions to be found in Cicero and a few other classical sources.[2] Interpreters of the tradition typically emphasize, with varying degrees of praise, the centrality of the Christian moral vision, both historically and theologically, in the development of just war thinking. Paul Ramsey provides a characteristically bold statement, writing that "'natural law' judgements do not proceed from autonomous reason alone, but are derivative principles in which *agape* shapes itself for action" (Ramsey 1961:33). Ramsey in particular emphasizes the centrality of Christian love in the development and application of the just war tradition, and in doing so he places much greater weight on Augustine's understanding of service to the neighbor as central to the moral life than on justice in any of its classical senses. (Cf. G. S. Davis 1991.)

The same cannot be said of the natural law tradition often associated with Catholic moral theology. Augustine certainly plays a major part in this tradition, although to his thought the burgeoning medieval tradition added that of Cicero and the Roman legal tradition and eventually added Aristotle himself. But whereas the Aristotelian tradition was appropriated by the mainstream of just war thought in the late middle ages, primarily through Aquinas and his followers, Aristotle remained in the service of Christian theology. Thus, from the start his influence was filtered through the concerns of Christian teaching, and as theology lost its privileged position in early modern and enlightenment moral thought Aristotle's voice was obscured as well. It is only recently that the Catholic moral tradition has regained a serious hearing in the world of secular moral thought.[3]

Those uncomfortable with the natural law tradition, but unwilling to adopt a "hobbesian," *realpolitik*, approach to justice in war, have been drawn, like James Johnson, to the developing tradition of international law. (Cf. Johnson 1975.) Although lacking the universal claims of divinity and a shared human nature, law at least offers the example of a generally binding system of entitlements, prohibitions, and sanctions justified by their role in securing social stability and the common good. The claims of justice may sometimes go unfulfilled, but they remain at least a standard recognized by all nations that would not be seen as outlaws.

This legal paradigm informs the most influential recent contribution to the tradition, Michael Walzer's *Just and Unjust Wars*. This attempt to replace religious with political consensus risks foundering, however, on the shoals of international conflict. Once a state opts out of what Walzer calls the "war convention," there is a rapid slide into national interest, supreme emergency, and other justifications for violating the rules. Walzer accepts this as the tragic limit of human moral endeavor. He closes his argument by reaffirming the primacy of rules if we are to achieve even a modicum of justice. "We must begin," he maintains, "by insisting upon the rules of war and by holding soldiers rigidly to the norms they set. The restraint of war is the beginning of peace" (1977:335). It remains an open question, nonetheless, whether and what sort of foundation can be given for such rules and how they cohere with the rest of our practical thinking.

In fact, the legal paradigm is a variation of the social contract and shares both the benefits and difficulties associated with that tradition. Part of its power is its refusal to indulge in divinity or metaphysics. Michael Oakeshott, in his introduction to *Leviathan*, remarks that "what stirs the mind of Hobbes is 'grief for the present calamities of my country,' a country torn between those who claimed too much for Liberty and those who claimed too much for Authority" (Hobbes 1960:xi). To still this grief, Hobbes elaborates a systematic account of political society grounded in observation of our material nature. Central to Hobbes's practice is the rejection of the Myth of the Garden, part and parcel of which is the metaphysics of the Fall. In the Myth of the Garden our first parents speak the language of nature, giving names to the animals and recognizing where their true good lies. Grasping the good allows them to understand the meaning and purpose of human life within the cosmos and thus to rank the various competing goods that present themselves in experience. Having ranked those goods, unfallen humanity can proceed to organize individual and political life in ways that generate rules of preference, obligation, and prohibition in accord with its natural dispositions.

Of this, Hobbes will have nothing. The state of nature, properly understood, places "all men in the condition of war" (Hobbes 1960:85) and at the same time compels them to accept limits on themselves as a means of securing protection from and restraint of their equals. In this way we produce a theory of justice. From the theory of justice we extract more specific instruction on such topics as social welfare, the right to privacy, and perhaps even the laws of war. Nature confers one principal right: to do anything one may "conceive to be the aptest means" for preserving one's life (Hobbes 1960:84). From this, Hobbes derives the fundamental law of nature, which turns out, with a certain air of paradox, to involve creating a complex of artificial constraints against the unfettered exercise of this right by others. He then turns, in the remarkable chapter 15 of part one, to a derivation of the laws of nature, which includes "A seventh, . . . *that in revenges*, that is, retribution of evil for evil, *men look not at the greatness of the evil past, but the greatness of the good to follow*" (Hobbes 1960:100; the italics are Hobbes's). As with the other laws of nature, the intent here is to moderate conflict. The goal of civil society is peace, "for a means of the conservation of men in multitudes," and when the laws of political community cease to function for this end they are voided. Thus, he writes that:

The laws of nature oblige *in foro interno*; . . . but *in foro externo*; that is, to the putting them in act, not always. For he that should be modest, and tractable, and perform all he promises, in such time, and place, where no man else should do so, should but make himself a prey to others, and procure his own certain ruin, contrary to the ground of all laws of nature, which tend to nature's preservation. (1960:103)

I have no stake in calling such laws "fictions" if that detracts from the seriousness with which Hobbes should be taken. But "laws of nature" that can properly be violated by the dictates of nature have a status distinct from those generalizations that describe and predict the workings of nature as well as from those dictates of conscience that other traditions of moral analysis have held binding come what may.

It was precisely this problem that exercised the later contractarian tradition and its more recent exponents, such as John Rawls. How is it possible to secure a foundation for political order that retains Hobbes's tough-minded insistence on political and psychological empiricism without licensing an unbridled consequentialism in circumstances of dire necessity? Of the various critiques of *A Theory of Justice* the most damning is that which accuses Rawls of importing an unacknowledged metaphysics of the good into the concept of right. His casual suggestion, for example, that there are natural duties which "apply to us without regard to our voluntary acts" (Rawls 1971:114) is difficult to sustain without a richer theory of the good than Rawls allows himself. Consider his remarks about killing. He rightly remarks that restraints on killing presuppose no antecedent promise, that to think so "is normally ludicrously redundant, and the suggestion that it establishes a moral requirement where none already existed is mistaken" (1971:115). But if the right to life is not a positive entitlement, how do we recognize the evil in killing, and how do we recognize circumstances wherein that evil becomes tolerable? It would seem that an adequate response must explain why we are obliged to refrain from killing even if that would further our otherwise best thought-out plan for achieving what we desire. One plausible answer seems to be that the other person's life is a good incommensurable with the good of our possible achievements and one we may not normally weigh in our own deliberations. But it is not clear how Rawls might be entitled to this good at the outset. Consequently, it is not clear how he is entitled to invoke "natural" duties and, to the extent that Rawls needs these natural duties to supplement the original position, his theory is undermined.[4]

A serious Aristotelian ethic will commend itself all the more to the extent that it maintains a commitment to naturalism, in the sense that its account of the good is continuous with our best account of humans as a natural kind. This doesn't require extensive technical knowledge, although it does imply an openness to the claims of anthropology and other studies of human activity, individual and corporate. Societies, after all, do not spring fully formed from the earth. I can admit, even with relish, that the coming together of hominids in extended groups can best be explained on Darwinian grounds. If such groups hadn't emerged, the species might well have been swamped in the evolutionary bump and grind. There is no reason, as Stephen J. Gould has made so elegantly clear, to believe that humans are biologically inevitable (cf. Gould 1989). But in acknowledging the Darwinian point I am rejecting the Hobbesian. There are no grounds for attributing to our protoancestors any judgments at all, much less ones about trading natural rights for communal security. This is just the way things turned out. That the species perpetuated itself is the mark of evolutionary success, but not much else. Of course, it seems to have worked so well that our protoancestors were enabled to sustain all sorts of other evolutionary innovations, not the least of which was the elaboration of language. In learning a language, we incorporate, literally, a complex network of skills and dispositions that presuppose various goods. To speak intelligently is to acknowledge that some things are inherently choice-worthy and others should be avoided. These are not decisions that we make in some prelinguistic vacuum but the outcome of the community's attempts to deal with itself and its environment. A language embodies the ecology of a community in ways that make it difficult, if not impossible, to distinguish the moral from the practical, and when we do make the distinction it will likely as not be misleading. (Cf. Hampshire 1989:81–110.) To be a language user is to be a moral agent.

Such a recognition manifests itself in the vocabulary we use in explaining action. In the prelinguistic world, explanation takes place in terms of physical structure, biochemistry, and instinct. Humans, of course, have all of these characteristics; thus, physical explanations of our actions will never, in theory, be irrelevant. But when we become language users we acquire the ability to formulate propositions and express beliefs. Some of these beliefs will register events as they overtake us; but others will reflect the goods acknowledged in our community, recognition of which we received as part of our learning the language. To the extent we are able, we consider our world in the light of these beliefs and take action to achieve many and various ends. Sometimes an analysis in terms of those beliefs and ends is sufficient to account for events, as when I say that I had been playing basketball, became thirsty, and stopped play so I could drink some water. Under most circumstances that is the explanation of the event. It depends upon human biochemistry and the like, but we know enough about that to let it pass. Of course, there might sometimes be a discrepancy between my proffered explanation and the facts. If, for example, we were in the middle of play and the other team was driving to the hoop, it would typically be inappropriate to call time. Am I *really* trying to keep them from scoring? Why didn't I get a drink after the last basket, or wait until a break? Am I taking unfair advantage of a friendly game? With the transition to language we are able, and sometimes required, to consider questions of motive, desire, intention, and the well-being of others. But these are precisely the characteristics to be considered in any stable, human social practice.

Any "theory" of justice that attempts to begin from neutrality about the good is bound to prove itself inadequate. Even to begin a discussion of justice requires recognizing an act as human, placing it within a complex web of ends and intentions, thus presupposing a full-bodied set of goods and their interrelations within a human life. Whatever else they are, humans are a natural kind, and in sustaining life it is necessary for any human community to reach some degree of ecological balance with its surroundings. The alternative is extinction. In reaching this balance, a community naturally divides labor in ways that facilitate achieving relevant goods, and, except in uncommon and usually mythic circumstances, these divisions of labor generate practices and disciplines that are then transmitted across generations. In perpetuating such practices, a culture inculcates a language of description and evaluation which reflects the ways that culture has found to establish for itself a form of life which nurtures its constituents and which they deem worthy of sustaining.

But the situation is still more complex. A language, as Wittgenstein suggested, "can be seen as an ancient city: a maze of little streets and squares, of old and new houses, and of houses with additions from various periods" (1958:1, 18). From one perspective we may be inclined to praise an individual or a policy, but from another it appears misguided. And this despite both ways of speaking "living," in seeming harmony, in our everyday language. We have no simple way of summing praise and blame across roles to produce a single judgment. Take, for example, Okonkwo, the protagonist of Chinua Achebe's *Things Fall Apart.* By turns a callous brute and concerned father, Okonkwo is a congeries of conflicting desires and fears, all of which reflect the interplay of individual and culture. He accepts a young hostage into his family and treats him with absolute fairness, but when the oracle judges that the boy must be sacrificed Okonkwo "drew his machete and cut him down. He was afraid of being thought weak" (Achebe 1959:59). Nonetheless, Okonkwo spends the next few days drunk and sullen in his own hut. The twists and turns of Achebe's story present a character whose stock is volatile, who rises and falls and rises once more in the reader's esteem. Thus, while not exactly wanting to *be* or *be like* Okonkwo, it is possible to agree with his friend Obierika that he "was one of the greatest men in Umuofia" (1959:191) and that his suicide is a tragedy the colonial authorities are too shallow to understand. We know this because we have entered into the story and been caught up in the complexities of judgment and choice in a community where standards are contested and expectations have become uncertain. Theories of justice, however, try to settle the judgments before the story has been told, typically by isolating a particular perspective and according it a privileged status. But as soon as we try to put the theory to work, it clashes with the details. To isolate one strand in the story as the key to a judgment on Okonkwo, for example, is not merely to give an unjustified reading of the novel, it is to say what is manifestly false on the basis of all the available evidence.

The rejection of theory building, however, puts the Aristotelian at something of a disadvantage. Granted that serious ethical discussion always takes place *in medias res*, we still need an entry into the subject. Perhaps it will be useful to stand Rawls on his head, so to speak, and begin with an experience common in any fully developed society: that of being cheated. I may not know what's fair in a particular situation, but I will usually recognize cheating when it occurs. When I say that a person is cheating or that I have been cheated in a given instance, what is presupposed? First, I make the claim in the context of a particular practice, directed toward a particular end. That end may be more or less specific and governed by more or less well-defined rules, but there is usually the presumption that all the parties, insofar as they are active players, acknowledge the point of the enterprise and that some outcomes are generally unacceptable. We need to distinguish "unacceptable" from "undesirable" to include those outcomes, such as losing a well-played game, where the loser can accept his defeat as merited without finding it in the least bit desirable. When cheating occurs, the outcome is neither desirable nor acceptable. All human communities incorporate activities in which, however upright the negotiants, it is *possible* to be cheated. What constitutes this possibility? I've already suggested that cheating is a breach of decorum in some practice where participants are led to expect that if their actions are appropriate to the practice in question and if all other participants proceed to the accepted end of the transaction, they will receive an anticipated good. The good can be strawberries, money, or applause; it doesn't matter. As long as there is agreement on the nature of the activity, then something is due the person who successfully participates.

For a practice that involves multiple agents to perpetuate itself requires what I'll call the habit of fairness. Even when we cannot give a theoretical account of why cheating is malicious, we recognize it as contrary to the ordinary and expected way of doing things. Such a recognition impresses itself on us because our expectations are now thwarted in a very disturbing way. If the practice in question is central to our daily routine, then ordinary life has been put in jeopardy. If we're doing something recreational, playing softball for instance, the danger is slight but the disappointment is, if anything, greater, for now there is no "existential" excuse for cheating and to do so just wrecks the game. Since we were playing the game for its own sake and the pleasure of doing it together, that kind of cheating deprives us of not just what we need but what we want and look forward to.

Occasional instances of cheating can be tolerable, but only if most people, most of the time, interact fairly. Regular cheating destroys a practice, making it pointless to work with the cheater and, if everyone cheats, pointless to do it at all. If, for example, adultery were to become the norm, that would be an end to the institution of marriage as we know it. Perhaps that would not be fatal to the community as a whole—although the consequences would perhaps be more devastating than we imagine—but it would mean a major shift in how the members related to each other and the world in which they operate.

(Cf. Hauerwas 1974:117–22.)[5] Because our practices reflect the social ecology of our community and because cheating disrupts the functioning of that world, fairness is the path of least resistence and that is why it is a habit. That fairness is a *habit* leads to yet another point. Habits relate perception to nature to action. To have a habit is to be disposed to act one way as opposed to another when presented with a particular state of affairs. If fairness is a habit of any stable institution or community, the members of the community will be disposed to respond to an action or state of affairs in terms of what they see as fair. If someone does X there will be a natural inclination in others to render the appropriate response. To cheat is not simply to fail but to refuse to render others their due.

This last phrase has a familiar ring. It is, in fact, the classical characterization of justice as that habit of action which disposes one to render each his due. To cheat is to act contrary to one so disposed, and in so doing to subvert the standards of the practice. It turns out, in fact, that cheating is the general form of injustice. From this, it follows that the concept of justice is part and parcel of any community that must organize itself for the pursuit of goods, and this, I take it, means any community this side of heaven. A theorist such as Rawls is not so much mistaken in what he takes to be the specifics of justice as in how he delineates the relation of fairness and rational choice. Rational choices are only possible in the context of a situation that enables individuals to weigh operating within one set of institutions as opposed to another, and this presupposes the habit of fairness. There is, thus, no need for a separate "principle of fairness . . . to account for all requirements that are obligations as distinct from natural duties" (Rawls 1971:111). It is not just that the original position is an explanatory fiction, it is analytically irrelevant. To put it still another way, the habit of fairness suffices to ensure that any coherent community exemplifies justice; it's the character of the society and the goods it pursues that can be contested. For even the lotus-eaters of *Odyssey* 9 cannot tolerate one of their number wantonly destroying the "honey sweet fruit." Odysseus's objection to the lotus-eaters is not, as it will be to the Cyclopes, that they lack justice but that the form of life they live is unbecoming to responsible Achaians.

Cheating as a point of departure, then, has several benefits. First, it allows me to postpone, in developing the concept of "justice," entering the metaethical swamps of "right and wrong" or "good and evil." I may not be able to articulate exactly what makes an act of cheating wrong, but this limit to my articulateness does not legitimate some-one's cheating me. I'll look in more detail at the relations of fairness to virtue and the good in subsequent chapters. Cheating also provides an entrance into problems of moral epistemology and philosophical method, for reasonably adjudicating the competing claims of various goods requires a commitment to what we can call, albeit hesitantly, moral realism. At the same time, familiar philosophical arguments in-cline me toward a realism both antifoundationalist and antirelativist. It consists, to oversimplify, in the view that claims about human good and the best options for carrying out human interaction can be true in the absence of any metaphysical grounding in the "right" or the "good." Here again I take myself as following a path opened by Aris-totle.

That truth in ethics can be had without metaphysical or, for that matter, any other kind of foundations is a point made forcefully more than once in Aristotle's *Ethics*. In his characterization of the "mean," for example, the Philosopher notes that "not every action nor every passion admits of a mean; for some have names that already imply badness, e.g., spite, shamelessness, envy, and in the case of actions adultery, theft, murder" (*Ethics*:1107a). Anyone sufficiently mature to know the meaning of the words knows that such characteristics and actions are bad. This goes equally for philosophers and corner gro-cers. In fact, corner grocers may well be more trustworthy here since they are not inclined to engage in debate for its own sake. They know, just the way that the audience of Aristophanes' *Clouds* knew, that no amount of sophistry can justify murder or, more generally, make it ac-ceptable to subvert justice. Consider, for the sake of example, Aris-tophanes' exchange between Right and Wrong. Discoursing on the dangers of embracing the tricks of Wrong, Right sings:

You will sing the trendy song, "Wrong is right and right is wrong/There's no difference, there's no Justice, there's no God"/And you'll catch the current craze for Antimachus'/ways—/Or in plainer language, you'll become a sod.

To this, Wrong replies, with encouragement from the leader of the chorus:

Don't worry, ever since he began his speech I've been bursting to blow it to bits. That's why the people here at the Thinkery call me Wrong; I was the one who invented ways of proving anything wrong, laws, prosecutors, anything.

Isn't that worth millions—to be able to have a really bad case and yet win? (Aristophanes 1973:154–55)

The answer, of course, is "no," because when Wrong wins out the entire fabric of the community is torn apart and the goods pursued cannot be achieved. Cannot, I should say, be achieved through purposeful action. For it is within the realm of possibility, or at least comedy, that we achieve our ends despite the injustices perpetrated against us. When we do, however, it is a matter of good luck and not as a consequence of our best deliberations and choices of action. Grocers, however, don't wish to trust in luck; they want, if at all possible, to eliminate the uncertainties and conflicts that would render their business successes a "lucky break." But luck would be the only hope for happiness in a society ruled by Wrong. Long-range planning and diligence would be self-defeating, because as soon as they began to pay off I would become a ripe target of attack. So-called philosophers who encourage or pave the way for the victory of Wrong are a danger to the community, and it doesn't take specialized theoretical, much less philosophical, argument to see this. If the philosophers attempt to impose their games on the day-to-day activities of the polis then grocers and their friends have every reason to reject them. And Aristotle would agree. The bases for the good life are not laid by playing philosophical games but by doing what needs to be done in the context of a particular activity. Those who neglect sound practice are like people "who take refuge in theory and think they are being philosophers and will become good in this way, behaving somewhat like patients who listen attentively to their doctors, but do none of the things they are ordered to do" (*Ethics*:1105b).

The analogy with the doctor is important to Aristotle's understanding of method in ethics. Doctors inherit a tradition of medicine that has been built up over generations. In the practice of their craft they bring this accumulated wisdom to bear on particular cases, which may be the result of specific causal sequences not previously encountered. Nonetheless, doctors look for relevant similarities and analogies and attempt to address the problem. When they succeed, well and good; when they do not, the opportunity arises for investigation and innovation. If the innovation proves successful it may enter into the body of medical tradition that will pass on to future generations. What doctors cannot do is make a person well just by saying so. The corpse will soon raise an unmistakable stink. Serious philosophers, as opposed to Aristophanes' sophists, are not unlike doctors. They start with what any-one can plainly see and attempt to explain it and solve the problems it might pose. That they cannot provide a metaphysical foundation for their craft does not mean that we should forgo their services; that would be foolish. Why should we demand other from the philosopher doing ethics? If someone does not know the meaning of "murder" then he is not yet mature enough to undertake philosophy, and if he does know its meaning then to ask the philosopher for more is unrea-sonable, for we learn things in many different ways, Aristotle notes, and we shouldn't assume that all can be reduced to a single method. The world is more complex than that. If the fact is established, then we should investigate it in whatever manner "is appropriate to the in-quiry" and not foolishly demand that butchers be mathematicians or doctors, geometers. To agree that murder is bad is to agree that we are mature speakers of the language; and this is the presupposition of ethical inquiry, where "we must consider happiness in the light not only of our conclusions and our premises, but also of what is com-monly said about it; for with a true view all the data harmonize, but with a false one the facts soon clash" (*Ethics*:1098b).[6] The sophistical attempt to deny the wickedness of murder represents, in fact, a refusal to engage in ethics, for it demands of us that we give up our language; and once we do this we can no longer formulate the reasons that led us to inquire in the first place. Metaethical theories that attempt to im-pose on moral judgments strictures drawn from other fields doom themselves to failure "by asking of their methods," as William Gass puts it, "answers that their methods cannot give" (1971:236). To ask, in short, why murder is wrong displays either ignorance or petulance, neither of which is an argument, and to ignore such a question is intel-lectual good sense, not lack of rigor.

There is, then, no foundation for ethics beyond what any reason-able member of the community can be expected to know. But to be "antifoundationalist" in this sense is not to embrace relativism, "fide-ism," or the modern "emotivism" dissected so devastatingly by Alas-dair MacIntyre (1981:chaps. 2–3). There is a simpleminded but fun-damental distinction to be made between true statements and the ways in which I come to know them. Pluralism about how we come to know propositions is distinct from the manifestly absurd claim that we don't know anything at all. Confusion here usually stems from one or an-other party in the discussion being wedded to the view that only some methods of inquiry are capable of producing justified statements and that only statements justified in those particular ways can rightfully claim the mantle of truth. But such a position is simply mistaken. To speak the truth, as Aristotle put it, is "to say that that which is is and that which is not is not" (*Met.*:1011b). How I come to know and say what I do is another matter. It is true, for example, that my mother loves me, although I'm not sure I could give a full account of how I came to know this or whether those things I say in justification of it are sufficient. It is true, nonetheless.

This seems to put me at odds with MacIntyre, whose most recent work suggests that the conflicting accounts of justice found in contemporary debate are not only incommensurable but also call into question the very possibility of making claims for truth in ethics. MacIntyre's emphasis on history as essential to determining rationality leads him to relativize criteria of truth to particular traditions of moral assessment. This in turn inclines him to deny the translatability of claims across traditions and to insist that, if they are to be understood, moral claims require the ability in their interpreter to inhabit the tradition in question. This would seem to mean that the claim about my mother's love is acceptable only to the extent that the audience for that claim shares my tradition and the criteria which constitute it. It appears that my "absolutism" with regard to truth flies in the face of MacIntyre's historical critique and probably reflects a uniquely modern liberal situation that is unaware of its own limitations (MacIntyre 1988:chaps. 19–20). But the appearance is, I think, only skin deep, for MacIntyre and I can agree that there is no clear line between the material and the conceptual ecology of a particular community and that the practices it develops will be relative to its environment. We can, moreover, agree that a community in one environment may come to have a different understanding of the way the world is from that of a group in a substantially different area, with consequent differences about what goods are appropriately pursued and how this is best done. But these relativities are contingent and amenable to discussion, at least in principle.

Neither MacIntyre nor I believe, if I read him correctly, that there is any *a priori* argument proceeding from self-evident premises to a conclusion about justice and the good which must be acknowledged by any rational intellect. Nor do either of us believe there is a single method for bringing discussion to a conclusion, nor any neutral standard of rationality against which we can measure that conclusion. But these are obstacles to reasonable argument only if we believe that the

paradigm of rationality is calculation of a fairly straightforward alge-
braic sort, that there is some single method of discovery called "scientific method", and that through applying scientific method we can
come to know the way the world is in something like the way we come
to know propositions in algebra. It's not necessary to be a methodological anarchist a la Paul Feyerabend to admit that none of these propositions are plausible.

We are left with what I'll call "investigative pragmatism." Ethics is
reflection on the good life, and there is no neutral standpoint from
which reflection can take place. Nonetheless, what we are inclined to
say about the good life turns out to be the best available evidence because what we say is intimately bound up with what we are disposed to
do, and as free agents what we are disposed to do speaks directly to
what we find most choice-worthy. Since we are natural beings and
must reach some ecological balance with the world, the choices we are
inclined to make will, unless we've become pathological, be tied closely
to the nature of that world. Being wildly wrong about what contributes to the good life is as difficult to make sense of as being wildly mistaken about the way the world is. (Cf. Davidson 1984:chap. 13.) Approaches to ethics which trade on the assumption that our practical
judgments could be thoroughly other than they are are as confused as
their epistemic counterparts. The rejection of foundationalism leads
to nothing more than methodological fallibilism.

Methodological confusion about rationality and argument in ethics
is not only unfortunate in itself but also obscures a much more important problem. Fallibilism in science suggests that theories can be well
developed, brilliantly formulated, and justified by all the available evidence but nonetheless wrong. Pragmatism in ethics, if I am to be consistent, would seem to imply something similar. But although I am
willing to applaud the Ptolemeans of late antique astronomy for their
determination and ingenuity, I am not similarly inclined to embrace
their moral counterparts who willingly adopted coersion and torture
in judicial proceedings, slavery as an economic necessity, and the
quest for empire as a privilege of power. These are not merely "theories" about the moral world, they are practices that, as we understand
them, are shot through with injustice. It just won't do to note them as
quaint relics of a bygone era. Something needs to be said about how it
happens that members of other cultures, and of our own at earlier
stages, can condone and engage in activities that strike us as horribly
barbaric. Here, I don't mean those cases where justice is clear but can-

not be achieved, as when a bystander is unable to help the victim of a crime. Instead, I mean those cases where it seems that one group is completely blind to the moral nature of a particular act or policy. We wonder how in good conscience they could be a party to such activities.

Talk of conscience should not be construed as introducing some jejune faculty of the soul. Knowledge, however obtained, is at least justified true belief. "Practical wisdom," in Aristotle's account, is a form of knowledge, and hence it must meet those three minimal conditions; but it is also "a reasoned and true state of capacity to act with regard to human good" (*Ethics*:1140b). Conscience needs to be distinguished from practical reason because we take responsibility for our actions, and when we perform them they are particular, not generic. Conscience differs from practical reason or prudence in general in being both particular and indexed to the first person. Thus, practical reason condemns murder as wicked, but it would be confused to say that my conscience bothered me about a murder with which I had nothing to do. If I knew something that might have prevented the murder but neglected to act, or acted irresponsibly, then conscience might condemn me, even if I was not properly responsible for the murder itself. And when I contemplate some act contrary to conscience, I don't simply recognize that such acts are wrong, but am aware that the particular act under consideration is wrong and that I would be responsible for the wickedness should I do it. Thomas Aquinas makes this point with customary clarity in denying that acts can be neutral in the individual case. If an act is of sufficient weight to be attributed to deliberation, as opposed to stroking one's beard or shuffling the feet, then it will be either good or bad. To take a walk, for example, is generically neutral, but walks can only be taken at particular places and times; thus, they must be the objects of deliberation, unlike, say, pacing the waiting room. When an action results from deliberation, then the particular circumstances that surround the event modify its reasonableness. To take a long walk, for example, when I know that my wife is getting very close to delivery is probably inappropriate. To do so at 1:00 in the morning, when she is having regular contractions every seven minutes, is thoroughly irresponsible. In short, since all actions must be "either directed or not directed to a due end . . . every human action that proceeds from deliberate reason, if it be considered in the individual must be good or bad" (Aquinas *S.Theo*:1a2ae, 9). Conscience registers the judgment of the agent on the act contemplated.

We usually do not have to engage in extended debates *in foro interno*; we simply act. But all this means is that most of the time most of us are acting reasonably. Our conscience comes into play either when there is a tension between our general sense of the human good and an act we are contemplating or when having done the deed we begin to wonder whether it is consonant with what we know about that good and what we should have considered about the particular act.

Perhaps some examples are in order. In Achebe's novel it is taken for granted that the community's oracle constitutes an unassailable authority and that pronouncing death on the young hostage, Ikemifuna, is in accord, sadly, with the workings of the cosmos. This is not a casual attitude but constitutive of the moral and social fabric of the society. To do the bidding of the gods is central to living well and acting responsibly, and Okonkwo upbraids his friend Obierika, saying, "I cannot understand why you refused to come with us to kill that boy" (Achebe 1959:64). When his friend responds that he had better things to do and that the burden was not explicitly appointed him, Okonkwo retorts:

"But someone had to do it. If we were all afraid of blood, it would not be done. And what do you think the Oracle would do then?"

"You know very well, Okonkwo, that I am not afraid of blood. . . . If I were you I would have stayed at home. What you have done will not please the Earth. It is the kind of action for which the goddess wipes out whole families."

"The Earth cannot punish me for obeying her messenger," Okonkwo said . . .

"That is true," Obierika agreed. "But if the Oracle said that my son should be killed I would neither dispute it nor be the one to do it."

They would have gone on arguing had Ofoedu not come in just then. (Achebe 1959:64–65)

This is a model example of moral dispute internal to a community. Most of the time our responsibilities are fairly clear, and we know the proprieties from long acculturation. But every now and then a situation arises that throws us into a quandary. As the guardian of the boy, Okonkwo had committed himself to protecting the child; but as a member of the community, he had a commitment to acting in its best interests. There is no single set of rules or principle of decision that could resolve the problem from some neutral perspective. Obierika's conclusion carries the conviction of an unbreachable barrier to action, but it rests on no firmer foundation than his general sense of how things are and should be. Were the argument to continue, Okonkwo would no doubt insist that his friend was simply mistaken regarding both judgment and fact. Something has to be done, but even best friends are unclear on how they should balance competing claims.

But suppose we are investigating the Dogon of Mali, who believe that humans were initially intended as sexually whole, androgenous beings, but also believe that this order was broken, with dire consequences, in the beginning of things. (Cf. Griaule 1965:17–23.) As a result, people must become either male or female and seek completeness is in the social institution of marriage. Nonethless, they retain at birth the remnants of their intended androgeny, a partially independent sexual counterpart. The male foreskin and the female clitoris house these residual and potentially conflictive sexual counterparts, and on maturity it is necessary to excise them so that development can continue apace. Failure to do so jeopardizes the later welfare of the individual. Circumcision of the male, I might think, is neither here nor there. I don't share the Dogon's sexual anthropology, but I have no particular reason to be dismayed. But in the case of the young girl, I could plausibly believe that excision of the clitoris seriously impairs her later possibilities for fulfillment. I may even recall Alifa Rifaat's story of Bahiyya the peasant girl, who still remembers in old age "a wound in my body and another wound deep inside me, a feeling that a wrong had been done to me, a wrong that could never be undone" (Rifaat 1983:9). Can I in good conscience stand by, much less record in detail the steps of ritual excision, knowing what I know? There is no more an easy answer to this than to the dispute between Okonkwo and Obierika. Depending upon the importance I attach to sexual fulfillment, I may inquire as to the propriety of the ritual, suggest objections, or perhaps kidnap the girl. But the magnitude of my act must be matched by thoroughness of deliberation and imagination in spelling out the consequences of my action. For example, the sort of sexual life anticipated by Dogon women is not that of a contemporary California teenager. From the Dogon perspective, my intervention threatens the order of things, the girl's future with her people, and the ability of the community to pursue the goods it has come to hold worthy. If the girl held the same views about life and sex as an American adolescent, and if she were inclined to sacrifice her life among her people to pursue a different set of goods, then I might allow myself to be enlisted in aiding her flight. Although I needn't. After all, I know the limits and miseries attendant upon contemporary Western sexuality. She may not.

Sex, however, is one thing; death is another. Had there been an anthropologist among Achebe's Ibo, should he in conscience have felt it necessary to intervene to save the boy? I don't think so. The magnitude of the act and the level of reflection attributed to the characters clearly indicate that the killing of Ikemifune is no casual or wanton cruelty. It is not an act of passion nor in any way self-serving. The sacrifice has more in common with an execution than a murder, although there is no element of punishment directed against the boy per se. And while we differ among ourselves as to the good of capital punishment, few of us would bring down the fabric of the society to prevent an execution. We engage instead in the same sort of argument and refusal undertaken by Obierika. There is no failure of practical reason here—quite the opposite. The boy is surely frightened and would flee death, but the elders of his own community knew that he might suffer this fate when they surrendered him to Okonkwo's village.

It is difficult to see how the anthropologist could be entitled to assert his own judgments here over and against those of the participants. When deliberating about the possibilities for action, he must consider where those acts might figure in the pursuit of genuine goods, and once he does this the anthropologist comes up short. What he hopes is that the Ibo revise their views, but an attack on their practices does not foster that end. He might save a particular victim, but in doing so neither changes the structure of Ibo institutions nor helps them come to a point where reflection becomes self-criticism. In fact he forsakes his own professional calling to make a gesture. It would be nice if the gesture brought about sudden and complete conversion, but that's just wishful thinking and any account of responsible action must distinguish wishful thinking from practical deliberation. (Cf. Aristotle *Ethics*:1112a–13a.) I needn't be happy about the death of the boy, but then that's true of the Ibo themselves. We can all acknowledge the *lacrimae rerum* without acting contrary to conscience.

When we bring such arguments home again the situation alters. First and foremost, we expect there to be much greater agreement as to the nature of things. We already share with the Dogon a vast agreement about simple objects and events, not to mention the psychology of human action. We disagree in a few, albeit crucial, areas concerning the principles of human flourishing, and frequently those areas of disagreement account for our disparate judgments. But back home the scope of that disagreement becomes even narrower. Thus, the believer and nonbeliever at odds over the justice of abortion agree with each other on the status of Western medicine, the blanket rejection of human sacrifice, and the innocence, morally and legally, of children under seven. Given the restricted scope of our disagreements, some disputes that would be reasonable in our dealings with the Dogon would be unjustified in contemporary Beverly Hills. To put it the other way around: since we can have reasonable disagreements in conscience even with our close neighbors, we should not be surprised to discover them in communities farther removed.

But I still haven't spoken to the question of action. If our pursuit of the good depends in large measure on our views about the world and if there remains at least some scope for disagreement here, then our actions may occasionally bring us into conflict with our friends. There may, furthermore, be no simple method for resolving the conflict, and we may need to choose among several uncertain paths. In our making such a choice, right reason dictates pursuing the most pressing good, and that aspect of our moral psychology which responds to the claims of competing goods is conscience. Consider the debate over abortion and public policy in late twentieth-century America. The conservative Catholic woman does not think merely that abortion is a tragic decision likely to have unfortunate consequences for the individual and for the fabric of society, she thinks that it is murder, and the sort of crime which she must intervene to prevent if that is at all possible. Were she to acquiesce in a liberal policy that incorporated the funding of abortions into public policy, it would be as though she had cast her lot with a crew of murderers. And as long as she believes that abortion is murder, her conscience cannot and should not be stilled.

For my anthropologists, the clash of judgments about the way the world is, and what to do about it, creates an impasse for action. For the antagonists in the abortion debate, the impasse is even greater. The anthropologist will eventually move on; members of our own community typically do not. In the case of abortion, judgment for one side amounts to rejection of the other, and whichever way the judgment goes the nature of the community will be altered. There is no inhabitable middle ground within the community. A commitment to moral realism implies that at least one side in the debate is operating with a mistaken conscience. And since practical judgments of this magnitude affect the overall worthiness of life in community, it is important to attempt to correct the mistake. This, in turn, means actively interfering with the plans of others in ways which, as we frequently see, create yet further conflicts within the social fabric. Might it not be better to let well enough alone, as Mario Cuomo, for example, has suggested and allow individuals to exercise the promptings of conscience free from any intrusion of religion or ethics into the public order?

The answer, of course, is that such a move does nothing more than default to the consciences of a particular group. If ethics is the investigation of the good life and if that good life consists in large part of life in a community, then it will be impossible to keep ethics or religion out of politics. To do so would be to place an unjustifiable burden on conscience, which even in error is binding on the agent. It will repay the effort to see how this is so.

Suppose that Marcus owns slaves, that his family has owned slaves for generations, and that he is a member of the legislature of his state. His background is such that the presence and command of slaves is natural to him. It is reinforced every day and incorporated into the institutions of his community. Not only that, his work in the legislature has forced him to reflect on the role that slavery plays in the economy and social life of the larger community. Beyond that, when confronted with the arguments of others, Marcus has gone on to develop arguments about the persistence of slavery throughout history and the sovereign rights of states to establish the laws internal to themselves. His conscience is as clear on this matter as any of his compatriots.

Nonetheless, slavery is wrong. It deprives a person of liberty for no other reason than that someone else wants to and has the power to do so. But this isn't a good reason. It depends upon the vagaries of strength and technology, and takes from someone what they have done nothing, in themselves, to merit losing. It is unjust. Shouldn't Marcus be constrained from perpetuating this injustice? There are, in fact, two questions here. The first might be rephrased: shouldn't those who recognize the injustice of slavery make every effort consonant with justice to change the situation and end Marcus's slaveholding? The answer to this is "yes." But another question might be: should we work to prohibit advocating and working for the continuation of slavery in those states that desire it or the propagation of such views by people who think we *should* desire it? Here the answer is "no," even when we have no doubt about the wickedness of the view. For although Marcus is mistaken, and perhaps culpably so, he judges slavery to be appropriate and attempts to act on that judgment. (Cf. Aquinas *S.Theo.*: 1a2ae, 19.) He deems slavery is a good, and in accord with right reason he pursues that good. Were he to do otherwise, Marcus would be willfully forsaking the good as he understands it and would be entering into malice. That, after all, is what it means to be malicious: to pursue what you have every reason to believe is wicked. Marcus finds himself in a tragic situation; both his options are grossly defective. Pursuing slavery perpetuates a gross injustice. Acting maliciously is wicked. Nonetheless, we can give a sympathetic account, explaining how Marcus sadly, but through no blame of his own, came to be mistaken. Acting maliciously undermines the very fabric of conscience and character and is likely to render him unfit for community under any circumstances. If Marcus, or anyone, is to remain of decent character and be worthy of the community, he must treat conscience as binding. And that means we should as well, even when it exacerbates the conflicts that arise among us.

The conclusions of this chapter remain somewhat tentative, and the work of subsequent chapters will be to amplify and extend these suggestions through application to cases. Still, we've made a bit of headway in laying out the alternative vocabulary the Aristotelian proposes for moral analysis. First, it is important to insist that humans are a part of nature and, as such, will be subject to the same sorts of analysis as the rest of the cosmos, and particularly the more advanced nonhuman animals. But humans are distinct in the extent of their ability to formulate the possibilities for action in pursuit of a wide variety of goods. They can, if suitably trained, deliberate about the reasonableness of one course of action over another; and if they are not constrained by ignorance, external force, or some defect of body or character, they may be successful in achieving the goods they pursue. These are the hallmarks of practical rationality. This, for Aristotle, is what ethics is about.

Practical reason always begins *in medias res*, presupposing an elaborate understanding of human goods keyed to a concrete historical community. There is no point in the quest for a theory of justice: any set of claims sufficiently general to meet our ordinary use of "theory" would be too thin to have much impact on practical reason. A "theory" rich enough to make susbstantive claims would have to depend upon our ordinary practical judgments to a greater extent even than do physical theories. A "theory of justice" in this sense would amount to a dispute about the very judgments we make, and thus lack the level of rudimentary agreement necessary for theoretical discussion. None of this, however, should lead anyone to believe that we do not make practical judgments or that those we make are somehow arbitrary, "subjective," or lacking in truth. They are, as Aristotle suggests, more like the judgments of a doctor than those of a mathematician; and despite those limits, the doctor's judgments are very much a matter of the way of the world, either true or false. Not only this, but just as medicine may progress, so may our ability to make practical judgments in general. Aristotle's frequent quips about the impropriety of ethics as an investigation for children may hold for some societies as well. Justice, as the overarching virtue necessary to any communal life, is presupposed by any group with a set of institutions sufficiently complex and stable to be called a human community. This is not because we have some mysterious inbred sense of justice or natural law, but because for any institution to function over time there must be a shared set of expectations and standards of performance that make it possible to incorporate the institution into the life of the community. Stanley Cavell once asked the question, "Must we mean what we say?" and answered it in the affirmative. To mean something is, among other things, to handle the tools of language in recognizable ways, and this means ways that our interlocutors can be expected to acknowledge. The same holds true for other institutions and the tools and practices through which they are constituted. "Justice" in practical activity bears much of the same primitive burden as "truth" in language.[7]

But, that judgments of practical reason are either true or false doesn't imply that those judgments are not indexed to speaker and culture, nor that there is any simple set of identities licensing the move from "X is unjust" to "Y is not justified in doing X" to "Y's act X is wicked." Our judgments of praise and blame are distinct from our judgments about practices and institutions in general, and I made this point in the discussion of conscience. Acting justly requires acting in accord with conscience, and when conscience conflicts with the justice of an institution we have the makings of tragedy. There is no theoretical way to avoid this because there is no theoretical way, for the Aristotelian at least, to achieve the god's eye view that turns everything into comedy.

Practical judgment, like all human endeavor, is a risky business. Indexed as we are to time and place, limited in knowledge and constrained by the need to act, our practical judgments are shot through with fallibility. But trying to be infallible is no more rational than trying to grow wings. (Cf. Aristotle Ethics:1112a–13a.) If the search for theory in ethics reflects the unattainable desire for certainty, then it is not only fruitless but also irrational. It stifles serious, if perhaps more piecemeal, thinking about the particulars of practical life. Better to get on with it and make an effort to see how a mature member of our community might respond to situations of conflict. It is in the hope of demonstrating the ability of an Aristotelian approach to provide guidance in such situations that I turn to the practical analysis of war.

Notes

1. This is too obviously, and intentionally, a caricature to need remarking, but a caricature with that necessary resemblance to the principals. But what's really at stake is not the details of Hume or Kant exegesis. It's rather the preconceptions at work in the bulk of Anglo-American academic moral philosophy. This is not the place to launch a full-scale review of modern moral thought and its critics, but I should give some account, at least, of the critics who have most influenced this essay. Without making it his principle business, everything Stanley Cavell writes is a critique of academic ethics and philosophy in general. Part four of *The Claim of Reason* is, to my mind, the most brilliant account of what it means to be human, and thus a moral agent, to be found in the recent literature. But Cavell's work is, perhaps, too personal to have the impact it deserves. A more traditional, though rich and subtly argued, critique of the status quo is Bernard Williams's *Ethics and the Limits of Philosophy*. His sense that "the demands of the modern world on ethical thought are unprecedented, and the ideas of rationality embodied in most contemporary moral philosophy cannot meet them; but some extension of ancient thought, greatly modified, might be able to do so" (1985:vii) captures well the feeling that sent me in the direction of Aristotle. Much the same can be said for the work of Stuart Hampshire, who is but one of the insightful critics of modern Anglo-America represented in Hauerwas and MacIntyre's collection, *Revisions*.

2. The literature on this topic is truly vast, even when restricted to works in English. Russell (1975) studies the sources in detail and provides a sound scholarly bibliography. Johnson (1975, 1981) range over more material and are more controversial, although perhaps less precise. Sheils (1983) contains a number of very interesting topical studies. Stein (1961) remains a model of philosophical rigor in its statement and application of the traditional Catholic just war theory, and Ramsey (1961) is seminal for its interpretation of Augustine and Aquinas and its attempt to introduce the tradition into Protestant social ethics. Finnis et al. (1987) traces its parentage to the Stein volume, and despite the erstwhile restriction to nuclear deterrence it develops and applies a general natural law version of the tradition. Johnson (1984) represents a contemporary development much influenced by Ramsey. The most influential

secular analysis has been Walzer (1977). All of the above offer further guidance in the literature.

3. There is an interesting story to be told about the fall and rise of the natural law tradition, but I'm not the person and this is not the place to tell it. In England it runs, in part, from Elizabeth Anscombe and Walter Stein to John Finnis, whereas the American story runs from John Ford to Paul Ramsey to the American Catholic bishops, both strands converging in Finnis et al. (1987). More of the details emerge in the discussion in chapter 3.

4. The best place to start assessing Rawls is, of course, with *Theory of Justice* itself. Very important reviews and criticisms, with bibliography, appeared in the original 1975 version of Daniels (1989). The reprint includes a new preface that reviews the main lines of criticism since 1975 and a substantial new bibliography. Of recent "communitarian" critiques, the most frequently noted has been Sandel (1982), although Sullivan (1983) is perhaps more suggestive of the place of Rawls in the liberal tradition and the limits of both.

5. For all his prolific writing, Stanley Hauerwas is at his best in his discussions of marriage, family, and friendship. From "Love is not All You Need" in Hauerwas (1974) to the essays on friendship (1990), he demonstrates a remarkable sensibility to the structure, importance, and fragility of these relations. In particular, Hauerwas recognizes the primacy of truth and honesty in sustaining these relationships, even when telling the truth will destroy a particular relation and the delusions that have been fostered by it. In his discussion of "open marriage," for example, he displays in fine fashion the ways in which the key issue is not sex outside of marriage but the transformation that would be required for us to remove "adultery" from the category of acts whose names, as Aristotle put it, "already imply badness." "On analysis," Hauerwas argues, "the person capable of open marriage turns out to be the self-interested individual presupposed and encouraged by our liberal political structure and our capitalist consumer economy," and a little bit of reflection should suffice to reveal how distasteful such a being is (1981:180). It is in coming to grips with the constitutive institutions of the community—marriage, family, religion, political participation, and health care, for example—that the limits of the contractarian tradition become clearest and Hauerwas's writings on these topics more telling in their critical implications than even the best of Rawls's more "philosophical" critics.

6. This is not the place to undertake an exposition of the account of truth implicit here. So far as I know no one has yet produced a complete exegesis of Aristotle's views on truth and method in the *Ethics* that takes adequate account of his remarks about truth elsewhere, notably in *Metaphysics* 4. The view of truth implicit there has, I think, close affinities with the account of truth and learnable languages advanced by Donald Davidson in the essays collected in his *Inquiries into Truth and Interpretation*.

7. It's impossible to extend this discussion here. Cavell (1979), Gass (1971), and Stout (1988) all approach these issues in ways amenable to my perspective, although from different directions. One way of making the analogy be-

tween truth and justice would be to note that just as we adopt a principle of charity in interpreting alien or nonstandard speech, so must we in interpreting practical action. The occasional deviation from accepted standards of practice may be tolerated as eccentricity or a minor vice, but major transgressions such as rape or murder are intolerable wickedness, and continual wickedness leads us to doubt whether the perpetrator is fully human. At the outer limit, linguistic and practical deviance converge. We call it madness.

2.

Pacifism as a Vocation

Most of us, most of the time, want to be pacifists, for most of us, most of the time, cannot consider war without focusing, with the eye of imagination, on the puzzled face of the first enemy we kill at close quarters. This, I think, more than the image of our own death, begets horror. Even the courageous, at the last moment, shut their eyes on their own death, and cowards never look at all. But the face of the victim demands, whether in memory or anticipation, its due consideration.

Soldiers needn't be particularly reflective to butt up against such thoughts. Fighting alongside their comrades cannot help but lead them into contemplation. The situation is only compounded by the knowledge, and perhaps the firsthand experience, of the ways that battle contrives to turn them from the decent sort they think themselves to be into killers, capable not only of defending themselves and their cause but also of vengeful slaughter, plain if not altogether simple. (Cf. Keegan 1976:45–52.) "But, say they, the wise man will wage just wars." This, Augustine notes caustically, is little consolation, "as if he would not all the rather lament the necessity of just wars, if he remembers that he is a man; for if they were not just he would not wage them, and would therefore be delivered from all wars" (*C.Dei*:19, 5). Modern methods of war make it possible to distance ourselves from the immediacy of death, not altogether unlike the way a supermarket distances us from the slaughterhouse, but this detachment is self-deception. We distinguish, in bad faith, the death from the killing in order to contemplate the conditions for and prosecution of war without the moral discomfort. But, as Augustine goes on to remark, should a person contemplate the miseries of war "without mental pain, this is a more miserable plight still, for he thinks himself happy because he has lost human feeling." The more decent the soldier, the more horrified at the prospect of killing. The soldier's predicament is not unlike Oedipus's as he confronts the consequences of his fate. E. R. Dodds is correct in insisting that Oedipus cannot, morally, be held culpable, but that this doesn't matter: "the great king, 'the first of men', the man whose intuitive genius had saved Thebes, is suddenly revealed to himself as a thing so unclean that 'neither the earth can receive it, nor the holy rain nor the sunshine endure its presence' (line 1426)" (Dodds 1973:73). In what ways does killing approach for us the repugnance we associate with Oedipus's unwitting patricide and incest?

Some acts, even when innocently done, undermine the ability of the society, and sometimes the agent himself, to accept that person as a full member of the community. To kill your father and then to commit incest are not simply infractions, but acts which cannot be incorporated into the fabric of society; and when Oedipus, the most thoughtful, just, and courageous of men, recognizes that these are his acts he rips himself, a loathesome pollution, from human society. The incest specially swims before the imagination: images of what was previously a delight now transformed into inescapable reproach. Similarly, as children, boys in particular, we revel in games of war, conquest, and heroic prowess, but as we grow and attain a clearer sense of the fragility of the body, the permanence of death, and how much there is to lose for someone caught up in violent conflict, the less comfortable we become with the naïveté of childish games. To imagine yourself a killer without feeling the enormity of the act is a sure sign of corruption. With his usual eye for contemporary analogy, Dodds notes (1973:72) that a driver who has, even innocently, killed another should feel the full weight of his act, regardless of any formal finding of guilt. There is a stain of homicide indifferent to responsibility or intent. If only because so few of us have ever been party to killing, homicide comes close to incest in its power to provoke not merely disapproval but revulsion, and this seems to be true even for soldiers engaged in a plausibly just war. Michael Walzer reports that "in the course of a study of combat behavior in World War II, S. L. A. Marshall discovered that the majority of men on the front lines never fired their guns" (Walzer 1977:138). Justification, opportunity, and need must be pushed to the extreme to overcome our deeply ingrained reluctance to mete out death.

We should, therefore, hold suspect anyone who is not drawn by the voice of pacifism. When conflict escalates to deadly force, I risk my person, which inspires a reasonable fear. But when I knowingly enter into such a conflict, I risk injuring and even killing another, which is a horrifying prospect. How can I take a life if I do not have the power to return it? I cannot reasonably answer for, or expect on my own initiative to transform, my entire society, but one step within my power is refusing to be a part of such conflicts. I say, in effect, that I am not and will not become the sort of creature who willingly risks the lives of others. But merely to say this, as Sophocles makes painfully clear, cannot shield us from the contingencies of human existence. As long as we share a communal life we risk implicating ourselves in those very acts that most horrify us.

For Oedipus, it is clear what needs to be done. Regardless of his intentions, relations existed between Jocasta, Laius, and himself that precluded certain further involvements. Specifically, Oedipus could under no circumstances undertake deadly force against his father or have sexual relations with his mother. In one sense, of course, he could because he did, but emphasizing the physical possibility of sleeping with a woman who also happens to be your mother betrays a modern narrowness of vision. For Oedipus, the consequences of action are more complex. The world is such that a patricide, even an unwitting one, puts him at odds with the fabric of life. He is no longer fit for human interaction; and if the community is to protect itself, then the offender must be cast out. Failure to remove the pollution risks destruction for the whole of Thebes. Not unlike present-day pollutants, Oedipus's transgressions exercise a corrosive force, invisible except to experts, that gnaws secretly at our very makeup, threatening unimagined future generations. The toxins must be removed. The distinction between the supernatural and the material, or between the divine and the secular, has no purchase here; that is just the way the world is.[1]

Made desperate, Oedipus removes himself from the society of others. The pacifist, horrified by the prospect of taking life, rejects war because it is the organized practice of killing. But war is not the only activity that makes up my life or the life of the community. If asked how my pacifism relates to the rest of my practical activity, what should I respond? The concept of pollution no longer plays the role it did in traditional thought. Recent moral theories elaborate the relation of the internal to the external act in different ways, but by and large they agree in emphasizing the importance of will and intention in ways that would interpret Oedipus's self-destructive despair as morally inappropriate. This seems, in fact, to be Oedipus's view in Sophocles' later *Oedipus at Colonus*. "How was I evil in myself?" he asks the chorus. "I had been wronged, I retaliated. . . . Then, knowing nothing, I went on" (*O.Col*:ll, 270ff). If revulsion at killing is, for some moderns, analogous to Oedipus's revulsion at fratricide and incest and if pacifism rests merely on this revulsion, then perhaps such pacifism is as misplaced as Oedipus's despair.

Such, at least, is Jan Narveson's argument. Take pacifism to be the position that recourse to war is wrong. What, Narveson asks, makes such action wrong? Some may be squeamish at the thought of killing and others may simply be unwilling to employ deadly force, but neither stance constitutes a moral position, properly speaking. These responses, so far, register nothing more than individual preference. Narveson (1965) rightly rejects appeals to violence in the abstract as in themselves irrelevant. Nor will it do to argue that war rarely achieves a good end. Particular failures are not by themselves arguments that a course of action is wrong. Unless it rests on a principle that establishes a duty independent of personal preference, it is not clear what would make war wrong as opposed to being messy or imprudent. It would surely be reasonable to adopt the rule that war is to be avoided as generally not in the best interests of the many. I suppose, in fact, that almost everybody already maintains something like this. For even Napoleon, as Clausewitz remarked, "is always peace-loving. . . . he would prefer to take over our country unopposed" (1976:370). But neither Napoleon nor Augustine, whose wise man wishes to be delivered from war, can properly be called a pacifist. Napoleon will certainly, faced with resistence, give up his irenic stance in order to subdue his prey and the bishop of Hippo will insist on the regretable necessity of war in order to protect the innocent against Napoleon's aggression. It is a Pickwickian pacifism indeed that can incorporate these exceptions.

To give moral weight to the idea, Narveson asks: what moral reasons might lead to someone becoming a pacifist? And he suggests that one response open to the pacifist is "that pacifism as such is a duty, that is, that meeting violence with force is, as such, wrong" (Narveson 1965:66). Only if violent response is wrong does pacifism move beyond the realm of habit or preference and constitute a recognizable moral duty. It is important for Narveson's argument that this duty cannot be one that applies only to a particular subset of the populace or be taken on voluntarily. Thus, for me to argue that I am a pacifist but that it is perfectly acceptable for others to defend their family and friends brands my rejection of force as preferential as opposed to moral. If a course of action is wrong, then it is wrong even for those who don't realize it. Similarly, should I as the erstwhile pacifist reject recourse to violence until there is a direct threat to my immediate family I am not, morally speaking, a pacifist. Restricting use of force to certain reasonably well-defined situations is not the same as rejecting it altogether. If pacifism is to be made plausible as a duty it must be shown to follow from our best analysis of justice. But among our most secure intuitions about justice is the view that defending self, family, and friends is not only reasonable but obligatory. After all, as long as my family and I have not otherwise violated the requirements of justice, why shouldn't I use whatever force is reasonable against an attacker? Whom do I have better reasons for defending? What kind of person would I be to just stand by? Thus, the pacifist must argue, against these intuitions, "that no one ought ever to be defended against attack. The right of self-defense can be denied coherently only if the right of defense, in general, is denied" (Narveson 1965:71).

Here Narveson's argument depends upon introducing the language of "rights." Rights seem to be of two sorts: those that acrue to individuals or groups by virtue of some acknowledged contractual relationship and those devolving upon someone by virtue of the sort of creature she is. Leaving aside, for the moment, how we recognize and from whence we derive these natural rights, we may agree that if something is a right then we are justified in maintaining and protecting it. One of our natural rights, Narveson suggests, is that to security of our persons against gratuitous attack (1965:72). It follows from this that should someone be attacked without cause she would be within her rights to exert herself against her attacker. But this seems to fly in the face of the pacifist's contention that defense is not a right.

Could, perhaps, the pacifist retreat to the weaker position that defense *with force* is wrong but that means short of force are acceptable? This won't do, for if the voice of reason and sympathy should fail, then recourse to force may be a last resort. Consider, for example, a woman confronting a would-be rapist. What more unwarranted attack could we imagine? Now suppose that she attempts to reason with her attacker, arguing that his action is vicious and a gross violation of her rights. What if reason fails? When he grabs her, is she duty bound not to resist? Two points. First, the pacifist cannot argue that it is a bad idea for her to resist, since it may provoke her assailant to greater violence. Perhaps it would, but this is not relevant. The pacifist must insist that resort to force is wrong, whatever the consequences. Second, it is equally beside the point that my victim may *forgo* any resistance. Perhaps she believes that rape is a symptom of a systemic social disease and that the behavior of the rapist is determined by social and biochemical forces over which he has no control. She might, in other words, be a Skinnerian behaviorist, capable of analyzing her assailant purely in terms of immediate stimulus and response. In doing this she would attribute to the rapist no reflection or responsibility beyond that of a rutting dog. But to be consistent she should attribute nothing more to herself. Thus, the pacifist appeal to duty, right, or the moral law is otiose. This is just her animal response. For her pacifist claim to be compelling, in the sense required by Narveson, she must view both herself and her attacker as bound by duties and hedged round with rights, and as yet she has not been given any plausible reason to forgo protecting her right to her person.

Suppose the pacifist retreats once again, to the still weaker position that *deadly* force is prohibited, but other forms of struggle are theoretically allowable. This position has two failings. First, it is not evident what should count as deadly force. If hitting him with her fists is acceptable, what about using the stick that happens to be on the path? It is a minimal weapon, but surely people have been killed with sticks. If the fortuitous stick is an acceptable instrument, what about the billy club she carries against just such eventualities? If the club, why not the knife, and so on? In short, if she is justified in using any form of force at all it would seem that there is no nonarbitrary way of drawing the line short of whatever "might be necessary" (Narveson 1965:73). Perhaps she may not justly intend to kill the rapist, but this is a different matter and the subject of the next chapter. The force she is driven to use may turn out deadly despite her best intentions.

But the pacifist has a more difficult problem than drawing the line between increments of force. If force of any sort may be employed in defense of rights, then why should the victim be prohibited *deadly* force if that is necessary to preserve a right? Perhaps some rights are not sufficiently important to justify such force; still, this admission leaves open the possibility that other rights, such as security against murder, rape, and being enslaved, are that important. All three attack my integrity as a person, and all three provoke a response similar to Oedipus's when first confronted with his patricide and incest. Being murdered, on reflection, seems to be the least revolting because as a victim I am no longer aware. The slave and the rape victim must live with the knowledge of that attack through which they were rendered objects, instruments for the will of another. This points up the importance of placing acts within the larger context of human interaction. Descriptively there may be no visible distinction between being raped and eagerly engaging in acts of sexual expression. But to pretend that there is no difference between the two is delusion, and to say that I have a duty to let myself be raped borders on the perverse. Thus, Narveson concludes that as long as we retain our basic moral vocabulary the pacifist's position is incoherent. It advances as a duty a principle of action which asks that we give up the very rights that make duties intelligible.

But how much has Narveson accomplished? Has he shown, as he maintains, that "the pacifist's central position is untenable" (1965:77)? I don't think so. His critique of pacifism works only if his antagonist grants the primacy of an ethics based on principles, rules, rights, and duties. Pacifists have the option of rejecting, as does MacIntyre in *After Virtue*, the vocabulary of natural rights as a philosophical fiction and belief in such rights as "one with belief in witches and in unicorns" (1981:67). Or they can adopt the position of chapter 1, that justice is, on the one hand, a prerequisite of any sustainable communal enterprise and, on the other, capable of progressive elaboration in ways that make the recognition of just practices nontransitive. Pacifists can then go on to say that although earlier societies did not achieve the rejection of deadly force, theirs has. Their awareness of the injustice of killing, they now argue, is analogous to my understanding of slavery vis a vis the eighteenth-century slaver. However elaborate they become, the slave-trader's arguments will not prevail against my clarity of conscience. That I, had I lived in the eighteenth century, might not have been able to convince the slaver of the injustice of his livelihood is not an argument in favor of slavery; it merely points up the limits of the 18th century moral vocabulary.

On the surface this strategy seems promising, for it emphasizes the capacity of practical agents to acknowledge that norms of action are supplied by the community and sustained by tradition while still being open to self-critical scrutiny. It rejects unargued metaphysical warrants for practical action and insists on a minimal level of pluralistic tolerance based on a pragmatic fallibilism. The nondogmatic pacifist can maintain that a rejection of deadly force is truly consonant with justice while admitting that the conceptual situation may be such that other reasonable and upright agents cannot be brought to see this fact.

But closer scrutiny reveals more serious problems even when we reject the vocabulary of rights. Justice, I've argued, renders each his due. Specifying the demands of justice in particular cases requires knowledge of fact and a mature grasp of the relevant social practices, values, and virtues. I granted that the agent in times of crisis, or the investigator caught between two social worlds, might find herself unsure about how to respond to incommensurable virtues and values, although I insisted, agreeing with Aquinas, that she was finally answerable to her conscience, and that that might mean acting against the prevailing norms of the community in which she found herself. The one thing that ensured a measure of continuity between communities, however, was the consensus that persons of practical wisdom consider the practices, virtues, and values of their community conducive to an acceptable quality of life. It is this last requirement that, when pressed, leads the pacifist into difficulties. Return to the rapist and his intended victim. Imagine that she *is* my pacifist. Then part of what she believes is that the good life for humans is such that it incorporates a disposition to refrain from undertaking deadly force against anyone, even if that means forsaking goods to which she might otherwise be entitled. Note here that the entitlement is a positive and not a natural one. It requires no warrant beyond the presupposition that my pacifist holds a particular position within a community and that part and parcel of that is the positive right to withold sexual favors. In the example given, the good of choosing her sexual partners is being set aside in favor of the greater good of refusing to undertake deadly force. While this is understandable, it is scarcely a demand of right reason; rape is so heinous an attack that a forceful defense is more than reasonable, it is what we would advocate were the situation to permit it. But perhaps her community has come to see the injury of forced sex as minor, not much different from being cheated out of five dollars in three-card monte. This would require a major transformation of human values, but it is not inconceivable. It would imply a dramatic shift away from our community's concepts of love, marriage, personal integrity, and the unimpeded pursuit of our own ends; but for the moment let's grant the point. We would then find ourselves in the position of the anthropologist. This is a remarkable and intriguing society, no doubt, but hardly one whose practices we have good reason to embrace.

Suppose, though, that the injury were not rape but murder. Confronted with an impending murder my pacifist might, I suppose, maintain that her assailant is being driven by forces that have obscured the ability to see what justice demands. She might then be willing to die rather than undertake the injustice of killing, forsaking herself in favor of the deluded other. But now she comes upon an unfolding murder that involves not herself as victim, but some third party. Staying her hand would seem to favor the life of the murderer over that of her innocent compatriot. Why is such restraint due the one and intervention not hers to offer the other? Is the one life more worthy?

Here, the following strategy may present itself. Her community, she might say, is one for which the use of force is inconceivable. She and her fellows could not even consider such acts. But what is the strength of this "could not?" It might come to pass that the community of rational beings achieved a presently unimaginable habit of justice, bringing it about that none of its number ever overstepped the bounds of justice. It might further be the case that, in the evolution of science, therapies had been developed which made it possible to cure all physical and psychological pathologies (they might even be the same) which led to inflicting harm on one's fellows. We might imagine that such a thirst for justice developed that even in cases of accident or unforeseen conflict the overwhelming inclination of community members was to redress any injury, forstalling resentment and deprivation. With the passing of time it might come about that no one ever thought to assault anyone. But even here it is possible to *consider* resort to force in the abstract. It simply doesn't occur as a live option in deliberation. If the resort to force were strictly incapable of being conceived, then the community would have passed beyond justice. It would no longer be able to consider the concept of attack. When confronted by my so-called rapist, a member of this community would either have to view the experience as rather like being caught in a summer shower or like being somewhat too close to an erupting volcano. The one is a minor discomfort and the other likely to vaporize me, but only a crude anthropomorphism would see in either an attack. An attack, to fall under the scope of justice, requires an object of pursuit and the intent to injure that object. It is only by extension from the realm of human experience that we say that a virus "attacks" the DNA of healthy cells or that a swarm of bees "attacks" an intruder to the hive. A community that lacks the resources for such contemplation lacks the resources for formulating the concept of justice. It would also, of course, lack a great many other concepts, such as "rape." In a sense, members of this community would not be able to recognize my rapist as a person, for he would be undertaking acts that *people* just don't perform. It is not difficult to see that this community would lack most, if not all, the concepts we typically consider ethical; and we would soon begin to wonder, appearances notwithstanding, whether we were justified in calling it a human community. Narveson makes the point more polemically, writing that, were we to discover a society such as this, "we should have to conclude, I think, not that this was a community of saints, but rather that this community lacked the concept of justice— or perhaps that their nervous systems were oddly different from ours" (1965:75–76).

Still, we haven't exhausted the options for a coherent pacifism. Under what circumstances, to follow up Narveson's hint, might a community of saints be justified in adopting pacifism, and how should this be understood? In a deliberately provocative extention of the meaning of the term, John Howard Yoder has cataloged various of the ways that "pacifism" has been argued. I say provocative because his *Nevertheless: The Varieties and Shortcomings of Religious Pacifism* extends the scope of pacifism to include arguments from justice (chap. 2), political strategy (chaps. 4 and 5), and what he calls "Utopian Purism" (chap. 8), none of which would traditionally count as forms of pacifism. Nonetheless, Yoder's own position is the most subtle and far reaching of any contemporary pacifism.[2] As such, it offers the most interesting available response to Narveson's claim that "the pacifist's central position is untenable." First, however, a little history is in order.

Christian pacifism has rarely, if ever, viewed itself in terms that would satisfy Narveson's philosophical presuppositions. Early Christian rejection of military service and the tradition of martyrdom, as opposed to armed resistence, do not seem to have stemmed from a rejection of war or violence as contrary to the principles of justice. In his response to the pagan Celsus, for instance, Origen insists that Christians are not, as his adversary claimed, antisocial and unpatriotic; they are merely following the law laid down for them by their Lord. Unlike the Jews,

for whom it was lawful to take up arms in defence of their families and to serve in the wars, the lawgiver of the Christians...taught that it was never right for his disciples to go so far against a man, even if he should be very wicked; for he did not consider it compatible with his inspired legislation to allow the taking of human life in any form at all. (1953:132)

This passage testifies to several important aspects of the early Christian rejection of deadly force. Central to Origen's understanding is the particularism of law. Jesus's prohibition of killing applies only to Christians. God left the Jews free to protect their community, and there is no suggestion that this is improper. True, all people would be better off if they embraced Christianity, but until that happens all may legitimately exist together. Furthermore, the prohibition, as Origen understands it, does not represent a rejection of political community. He seems to take for granted that political community is a necessity and that wars will occur. In this, Origen does not differ from his pagan contemporaries. What restrains the Christian from killing is discipleship, a special vocation that is not different in kind from the exemption granted pagan priests (Origen 1953:509). Christian prayers, in fact, serve as a first line of defense against the demons of discord.

By and large it is the sense of vocation that animates the Christian refusal to serve, even after military service becomes common. Later, in an era when bishops were known to lead men into battle, the monastic orders persevered in their pacifism, but it was a militant pacifism. Orderic Vitalis, recommending the foundation of a monastery, advises an earl to "look carefully at the things which are provided for you by trained monks.... Strenuous is the warfare which these castellans of Christ wage against the Devil.... The cowled champions will resist Behemoth in constant warfare for your soul" (Southern 1970:225). All life is a struggle, and the invisible struggles are the most difficult. The monk eschews physical force because he is in training for a more profound battle, with more powerful tools, and cannot risk the diminution of his energy.

The rejection of killing takes on a more exclusivist complexion among the radical Reformers. The eponymous founder of the Mennonite tradition proclaimed an acceptance of any secular involvement a capitulation with the prince of darkness, whose servants "are born to torture and corruption, for their hearts, mouths, and hands drip and reek with blood" (Holmes 1975:189). Despite their differences, all these positions on killing reflect not a theory of justice so much as an interpretation of Christian vocation. Christians are called out of the world because it can no longer house them. It is ruled by a lord of vengeance and destruction, and if we attempt to match him at his own game we cannot avoid losing our souls. The only refuge is with Jesus, and those who do not hear are, finally, beyond our help.

A vocation, obviously, is a calling, but a calling of a rather special sort. The person called is enjoined to take on a particular task and bound to the faithful pursuit of that task even should it lead into difficulties or require forsaking other goods. A vocation, thus, differs from a principle or duty in two distinct ways. Narveson rightly notes that principles, and the duties they generate, hold generally, regardless of whether we believe ourselves bound by them. Thus, if there is a duty to respect parents it is binding on me regardless of my beliefs about, or attitudes toward, my parents. It is this understanding of principles that leads Narveson to write of the person who holds "that only he himself ought not to meet force with force, although it is quite all right for others to do so," that "we may continue to call him a 'pacifist,' in a somewhat attenuated sense, but he is then no longer holding pacifism as a *moral* principle or, indeed, as a principle at all" (1965:67). To talk about adopting something as a "principle for me" is to misunderstand the concept. Principles are norms of a practice, not of the participants.[3] Narveson is wrong, however, to move from the insight that pacifism cannot be a principle to the claim that the pacifist's rejection of violence "is essentially just a matter of taste" (1965:67). This reflects an all too common blunder not unlike that made in epistemology when the only alternative to foundationalism (be it positivist or Cartesian) is thought to be an inexplicable relativism. Consider a paradigm example of calling, that of Moses called to redeem the Israelites. "But they will never believe me or listen to me," Moses responds in an attempt to beg off. And when that doesn't work, he protests that "I have never been a man of ready speech, never in my life, not even now that thou hast spoken to me" (Exod. 4:1–11). Despite running counter to his own inclinations, Moses cannot avoid God's call. When finally he acquiesces, Moses acts as someone who has voluntarily, if reluctantly, undertaken a task that must be seen to its end. A vocation once acknowledged has perhaps a greater power over the individual than action from principle or virtue because it involves accepting a task as his own, in which his identity and merit are involved. Moses accepts responsibility for leading the Israelites. The bodhisattva, to take a non-Western example, forsakes entry into Nirvana in order to help all other sentient beings free themselves from the rounds of Karmic suffering. Evaluating an individual and her vocation involves a rather different procedure than that appropriate to an ethic of principles and duties. Even if there is no compelling duty, the bodhisattva chooses a worthy task, and by persevering in that task becomes an example of greatness that creates not an obligation but an option for human striving. Accepting the kingship, Oedipus takes on responsibilities most cannot bear, and when he is crushed it is genuinely tragic. Imagine that Moses had weaseled out. He might have lived a perfectly decent life herding sheep in Midian, but he would not have merited a special place in the sacred books of the Israelites.

A vocation, then, is felt by an individual to be personally binding, regardless of the position of others, and in this it differs from a principle or a virtue. By the same token a vocation requires the forsaking of genuine goods that remain available to others. A mafioso cannot, this side of farce, forsake the mob, although he can leave it, and risk the consequences. To forsake a particular goal, status, or enterprise is to acknowledge its legitimate claims and allures while nonetheless choosing to distance yourself, perhaps forever, from them. Familiar examples are not hard to find. How much did Schweitzer the scholar, musicologist, musician give up to work in Africa? To think that these other pursuits did not matter is to miss the impact of Schweitzer's choices.

When it comes to pacifism, at least three goods are being forsaken. Least of these is my person, but it is a good nonetheless. My ability to pursue reasonable ends without undue fear of attack is a presupposition of social life. Protecting myself from the occasional attack is a regretable eventuality, but in accord with reason should the attack be unwarranted. Who, after all, would it be more reasonable to protect? One answer, and a second good the pacifist wishes me to forsake, would be my family and friends. Unlike certain theorists of the natural law, I don't believe that individuals have functions by nature which impell them toward any particular form of sexual activity or which lead naturally to forming certain kinds of socially recognized bonds. This having been said, there are, nonetheless, goods of fellowship, child rearing, sexual satisfaction, and friendship that marriage and parenthood are well designed to serve. Not only this, but one of the best candidates for genuine moral progress in recent centuries is the changing status of relations in marriage. It is true that Aristotle maintained that "between man and wife friendship seems to exist by nature.... Human beings live together not only for the sake of reproduction but also for the various purposes of life.... they help each other by throwing their peculiar gifts into the common stock" (*Ethics*:1162a). Still, for the most part, this view of married virtue seems more a peripatetic ideal than a practical reality.[4] But relations between men and women, at least in much of the modern West, have reached a level at which it is at least possible to imagine friendships of genuine virtue arising between husband and wife. Marriage and parenthood are goods; the friendship that can emerge between family members is a good in which individuals acknowledge the intrinsic worthiness of others. Having entered into these relations and invested self and energy in fostering their attendant goods, I am henceforth disposed to maintain and protect them. That's part and parcel of achieving a lasting good. When my family is subjected to attack, the reasonable thing would be to protect it. Failure smacks of cowardice or indifference, and these are attributes of character that render me unworthy of the relationships themselves.

Pacifists, then, want me to forsake both the goods attendant on my person and the family that I love. They ask me to do this in the name of an abstraction, "human life," which I encounter only as embodied by individuals whom either I love, am indifferent to, or view as actively undertaking to injure those I love. Not only this, but the pacifist is asking me to draw no distinction between these classes. This seems to run contrary to right reason.

A striking aspect of John Yoder's pacifism is his willingness to embrace this conclusion. Sensitive as he is to the demands of consistency, Yoder does not attempt to argue that his Mennonite pacifism meets the demands of justice and right reason in anything like the common-sense meanings of the terms. Instead, he argues that Jesus initiated a revolution, Yoder's "original revolution," in which the participants acknowledge God's call by giving themselves over to His providential will. Part and parcel of this response is forsaking the traditional human ways of coping with an unjust political order. Rather than attempting to impose order and justice on the social world, Jesus called His followers to leave that world and enter another:

He gave them a new way to deal with offenders—by forgiving them. He gave them a new way to deal with violence—by suffering. He gave them a new way to deal with money—by sharing it. . . . He gave them a new way to deal with a corrupt society—by building a new order, not smashing the old. (Yoder 1977:29)

To say, however, that Jesus invites his followers to form a new community is scarcely the end of the matter. We need to investigate the nature of this community and the structure of the vocation to which its members are called. For the sake of clarity, we can divide this into three related questions: What, morally speaking, is the nature of this community; in what ways can that community effect the political life of the society it rejects; and what is the relation of the pacifist community to those communities or individuals who at least profess a desire for justice?

To answer these questions means introducing a new and unfamiliar vocabulary. Central to the very idea of Christian pacifism, as Yoder understands it, is an eschatological perspective. To be a Christian is to proclaim that Jesus is the Christ and that Christ is Lord of creation. To acknowledge that Christ is Lord is to admit that human life can only be understood in terms of the Lord's intentions for creation, and in Yoder's reading of the gospel message this means perceiving Jesus's activity for the world as pervaded by *agape*. Christ's *agape* is non-resistent, seeking neither justice nor results, but reveals itself instead "in the uncomplaining and forgiving death of the innocent at the hands of the guilty" (1977:56). Individuals responding to the call of Jesus take upon themselves the burden of forgiving the guilty, even when what is attacked is what they most love. True, there is the promise of eternal life, but, as Yoder notes, "before the resurrection there was the cross, and the Christian must follow his Master in suffering for the sake of love" (1977:57). Jesus displayed, in willingly accepting the cross, the nature and depth of his love, and from this love he issues his call to repentence. The would-be disciple must repent the sins of the past and prepare for the Kingdom (1977:37–38). Accepting this message is primary, and it is a message that refuses to be judged by the standards of the world; the old standards no longer apply.

It should be clear that Jesus, as Yoder interprets him, advocates pacifism neither as a strategic means to an end nor as obedience to principle. Yoder takes great care "to combat one of the most widespread interpretations of the contemporary pacifist commitment," namely, that it is "a logical, deductive, impersonal kind of legalism taking certain biblical texts or certain ethical principles with utmost rigor, without asking whether it be possible or not to live up to such demanding ideals" (1977:34). The world is not made just in Christ's crucifixion; it goes on pretty much the same as always. Nonetheless, the Christian is called to persist in love, even when it is rejected. This is a pacifism, in other words, based not on principle but on the desire to live in a way that reflects the life of the master, regardless of any practical achievements in the world. In any case, only an ethics wedded overmuch to Kantian universalism would be tempted to deny that Yoder's is a compelling moral vision.

To undertake discipleship means to live in a way that reflects Christ's lordship and to rejoice in Christ as Lord (Yoder 1977:39). Honesty requires that entry into this way of life be voluntary. This requires reflection on and interpretation of Jesus' career, as opposed to mindless emulation; but central to that career is the belief that God's will does not go unfulfilled. True disciples, in fact, have undergone a transformation at Jesus's hand, a healing that enables them to fit, to be "at home" in God's kingdom (1977:40). When they feel at home they find rules and rewards irrelevant. Having been healed of the ills of the world they strive to resemble God in the character of their love (1977:47). Part of this means rejecting preference and calculation and striving to love the other person, even should he be her enemy.

This is indeed, as Yoder insists, "an ethic of excess" (1977:49), but it is one to which the Christian is now disposed as a matter of character. In confronting a situation, disciples of Jesus do not ask what principles of Christian morality apply or what duties they are called to perform, but rather how to "reach beyond available models and options to do a new thing whose very newness will be a witness to divine presence" (1977:49). Or, as Yoder pithily puts it: "We do not, ultimately, love our neighbor because Jesus told us to. We love our neighbor because God is like that" (1977:51).

The vocabulary of this new community, then, rests heavily on such terms as "repentence," "discipleship," and "love." But how do these concepts come together in social action? Answering this question requires the addition of a third vocabulary entry: "Witness." Members of the new community seek to perform acts that "witness to divine presence," and it behooves us to recall the Greek background in the term "martyr." To be a martyr is to witness, in the most active fashion, to the consequences of belief. The martyr testifies to the transforming power of God; and given the historical resonances of martyrdom and persecution in the Christian tradition, the concept of "witness" establishes the central connection in Yoder's pacifism between putting forward the evidence of Jesus's healing activity and accepting the unjust suffering imposed upon the disciple by an unbelieving world.

To make sense of her actions, the witness must take an eschatological perspective on the world. This perspective must be a minority one, and the consequences of its being true must be sufficiently profound to bring its adherents into conflict with the majority. If the likelihood of the minority belief being true is unimpressive or if the consequences are comparatively unimportant, then witnessing in a manner approaching martyrdom is remote. Here I'm not making a sociological prediction about the likelihood of believers dying for their beliefs. Suppose that, proclaiming their position at the local airport, the Christians sufficiently aggravated travelers to the point that irrate fliers started shooting them in order to proceed unmolested to the shuttle. This would be an aberrant form of martyrdom, for the commuters are indifferent to the beliefs involved; they just don't want to be bothered. What makes it possible for Christian pacifists to be martyrs is that the majority culture takes seriously the import of their belief, rejects it, and expresses a willingness to impose some form of sanction or injury on them as a consequence of continuing to maintain the belief.[5]

Yoder's Christian is a "pacifist" not by design but by default. Were the majority, and hence the political organization that represents the majority, to acknowledge the lordship of Jesus and to reject recourse to violence in favor of Christlike *agape*, then there would be no special vocation for the disciples to adopt. There would equally be no special witness for them to make. For should everyone adopt the Christian perspective on history there would exist a consensus that all things serve God and that, appearances to the contrary, the Lamb did indeed triumph in the Cross (1977:58–61). Under those conditions the state would not be demonic and thus not be a power over and against which Christians needed to affirm the *agape* of Jesus.

It takes no particular historical knowledge or sociological acumen, however, to recognize that such is not the case. If Jesus is who Yoder says he is and if his will is even remotely like Yoder suggests it is, then the state remains a power to which the disciple of Jesus must remain opposed. This is not the place to assess the quality of Yoder's biblical exegesis or the details of his account of the falling away of the church from Jesus's original revolutionary vision.[6] Nonetheless, it is important to sketch the steps of "demonization," if only because they come to represent the paradigm form of temptation for those who lose sight of the revolutionary nature of Jesus's message.

When, for reasons of history and social affiliation, the Roman Empire gave up its persecution of the Christians and when the Christian community came to incorporate within its ranks members of the political and intellectual elite, it became natural, as Yoder sees it, that "the next step in the union of church and world was the conscious abandon of eschatology" (1977:66). It is a virtue of Yoder's analysis that he can present this move toward "disavowal and apostasy" (1984:144) as undertaken by Christians of good faith, such as Augustine. Transformations in ecclesiology, social expectation, and even metaphysics (cf. 1984:136–44) need not be seen as the machinations of demagogues and heresiarchs, but may be accounted for in social and historical terms sufficient to explain how such changes, when noticed at all, could be viewed as the natural consequences "of time and organic development" (1984:144). Augustine, on this account, can be absolutely clear on the pervasiveness of sin and still see the Roman Empire as providentially ordained. If Augustine's thought constitutes a watershed, and later a fountainhead, for interpretations and movements contrary, as Yoder would have it, to the original Gospel message, it is not because the saint fails to recognize sinfulness, but that "he seriously overestimated the adequacy of the available institutional and sacramental means for overcoming it" (1977:66). Fourth-century Christians were no less men and women of their time, and their interpretations of their Christian commitment were no less dependent on the new and inherited forces that made their interpretations possible. This doesn't mean, however, that those interpretations are sound or that later generations must remain uncritically bound to them. If Yoder is correct, the heirs of the fourth century remain trapped in the "Constantinian" understanding of political life precisely because of the deforming powers of that interpretation.

Once the original eschatological vision is given up, what replaces it for the Christian community and what are the components of "Constantinianism"? First, no longer at odds with the state, the church loses the impetus to speak out against it. The church can even endorse the basic premises of political activity as part of God's providential order. As the relation between the church and the state changes so does that between the individual believer and the demands of the state. "After Constantine," Yoder writes, "not only is the ruler the bearer of history; the nonsovereign ethical agent has changed as well" (1984:139). The simple believer is called merely to do his or her duty and abide in the established practices of the church. In these changed circumstances the Christian finds it less immediately necessary, and then less plausible, to "witness." A new question, "What if everyone did that?" begins to intervene in deliberations, which "would have been preposterous in the early church and remains ludicrous wherever committed Christians accept realistically their minority status" (1984:139). Since the church has identified itself with the political order, the sort of witnessing envisioned no longer operates. It becomes, instead, "sectarianism." Christianity has ceased to be a vocation.

If pacifism as a vocation is no longer operative, Christians will need an alternative way of interpreting their role in political society. But however well-intentioned such alternatives might be, forces of sin work from the very beginning to undermine their efforts. As soon as the Christian community gives up its minority status, the state loses a powerful voice of criticism, which had previously acted as a check against easy self-justification by the political authorities. Given the pervasiveness of sin in the structures of human society, the state reinterprets the Christian message as endorsing its political agenda. The church, in its turn, risks being coopted into the establishment. Rather than testing the state, there is pressure toward first condoning and then advocating force in God's name. The consequences are first the rise of the crusader mentality and ultimately "a purely pagan view of God as a tribal deity" (Yoder 1977:71), represented on the field of battle by the armies of Christian Rome, for whom the church, as a matter of civic duty, provides a chaplain (1977:113–15). The mission of the Christian community becomes in this moment the mission of the state, be it Constantine's Rome or Reagan's America.[7] The church, in other words, has given up its minority status and in so doing directs itself to establishing an ecumenical and natural theology that makes evident the work of the state as God's work, carrying out a providentially appointed task. Once this transformation has taken place, Yoder suggests, the conviction of our own mission, as bearers of the burden of righteousness in history, becomes so pervasive that "the imperative itself 'Thou shalt make history come out right,' is so deeply founded in our culture that we cannot even perceive that it might be in need of verification" (1977:133). At this moment, both state and church become demonic because both are now bent on replacing God's will in history with their own.

Yoder maintains that a pervasive will to power continuously reasserts itself, in the state and in the individual (1977:135). Did Paul not write: "concerning the principalities and powers, those structures of the present world order in whose autonomy mankind has become enslaved" (1977:140)? In saying that we have been freed from bondage to these powers, the apostle implies that the followers of Christ are "freed from the temptation to sanctify the power structures" (1977:141). But since those powers continue, for the time being, to rule this world, the Christian must give up the quest for efficacy in history—that, after all, is God's business—and accept once again the minority function of witnessing, even to the point of martyrdom, to the original revolution in which humanity is called to acknowledge the absolute lordship of Christ (1977:175).

Yoder's biblical exegesis and his reading of Christian history may be contested, but they are not implausible nor without justification in the central texts of the tradition. Exactly how to go about shaping a life on the basis of this vocation is, of course, susceptible to various interpretations, but the particulars of the witnessing community are not the concern of this essay. Yoder himself clearly thinks that those possibilities are given the community by the contingencies of history, which are themselves shaped by the time and place in which people hear Christ's call. But he insists that the contingencies may be distinguished from the communal response to the essentials of Christ's message.

First and foremost, the community forsakes the person of the other. Despite the love that the disciple has for her fellow citizen she will not come to his aid with the offer of protective force. This is to forsake justice, and Yoder properly terms it the "scandal of the Cross." My family and friends do not, contrary to common sense, have a privileged status that should, morally speaking, incline me to protect them against injustice. Nor will I press the just attack against the aggressor, regardless of the scope of his depravity. Despite my love for family and friends and despite my reverence for justice, I do not merely avoid, indeed I actively refuse, to accept political responsibility for preventing evil. In short, when it comes to engaging political force against injustice, I deny that "letting evil happen is as blameworthy as committing it" (Yoder 1977:81). To be faithful to my vocation I must admit no exceptions, for God's claim on me, as on all of creation, is absolute and overriding.

These are harsh demands, but they must be met by the aspirant to pacifism as a vocation. And such pacifism is, unlike that criticized by Narveson, an intelligible stance to take in pursuit of human good. First, on the persuasive side of the issue, Yoder's pacifism of vocation is founded on divine revelation. God himself has, in the eyes of the believer, displayed His will for humanity and called people to acknowledge and faithfully to attempt to do His will. Not only this, but the Gospel in which this revelation is embedded tells the story of a loving God, a God, in fact, whose love is so unfathomably great that having taken on human nature He sacrificed himself for humanity. Here,

Yoder can explicate his point effectively through analyzing the Gospel narrative, for in the crucifixion the disciples of Jesus themselves lose heart and even Peter cannot sustain faithfulness. It appears as though at the moment of expected triumph all hope perishes, much as it must have seemed to Abraham, called to sacrifice his son. The question becomes, as Yoder puts it, "'Can I obey God when He seems to be willing to jeopardize His own purposes?' The answer, 'God will provide,' is thus a reassurance not of our own survival or comfort, but of the rationality of obedience which seems to jeopardize God's own purposes" (1977:96). God is loving beyond what human beings could reasonably hope and, even when submitting to God's will, seems contrary to love and right reason, He nonetheless provides. What better grounds could be asked for my persistence in faithfully doing His will? As pacifist I do not paradoxically claim that I have discovered a principle which demands that I act contrary to a well-established principle, but that I have discovered a power for good which can achieve ends I could never have imagined and which is willing to welcome me among the flock if only I will serve in strict obedience to divine will. Once I am convinced of the will of a benevolent deity, it is hard to imagine what further requirements I might have for acting in accord with that will.[8]

Nevertheless, to the extent that discipleship rests on faith, it seems not just to supplement what can be discovered by any reasonably intelligent person but to go beyond what the consensus of the community maintains about the way the world is. Here the Christian risks falling into a trap in many ways analogous to the pacifist caught up in the language of rights. It is true that Yoder's disciple is the member of an embattled minority and that this group proclaims foolishness to the larger world, but he need not admit that "that wider society is itself the universe, or that its ways of testing validity beyond the provincial have succeeded, by dint of a harder and more thorough hauling away at one's own definitional bootstraps, in transcending particularity" (Yoder 1984:49). If believers allow themselves to be saddled with secular standards of believability, by which religious belief is presumed incredible unless it meets conditions to which the secular culture never holds its own analogous beliefs, then they will always be found wanting. But why do this? (Cf. Wolterstorff 1976.) Outside the limited arena of technological proficiency, the establishment vocabulary can make no claims to universality or *a priori* justification. Just the opposite. The inflated claims for "scientific method" have not shown themselves resilient to criticism. The various reductive "isms" have all been

found to have feet of clay or to fail to address the real issues motiva-
ting religious life and thought. When placed within the context of its
historical particularity and the tradition through which it develops,
Christian belief is a rival to, not a subordinate of, economics or biology
in its account of "wholeness, coherence, happiness [and] self-fulfill-
ment" in human life. If it is currently a minority position, that need
not be the result of any incoherence; it may as easily be that the failure
to believe on the part of the majority reflects their own waywardness
and desire to serve their own inclinations rather than God's will. That,
at least, is how the Christian story interprets the situation. And while
granting that there is room for honest dispute, the Christian tradition
is under no obligation of reason to proclaim itself "a hypothesis needing to verify itself by someone else's standards" (Yoder 1984:58).

Yoder concludes that the "real issue is not whether Jesus can make
sense in a world far from Galilee, but whether . . . we want to follow
him" (1984:62). The aim of this chapter has not been to advocate following Jesus, though even in dissent I believe that doing so is a live option in William James's sense of the term.[9] As long as Christian belief
remains a live option, the burden of proof in contests of rationality
will lie with the nonbeliever and it is one I do not wish to pick up. My
goal has been to show that the only morally acceptable form of pacifism, properly so called, is pacifism as a vocation. Pacifism as a strategy
rises and falls with the likelihood of success, like any other means to an
end. Pacifism as a principle cannot be made coherent; Narveson is
right about this. But if ethics is about living that life which is best for
people, it remains a possibility that God will call and that people will
listen to that call. If it is God's voice, they would be foolish to ignore it.
Nonetheless, pacifists should not be allowed to forget the enormity of
what they forsake in heeding that summons. In renouncing any recourse to killing they willingly forsake their physical selves, their families, and their friends. They abandon as well their moral selves to the
extent that they will not raise their hands against rape, slavery, torture, and oppression. Thus, pacifism represents, from any view other
than the disciples', the forsaking of justice and all that implies. This
Yoder rightly acknowledges as scandal. To ignore the ties of family
and community goes beyond any particular act of wickedness, for it
turns its back on the very relationships that constitute and sustain any
human community. This is the worst of scandals, only tolerable so
long as it can be viewed as a genuine response to a good even more
worthy than the justice of human community. The only good that

presents a plausible claim to such transcendence must be divine. Yoder must couch his pacifism in the larger picture of disciples following a god who not only comes among them in human form but also sacrifices himself on the cross out of love. The disciples of *this* god act as they do in acknowledgement of that sacrificial love which alone makes it conceivable that they should give up what they do. The Gospel narrative and Yoder's way of reading that narrative are indispensible to the moral integrity of discipleship, and they must, to sustain that integrity, be true in all essentials. Pacifism as a vocation stands or falls with belief in Jesus and the substantive historical truth of something very like Yoder's interpretation of that truth. In the absence of a story about human relations to the divine that provides a context for such renunciation, pacifism itself is a source of pollution altogether on a par with the crimes of Oedipus.[10]

Notes

1. The limits of such distinctions as "natural/supernatural" and such analogues as "moral/physical" are familiar to anyone who has spent much time reading non-European, or premodern European materials. Mary Douglas's classic *Purity and Danger* sheds much light on the complex ways in which peoples understand their worlds and the interrelations between practical reasoning, self-perception, and cosmic order. Jeffrey Stout has employed Douglas's work to illuminate ethical debate in "Moral Abominations," reprinted in Stout (1988) as chapter 7.

2. While I don't intend to justify focusing exclusively on the pacifism of John Yoder, some explanation is in order. It is not, I hope, Western parochialism that leads me to center on the Christian tradition. The superficially obvious alternatives of Gandhian nonviolence and the Buddhist tradition must be approached with caution. Gandhi's movement is idiosyncratic within the Hindu tradition, although it has garnered many Western adherents. Within the context of the present discussion, Gandhi's strategy of nonviolent resistance is just that, a strategy, and lacks a grounding in any independent reason for judging resort to deadly force reprehensible. The doctrine of the *Bhagavad Gita* is more representative of the Hindu mainstream. The Buddhist doctrine of *ahimsa*, or "no-injury" is bound closely both to the various theories of Karma and causality and to the ideal of the bodhisattva as striving for the release of individuals from the cycles of suffering. Both lack the standard Western association of pacifism with the rejection of war in principle. Yoder himself restates most of the classic Christian alternatives and it would be to no

point for me to repeat them. To the best of my knowledge, pacifism has been a fleeting flirtation for Judaism and Islam, when it has surfaced at all.

3. I should note that the same would hold for virtues as excellences of a practice. Participants either achieve or fall short of virtues in much the same way that they abide by, or fail to act in accord with, the principles of a given activity. Nonetheless, there are many things about the ethics of principles, rights, and duties that don't sit well with the ethics of virtue. Some of these problems will occupy us in chapter 4.

4. The history of marriage provides a particularly instructive introduction to the concept of progress in ethics. Brooke (1988) presents an overview of the changing concept in the Middle Ages. Much fascinating information and analysis on marriage is to be found in the volumes of *A History of Private Life*. The discussions by Paul Veyne and Peter Brown in Veyne (1987) are extremely interesting. Marriage from antiquity to the recent past was more often than not a matter of establishing alliances, concluding financial transactions, and ensuring the continued exercise of power through wealth passed down to progeny. The interaction of powerful characters that engenders affection and self-knowledge between Jane Austen's Emma and Knightley would have been uncommon to the point of unbelievability for much of history. More indicative of the status of marriage is Duby's account of the ways in which women were promised, taken back, and reallotted among the barony of medieval England. (Cf. Duby 1985:118–37.) Many recent studies of women and the family in Islam provide an illuminating comparison. Of contemporary writers on marriage and the family, Stanley Hauerwas seems to me consistently the most rewarding.

5. It is this, more than the absence of any prior pacifist tradition, that would have made Jewish pacifists anomalous martyrs in the context of the holocaust. The intention to commit genocide, as opposed to "religiocide," renders pacifism pointless. Hitler's final solution was directed at race and consequently indifferent to principle, virtue, or vocation. For their pacifism to be meaningful, paradoxically, Jewish pacifists would have had to take extraordinary steps to flee the holocaust.

6. The primary source for Yoder's interpretation of Jesus is his 1972 work. Several of Yoder's historical essays on the transformation of the tradition and its relation to the radical reformation are reprinted in his 1984 work. See especially part 2, "History." The notes contain a useful bibiliography.

7. Yoder's remarks on America as a surrogate church (1977:119) are even more apposite to the 1980s perhaps than they were to the late 1960s and 1970s.

8. Implicit in these remarks is a rejection of most variations of the "Euthyphro dilemma." If you have been apprised of the will of God and if this god is not nasty, capricious, or demonic in its behavior, then it is no more reasonable to question its authority than it is for a child to question the authority of a parent who has proved to be faithful and caring. On this point see Peter Geach (1969). Robert Adams (1987) has incorporated the nature of God into his attempt to elaborate a divine-command theory of moral action. For some problems with Adams's account of the status of moral terms vis a vis revelation, see my 1983 article.

9. See William James, "The Will to Believe" in his 1896 work.

10. This extreme way of putting the point can only be true if the Gospel narrative is false, and can only be false if it is true. For the nonbeliever, or for the Christian who does not endorse Yoder's reading, pacifism cannot become a genuine option without some sort of conversion. The theological presuppositions are that important. Consequently, it will always skew the discussion to attempt an analysis of pacifism cut off from analysis of Christian vocation in general. There seems to me no better contemporary argument for this view than that of Paul Ramsey and Stanley Hauerwas in *Speak Up for Just War or Pacifism*. It's unfortunate that failure to come to grips with the theological sources of Yoder's pacifism vitiates Ramsey's discussion (pp. 96–113). There is need for a more comprehensive account of Yoder's pacifism and its relations to his theology, hermeneutics, and social ethics as a whole. Despite refusing to participate in the political structures of the wider world, Christian love remains operative and directed toward that world. Furthermore, the good will directed toward the world continues to be formed by God's will. Thus, it is not enough to live as the Messianic community in moral isolation from others, although, as a matter of discipline, physical removal may be prudent. If Yoder's reading of the Gospel narrative is sound, then that community is obliged to witness to the world and to lead it to acknowledge God's sovereignty. Only in this larger context, for example, is it possible to understand how Yoder can speak against pacifism as strategy or principle in *The Original Revolution* while giving it a qualified endorsement in *Nevertheless*. The argumentative strategy of the latter volume is to present the pro's and con's of various ways of limiting war with an eye to undermining simplistic distinctions between pacifism and its rivals. This is a strategy dictated by Christian love because it paves the way for at least a gradual approach to God through approximating the kind of community He desires for humanity. If the Gospel narrative were not true then the varieties of pacifism beyond that of "the honest study of cases" would be no more than strategies for securing justice and would have to be judged in that light. (Cf. *Nevertheless*, chapter 2.) From the Gospel perspective, the just war tradition is, however, a strategy for containing human sinfulness, and this the pacifist of vocation desires as part of Jesus' love even when he does not believe that he is capable of achieving it himself. It is this position that informs Yoder's critique of current just war thinking in *When War is Unjust*, and thus ties the three volumes together. In general, there is a remarkable coherence to all of Yoder's work and a full analysis of it would repay the effort manyfold. James Gustafson, in *Ethics from a Theocentric Perspective*, and Thomas Ogletree, in *The Use of the Bible in Christian Ethics*, have already begun to recognize the power of Yoder's position, although as a worrisome rival to their own. Stanley Hauerwas has gone further than anyone in absorbing and expanding on the implications of Yoder's thought, not only in his writings on war, gathered in his *Against the Nations*, but also in *The Peaceable Kingdom*.

3.

Natural Law and the Credibility of the Just War Tradition

Those who do not hear, or cannot follow, Yoder's Lord must look elsewhere for an understanding of war in human society. When we come, however regretfully, to realize that we cannot sustain a secular pacifism as part of our character and self-understanding, the natural place to look is in the direction of the just war tradition. But in turning to the just war tradition, we confront rather different questions than we do in looking at pacifism. We will only briefly be occupied with whether the tradition can, in theory, meet the conditions of justice. Instead, we will have to ask whether those who undertake to uphold the tradition carry out their task rigorously or whether they allow the requirements of justice to be modified and diluted by the pressures facing them in the contemporary situation. If it turns out that justice is no longer being served by the principal upholders of the tradition, then we will have to look still further afield to see whether it can be sustained at all.

I sketched a bit of the background to the just war tradition in chapter 1, without going into the details of what have come to be called the "just war criteria." Thus, it is important here to lay out those criteria and get a sense of how they function in practical reasoning about justice in war. As generally interpreted there are two distinct sorts of criteria generated by the tradition: those dealing with the justice of going to war—*ius ad bellum*—and those that must be satisfied in the prosecution of war—*ius in bello*. The particular list differs from writer to writer, but the following minimal list is common to all. Although I have drawn the following criteria from various sources, the justifications I'll provide are those I take to be consistent with, if not directly derived from, Aristotle and Thomas Aquinas:[1]

Ius ad bellum
  1. Proper Authority
  2. Just Cause

53

3. Just Intent
4. Last Resort
5. Reasonable Hope of Success

Ius in bello

1. Discrimination
2. Proportion

Despite the often convoluted discussions these criteria receive, their propriety is uncommonly clear. War is an organized, communal action and, as such, can only be undertaken on the authority of the community. Justice makes no distinction as to how the community is constituted or where the authority lies, but unless those authorities undertake the war in their capacity as public officials, under constraints recognized by the community, the action is illicit. Private individuals may feud, wreak vengence on each other, and undertake vigilantism, but none of these is war, and they are all contrary to justice and the common good. Some qualifications may have to be made later, in discussing revolution, but the fundamental point stands.

As a condition for acting justly, just cause is self-evident. To act without it manifests indifference to justice. Intent is somewhat more complicated, for it plays a dual role. On the one hand, it describes the relation of the agent to justice in the sense that the desire to secure and protect the good fairly, with an eye to the general betterment of the community, must be characteristic of the agent, and from the outset. On the other, the agent can be generally just in his intent without being clear about where justice lies in the prosecution of a war. Thus, there is a second sense in which just intent is secured by the reflectively held disposition to abide by the just war criteria considered collectively. To put it another way, in keeping with the vocabulary of chapter 1, the criteria emerge as the requirements of fairness in resorting to and prosecuting a war and a failure at any point renders the entire effort defective. Last resort and reasonable hope are in this sense subordinate to just intent. Should we undertake war as anything other than a last resort, doubt would be cast on our motives. Are we merely looking for an excuse? Do we secretly hope to gain some further advantage? Are we willing to use war, with all its risks and losses, for something less than a just cause? Much the same holds, in reverse, for reasonable hope. Does a hopeless war make sense? Can we rationally throw away our own lives and those of others without believing a commensurate good can be achieved? None of these possibilities is consonant with right reason and the just person will reject them all.

The *in bello* conditions are also clear requirements of justice. Failure to distinguish those who are subject to attack from those who are not amounts to willingness to injure whomever in pursuing your ends, and that is the opposite of justice. If war is to be just, it must be the organized attack of one public body on another, with the instruments recognized as appropriate. Anything else is difficult to square with the conditions for public life. Here I mean something fairly specific. Wars are assaults of one community on another, and just wars are those undertaken to preserve the integrity of a community and intercommunal relations. When I prosecute a war, it is because I, in my public capacity, have received some injury which I deem unwarranted and which is sufficiently grave that it needs redress. My intent is to secure that redress; otherwise, our ability to function as independent and integral communities, seeking the good in public intercourse, will be jeopardized. I have, if my war is just, made all reasonable efforts short of bellicose acts to get you to redress the grievance of your own accord and, having failed, I decide to take more severe measures. But even here my argument is with your state, not with any private persons. They may, in their private capacity, be as malicious as you like, even depraved, but their private lives are of no communal interest to me. The state has offended against justice, and my actions are directed against the offender. If you resist with an army, then I will attack that army as an instrument of your community, and this means attacking the soldiers as soldiers, not as Fred, Frieda, and Robin. If and when they cease being soldiers, they cease being objects of legitimate attack. They lose their public status. This is not to say that there are no borderline cases, there are. Nonetheless, as John Ford wrote many years ago, the burden of proof falls on "those who want to increase the number of combatants, and include large numbers, even the 'vast majority,' of the civilian population" (Ford 1944:20). Some occupations, even when they are crucial to my enemy's efforts, may prove immune from just attack. But soldiering is not one of them. I can directly attack soldiers, but I *must* discriminate them from civilians.

Even a discriminate attack is not perfect, though; we cannot require both justice and perfection. Thus, my discriminate attacks must be weighed against the evil that will result, the unintended loss of life and livelihood that may attend even the best executed actions. I have, then, the burden of ensuring not only that my actions are necessary to securing justice but also that the good achieved is not outweighed by the attendant misery and loss. Even in otherwise just actions, proportion must be observed. It is important to keep in mind, however, Aristotle's remarks about the mean. "A master of any art," the Philosopher writes, "avoids excess and defect, but seeks the intermediate and chooses this" (*Ethics*:1106b). By "intermediate" he does not mean an average. The mean is that path which best avoids defect, and this requires being accomplished in a practice as well as being able to situate that practice relative to our other activities. There is no simple calculation that can determine what miseries are acceptable in the pursuit of which goods. As with all practical action, prudence must be fully operative, discerning what is and what needs to be done. Thus, determining whether the good to be achieved is proportionately greater than the damage being risked can never be a matter for technicians, but must, as with all the just war criteria, be undertaken by agents fully grounded in the virtues.

The above criteria, as conditions for justice, are individually necessary and only conjointly sufficient to secure a just war. They are like dominoes; when one falls they all go down. Failure to observe proportionality *in bello* registers indifference to discrimination, which calls into question your intent. This, in turn, introduces some question as to cause: is the injury merely an excuse for doing what you wanted but could not justify? Should this be the case, a possibility explored in chapter 6, the authority for acting would lose its legitimacy. Individuals pursuing justice will find each successive criterion a barrier to action, and must seek to satisfy their consciences before continuing. This holds even of soldiers. While I must view them as the instrument of my adversary, they cannot pretend to be automatons. Their actions remain voluntary and their conscience can no more be forsaken than their sight.

Here, I come up against a powerful objection, captured in large part by Martin Luther's injunction "not to weaken certain obedience for the sake of an uncertain justice" (Holmes 1975:159). Soldiers have, inescapably, a dual aspect, at once as members of the military machine and as individual practical agents, responsible for the consequences of their acts. The two must be balanced somehow if reasonable and conscientious policies are to be implemented. Military efficiency requires that the individual components be welded together as a coherent unit, and if individual conscience allows itself whatever freedom it deems necessary to satisfying the demands of conscience, we risk erecting an insurmountable barrier to corporate action. All things being equal, we should welcome serious reflection on action by the members of our community—it could only make us better—but our ability to tolerate individual reflection is inversely porportional to the gravity of the situation and the immediate need for action. So the uncertain conscience of the individual soldier must be subordinated to the coherent action of the military if we are to defend the common good, and since that's the only good and just reason for taking military action, justice would seem to require that the conscience of the soldier be in certain ways constrained by the demands of military discipline.[2]

It is important, of course, to be clear on the nature of this constraint. The person committed to justice, when he becomes part of the military, does not give up the pursuit of justice. It should, rather, be the other way around. He gives up the independent exercise of conscience *because* that is necessary for the pursuit of justice. Thus, it remains an act of virtue to the extent that he knows and retains control over the act. He must, in conscience, believe that those who direct the military and those who plan the strategies can take over while his conscience is constrained. He should have a reasonable certainty that his leaders will act in ways and for purposes that he could condone, were his energies not engaged elsewhere. Thus, soldiers are dependent upon the consciences of their superiors, both military and political, and it must be part and parcel of the just war tradition to insure that those consciences are well grounded in justice and disposed to act accordingly.

It is precisely at this point that John Yoder has recently challenged the health of the tradition. Regardless of their formal adequacy, he has argued, historical precedent and moral predispositions of contemporary society have rendered the just war criteria inoperative. Yoder goes further still and suggests that in its current state the remnants of the tradition actually constitute a barrier to thinking honestly about justice in war. The continued invocation of the just war criteria leads us to believe "that there is no *carte blanche*; there are some things one would never do, even for a just cause. But then when we ask about the firmness with which the criteria apply, we discover that they keep sliding farther down the scale" (1984:70). He concludes that the tradition currently finds itself on a slippery slope, where even the pretense of justice will soon become impossible.

This argument is part of Yoder's strategy of demonstrating the limits of human justice in general, thereby displaying even more clearly the necessity for joining with Jesus in accepting the providential rule of God. But that is not a criticism of the analysis itself. The just war criteria come to life only when applied, and their application takes place in a concrete historical context. They are intended to ensure that a particular kind of political activity is carried out fairly, so that those who win are entitled to the goods thereby secured and that those who lose retain their place within the larger social and political environment. Contemporary political alignments are complicated by ideological as well as technological situations that, as Yoder rightly notes, tempt adversaries into dehumanizing their antagonists and using this as an excuse for behavior we would condemn among ourselves. Examples of such political rhetoric are legion. E. H. Gombrich provides a particularly insightful introduction by way of "The Cartoonist's Armoury" (Gombrich 1963), but examples, from the "godless empire" to "the great Satan," abound in the daily newspapers. Nonetheless, any attempt at removing the antagonist in principle from membership in political society is dangerously self-deceptive. Few, if any, of the most notorious of modern tyrants can properly be called mad. The more we discover about their motives and goals, the more their vicious brutality becomes explicable, albeit no less horrifying. John Keegan's rich and troubling chapter on Hitler, particularly when read as a contrast to his other subjects, is a model essay on the limits of the pathological (Keegan 1987). And surely the officers under the tyrant and the soldiers under them cannot plausibly be brought under the general umbrella of the inhuman. A political order in turmoil remains an arena of human contests. It is precisely these contests that called forth and fostered the just war tradition.

The task, then, is to see whether current advocates of the tradition put forward analyses and suggestions capable of providing practical guidance for makers of policy and at the same time securing justice for all parties, friend and foe. As a practical approach it will be convenient to focus on a single issue, nuclear deterrence, and specifically on the debate over deterrence as it has taken shape in the Anglo-American religious community. In contemporary discussions of war, the intersection of politics and morality is nowhere more evident than in the analysis and justification of nuclear deterrence. Since the advent of the nuclear age, politicians and citizens alike have been buffeted by the frequently conflicting claims of strategists and moralists. Critics from the natural-law tradition have provided far and away the most coherent voice for justice throughout the period. To follow the debate through that tradition will both clarify the ways in which just war criteria may be brought to bear on practical political questions. It will also bring out the limits of and prospects for that tradition. In trying to meet the responsibilities of pastoral guidance, Catholic and Protestant moralists have subjected themselves, often courageously, to precisely the tensions, pressures, and temptations that threaten the integrity of the just war tradition.[3]

There is, however, a preliminary issue to be addressed. Although the natural law tradition, which will figure prominently in the discussion, is most often identified with Catholic moral teaching, it applies in principle not only to Catholics but also to all rational animals. It is simply the Catholic tradition in moral theology that has most insistently advanced natural-law analyses. This is a point frequently misunderstood, by non-Catholics and Catholics alike. Mario Cuomo, to take a particularly visible example, gives voice to several popularly held misconceptions, remarking that

surely I can, if so inclined, demand some kind of law against abortion. But should I? Is it helpful? Is it essential to human dignity? Does it promote harmony and understanding? Does it divide us so fundamentally that it threatens our ability to function as a pluralistic community? When should I argue to make my religious value your morality, my rule of conduct your limitation? . . . I believe I have a salvific mission as a Catholic. Does that mean I am in conscience required to do everything I can as Governor to translate all my religious values into the laws and regulations of the State of New York or the United States? Or be branded a hypocrite if I do not? As a Catholic, I respect the teaching authority of the Bishops, but must I agree with everything in the Bishops' pastoral letter on peace and fight to include it in [political] party platforms? (Cuomo 1984:17)

Note two things about this passage. First, it presupposes a distinction between ethics and something called "religious values." As we saw in chapter 2, John Yoder's pacifism depends for its cogency on the truth of certain religious beliefs, namely that Jesus was incarnated God and that he enjoined us against political force. Thus, suffering and marytrdom are valuable expressions of religious conviction. In this sense, as I argued earlier, Yoder may argue that pacifism is a good while admitting that recognition of this good depends upon religious faith. But were he to give up the particularly religious belief that Jesus was God, Yoder would be hard-pressed to account for any continued pacifism.

Perhaps this is how Cuomo interprets the traditional Catholic rejection of elective abortion and insistence on justice in war. But this is confused; natural-law arguments per se do not depend for their cogency on the truth of any belief peculiar to the Catholic tradition. The tradition that comes to be called "natural law" attempts to sketch those standards of action and character which must be upheld and at least approximated by any reflective agent in pursuit of the good. This tradition insists that any agent of reasonable maturity can, with a bit of reflection perhaps, grasp as a fact that murder is always and everywhere wicked. The natural law is, as it were, the lowest common denominator that applies to pagan and Christian alike. Cuomo, on the other hand, seems to think that practical reasoning engaged in by Catholics applies only to Catholics, but this is just mistaken. If Catholic teaching about abortion is right at all, then abortion is murder, not some hybrid "murder for Catholics." For the natural-law tradition is nothing if not "realist" in the sense of maintaining that there are facts about good and evil independent of any human social orders or conventions. Such facts reflect the way the world is and the reasonable forms of human activity in that world. Although this tradition has roots both in classical Aristotelianism and stoicism, it need not require any particular belief about biology, cosmology, or human psychology. To discuss justice in war implies, for the natural law, facts about war and its conduct that render some acts wicked. Knowingly to engage in or to intend such acts renders the agent wicked, regardless of any particular religious beliefs, and the goal of the just war tradition is to provide criteria for distinguishing the wicked from the acceptable and to establish which actions must be rejected altogether by any reflective agent in pursuit of justice.

Second, Cuomo suggests a distinction between a private realm, wherein ethics and values operate freely, and a public arena of policies and platforms from which those private matters are properly restricted. But if "private" means "unique to me," then the distinction never gets off the ground. For part of what it means to be a value is for some judgment of good to figure in the claim that a particular activity or state of affairs contributes to human flourishing. Thus, to say that we value honesty is to affirm that in the human community we dub honest people worthy and their actions a positive contribution to the good we seek. If the realm of ethics were purely private, then all values would collapse into preferences. It would be impossible to attempt any general statements at all about how people should live or what activities the community should pursue.

Undoubtedly Cuomo intends something weaker. Perhaps he wants to indicate the distinctive goods and the various ways of ranking those goods, pursued by the ethnic, religious, and professional subgroups who perpetuate the traditions that make up our "pluralistic" society. It would then be in keeping with the argument of chapter 1 to maintain that these diverse traditions may be incommensurable and yet not violate our basic understanding of justice. We might, without giving up our moral "realism," admit that there is no present consensus on where justice lies. This would explain how we can disagree without ascribing malice to our partners in debate. Given the complexity of the issues and the darkness of the times, they may be recognized as worthy and acting in good conscience, without presenting a position compelling to others. Here, we have once again the dispute between Okonkwo and Obierika so nicely laid out in Achebe's novel. But that disagreement presupposed that there was a fact of the matter, that at least one of them was mistaken in conscience, and that it would be better for the entire community to determine if possible where the truth lies and adjust its behavior accordingly.

The natural-law analysis of nuclear deterrence, then, is not a uniquely Catholic debate. It concerns the nature and application of a moral vocabulary that makes demands on any rational agent. Central to the argument is the distinction, as Elizabeth Anscombe puts it, between war and murder. War pits one fighting force against another in a test of strength and ability on the field of battle. The measure of success is disabling the opponent, and this is accomplished by destroying his forces. Soldiers are trained to kill other soldiers. The killing is intended, planned, and practiced. It is, nonetheless, not murder. Murder, as Aristotle remarked, is always and everywhere recognized to be wicked, but no blame accrues to the soldier who kills because this killing is just, undertaken in support of a lawful authority. Living in community, as we've already seen, requires a division of labor, and one of the tasks that falls to the authorities is securing the good. Protecting it with force is sometimes necessary, even when that means killing. "It ought not to be pretended," Anscombe admonishes, "that rulers and their subordinates do not choose the killing of their enemies as a means" (Stein 1961:50). Part of the awful responsibility of the authorities is facing the need to kill, and this responsibility devolves from them to their agents, the police, and armed forces. To kill in the exercise of duty is just and courageous even though the recourse to war is tragic. Insofar as the authorities act responsibly, and the soldiers follow what they believe to be a legal order, there is no injustice; hence, the killing is no murder.

This distinction brings to the fore the doctrine of "double effect" as it has emerged within the natural-law tradition. The political authorities may directly kill because they are, in their public capacity, defending the community. But they may not overstep the bounds of justice. The private individual may not seek to kill another; capital punishment is reserved for the law. Nonetheless, the individual may defend himself and this may lead to the death of another. How can we rectify these seemingly conflicting claims? In asking whether a person may kill in self-defense, Thomas Aquinas concludes that "nothing hinders one act from having two effects, only one of which is intended, while the other is beside the intention" (*S. Theo.*:2a2ae, 64, 7). In particular, since defense of self is natural to all beings, when that intention properly describes an action the act is not contrary to reason and the natural law. This holds even when, as an unintended effect, the attacker is killed. This concept rests on the distinction between an act, its motives, and its consequences. If my intention is to defend myself and my acts are reasonably undertaken, then the death of the attacker is unfortunate, but it carries no malice. Hence, it imparts no guilt. The death is regrettable, and in a sense involuntary (Aristotle *Ethics*:1110b). If I had had a reasonable alternative, that would have been the action of choice.

Understanding the complex interrelations of intention, act, and consequence depends on the precision with which we can describe actions. What actually, as opposed to what might have figured into the act, determines its goodness or malice as well as the praise or blame deserved? An example outside the scope of war may prove useful. Suppose that my wife and I are inclined to make love. The act itself can be described as a particular sexual coupling at a particular time and place. The physical description, however, does not provide enough information for a judgment about goodness. We may have various motives for making love, and they can be different for each of us. And, just as many motives can lead toward an act, so can many consequences follow from it. Some of the consequences may be directly related to the motives, while others may be unexpected. We are not omniscient or even saints enough to intend all and only the good consequences of our acts. Determining exactly what was intended, and hence assessing responsibility, not to mention praise or blame, is often much more complicated than any simple physical description of an event. But this doesn't make our judgments arbitrary, "subjective" (whatever that means), or lacking in truth value. Whatever the relations between acts, motives, and consequences, they are nonetheless distinct, and their distinctness is crucial to our making the judgments necessary to an intelligible practical life.

It is with an eye to distinguishing the morally relevant aspects of an act that Thomas Aquinas makes the above distinction. For example, a sexual act may be a rape. How we determine this depends on the relations and intentions we attribute to the actors in the scene. Sexual acts voluntarily entered into by two mature individuals are not rape. Wherein would the injustice lie? There are borderline situations, of course, but these should not deter us. Even if a husband mistakenly believes that forcing his wife to have sex with him is not rape, he certainly does know that forcing anyone else to do so is wicked. Perhaps he thinks that marrying a woman entitles him to sex whenever he wants, regardless of the wife's views. This is a brutish view, but not an incoherent one. He is tragically, and perhaps maliciously, confused about the nature of the relation established by marriage. But to be reasonable, we measure the malice in the act against what we expect of each other in the analogous context. If I learn that this case took place on a peasant holding in the ninth century I judge it rather differently than I would should it occur in contemporary Brentwood. This doesn't mean that some rape is not wicked but only that we levy blame appropriate to the context and character of the agents.

The same holds true for murder, and for the intention to commit murder, even if that intention is never acted upon. If we determine that the killing was unjust and that the agent should in conscience have realized this, then it is a murder. And if we judge that a threat, seriously made, involves a murderous intent, then it is unjust as well and so is the agent. Double effect does not excuse or "justify" wicked acts. It explains what everyone encounters in the course of life: outcomes which are lamentable and tragic, but for which we cannot in good conscience attribute evil to the agent.

But what about actions intended to forestall the need for war, as in the case of nuclear deterrence? Deterrence, properly so called, seeks to prevent some enemy action through creating the fear of an unacceptable response. For the threat to be credible the deterring party must maintain an effective force and evince the willingness to use that force, even if reluctantly. In the case of nuclear deterrence, the goal is to prevent a nuclear exchange, and the strategy to ensure that, even were there an initial strike against your own forces or population, sufficient resources would remain to launch an equally devastating, hence unacceptable, strike against the enemy. As Lawrence Freedman recounts the development of nuclear strategy, by 1964 "unacceptable damage... was put at a loss of 20 to 25 percent of population and 50 percent of industrial capacity. There was little doubt that by the mid-1960s the United States could ensure destruction at levels much higher than this" (Paret 1986:758). It is to this developing strategic configuration that the contributors to the Stein volume respond. Unlike the legitimate use of armed force, nuclear weapons are by their nature indiscriminately destructive. The strategic arsenals of the early nuclear age assured their destructive capacity through the sheer size of the explosion, and this rendered it impossible to use them without incorporating the civilian population. Such an attack would be murderous and any policy based on it irredemably wicked.

The problem is not simply one of intention, for it is no response to say that the intention of the policy is to ensure that nuclear war be avoided. Double effect does not operate in this situation. The weapon itself, "if we discount the totally unreal, hypothetical case of use on isolated targets like ships at sea—for which nobody would dream of manufacturing H-bombs—is always evil" (Stein 1961:76). To use an indiscriminate weapon amounts to saying that you are more concerned with responding to the enemy than protecting the integrity of the noncombatant. But to take this position is to forsake justice in acts of war *and* to lose any claim to right intention in going to war. Hence, any strategy that requires a willingness to use nuclear weapons, even reluctantly, is unjust according to the criteria of the natural law. This being so, concludes R. A. Markus, we must hold ourselves and our elected officials to the standards of justice, for to do otherwise is "to capitulate to the forces that have gone so far to undermine our humaneness that we still speak the language of morals while consenting to exempt warfare from the realm of morality" (Stein 1961:87).

Markus rightly senses an inclination to exempt nuclear weapons from moral argument. Fear of nuclear annihilation tempts us to allow our leaders to do whatever it takes to keep us protected, even if that includes a willingness to murder. Deterrent strategies incorporate the willingness to commit murder because they involve indiscriminate weapons that cannot be reasonably deployed without targeting noncombatants. It is no justification to cite the end deterrence is supposed to achieve; the belief that the pursuit of justice requires violating the demands of justice reflects, in Walter Stein's luscious phrase, an "habitual moral squalor" (Stein 1961:39). A government undertaking such strategies renders itself unjust and must be opposed as a matter of conscience.

There have been, of course, attempts to avoid the conclusion of this argument, the most serious being that of Paul Ramsey in a series of papers reprinted in his collection *The Just War*. Ramsey admits the basic points of the argument, and acknowledges that a morally unusable weapon cannot figure into a rational and just deterrent policy. Nonetheless, he argues that some military installations are themselves city-sized and constitute legitimate and proportionate targets for strategic nuclear weapons. That there exist legitimate targets of the appropriate size means that the weapons are at least conceivably usable and hence legitimately possessed. Deploying strategic missiles against such installations is thus acceptable, despite the fact that using them would still result in potentially massive noncombatant injury. As a matter of deterrence, in fact, this risk of noncombatant injury should augment the already considerable sense of risk and incline the Soviets—the ostensible villains in all these debates—against unjust attack.

Understanding this step is crucial to grasping the ins and outs of just war reasoning. For while it is unacceptable to will injury to noncombatants, it is perfectly reasonable, in fact it is a matter of decency, to point out to opposing leaders the dangers of their own ill-considered acts. Even if we don't give a lick about noncombatant Soviet citizens, we can still hope that their rulers do. Consequently, we can hope that the risk to their own citizens deters the Soviets from attacking us and our allies. There is more. Just as we might consider the Soviets depraved warmongers, exporting revolution at any price, so they doubtless view us as slavering capitalist swine, willing to protect our repressive structure at whatever cost. Thus, nothing ensures that we do not, when provoked, step over the bounds of justice and train our bombs on civilian centers as well as large military installations. Of course *we* can't do that, Ramsey insists, but if their insecurity about the depth of our virtue has a deterrent effect, then so be it. In response to the strict natural-law position, then, Ramsey musters an ordered set of arguments. Use is possible, hence possession is acceptable; legitimate use has consequences that should augment the deterrent effect of legitimate possession; the deterrent effect of legitimate possession may, without malice on our part, find itself enhanced by the fear of illegitimate use in time of stress. Ramsey goes further, however, and suggests that although we cannot adopt a policy that targets civilians, we can refrain from telling our adversaries that we eschew murder; let them sweat it, he suggests.

With this in mind, recall the steps in the development of Ramsey's argument for deterrence:

1. Any direct attack on noncombatants is murder, a moral atrocity, absolutely incapable of justification.
2. Any counter–city use of nuclear weapons is a direct attack on the innocent, hence absolutely incapable of justification.
3. Any targeting of civilian populations with nuclear weapons constitutes a murderous threat, and hence is unjustifiable.

Up to this point he maintains continuity with the argument of Anscombe, Markus, and their compatriots. But given his claims about the nature of many military bases, on both sides, he moves on as follows:

4. Targeting large-scale military installations with strategic nuclear weapons is legitimate and thus establishes legitimate if limited grounds for possession of such weapons.
5. Recognition by the potential adversary of the inevitable collateral damage produced by a legitimate exchange of strategic missiles should have a deterrent effect.
6. Uncertainty about our resolve to limit weapons to legitimate uses only should increase the deterrent effect yet again.
7. Refusal on our part openly to declare that resolve adds yet another increment of deterrent.
8. Leading our adversary to believe that we would be willing to overstep the bounds of justice—though only a "bluff"—adds a final level of deterrence.[4]

Taken collectively, this amounts to a credible deterrent policy, consistent with the natural-law argument of Anscombe et al. Ramsey insists that a hard-and-fast line must be drawn at injustice; and the flip side of a just deterrent is to acknowledge that when we can no longer pursue either a deterrent policy or a war within the bounds of justice, we must accept defeat. If there is the possibility of elaborating a just deterrent, however, let us do so. But in his last work on war, as in his first, Ramsey insists "that the one thing Christian pacifists and just warriors have in common is that if anything is shown to be *per se* a moral atrocity, or to have no 'just cause' *now*, it should be given Christian endorsement *no moment more*" (Ramsey and Hauerwas 1988:52). This is the fundamental boundary established by justice, and once it has been reached the person of justice can go no further.

To understand what it means to issue an absolute and unqualified "No!" it is instructive to consider Ramsey's own self-criticisms. At every stage he provides arguments in support of deterrence, but he offers them as a moralist intent on guiding those charged with the dreadful responsibility of protecting the common good. The resemblance to Augustine, counseling commanders and analyzing the plight of the judge, is instructive. (Cf. G. S. Davis 1991.) As Christian moralists, both Augustine and Ramsey speak from within the church and from the perspective of their own, admittedly different, pastoral responsibilities. In a remarkable letter reprinted in *Speak Up*, Ramsey writes, regarding step 8 above, that his arguments

were insufficient, indeed disturbingly insufficient, within the year. The "bluff" was withdrawn from my analysis of a possibly moral deterrence. Again, my reasons were two: (1) one's *real* intentions (*not* to go to such use) will be found out; the "bluff" must fail to deter; and (2) even if our top political and military leaders were pure in heart, they *must* count on thousands of men in missile silos, planes and submarines to be conditionally willing, under some circumstances, to become murderers. One should never occasion mortal sin in another, tempt them to it, or enlist them for it. (Ramsey and Hauerwas 1988:207)[5]

From the just war point of view, the first failure renders step 8 ineffective, hence unacceptable. But for a Christian moralist, the second failure is decisive. Mortal sin is the gravest of states, and the person in that state risks what is most important, the chance for salvation. To tempt someone into sin runs counter to both charity and justice, and to counsel those in power to subvert the consciences of the soldiers whom they lead means to give up altogether any pastoral vocation. Thus, the tradition of just war in the Christian context must, as Ramsey sees it, proffer a final and unqualified "no" to any policy that would jeopardize the consciences of those who serve. The bluff of step 8 cannot be maintained, for as long as the bluff works the soldiers are in exactly the same position as their adversary: led to believe that their nation's policy is to overstep the bounds of justice should the situation reach last resort. If they are to follow the apparent policy of their commanders, they must form a willingness to attack noncombatants, to commit murder, should they be told to do so, and this is to form the intention to commit an atrocity. This being so, they must urge the political authorities not to resort to bluff and, thus, to limit deterrent policy to step 7. In sketching the possibilities for a just deterrent, Ramsey differs from Anscombe et al. in finding a legitimate purpose for the weapons and hence a legitimate, though limited, political strategy. But the limit, the unqualified drawing of the line, binds Ramsey and the British authors within the tradition of just war thinking.

Ramsey's conclusion, "that we ought never to *do*, or seriously *threaten*... or occasion another power to 'any act of war deliberately aimed at the destruction of whole areas and their populations' " (Ramsey and Hauerwas 1988:207), drawn as it is from the second Vatican Council, makes an apt transition to *The Challenge of Peace*, authored by the National Conference of Catholic Bishops. Issued in 1983, after several drafts and much intense debate, this pastoral letter of the American Catholic bishops generated more discussion of just war principles and application than any of its secular predecessors. Where, more than twenty years later, does the bishops' pastoral stand vis à vis the arguments of Ramsey, Markus, and Anscombe?

The bishops' condemnation of counter-population use is unequivocal. Equally clear is their rejection of any first-use of nuclear weapons, even were there a legitimate military target (1983:par. 153, but see note 69). They also appear to condemn reasoning from double effect as "a perverted political policy or moral casuistry" should it be invoked "to justify using a weapon which 'indirectly' or 'unintentionally' killed a million innocent people because they happened to live near a 'militarily significant target' " (par. 193). At the same time, they oppose development of weapons that would be discriminate because they raise the risk of crossing the nuclear threshold. Whereas countervalue weapons are inherently unusable, tactical weapons and their limited use are rejected because the limits of technology, communications, and the "weakness and sinfulness of human communities" (par. 152) render the likelihood of escalation very high (pars. 157–61). This position is in fact *stronger* than that of Anscombe and her coauthors; by ruling out the use of tactical weapons, the bishops appear to eliminate all use of nuclear weapons and hence all legitimate possession. But this would seem to rule out any deterrent policy. You can't justly threaten someone with something you don't legitimately hold.

It is surprising, therefore, that the bishops go on to cite John Paul II's remark that "deterrence based on balance, certainly not as an end in itself but as a step on the way toward a progressive disarmament, may still be judged morally acceptable" (par. 173). Such interim deterrence is provisional only, but it remains nonetheless very puzzling.[6] It is not, however, incoherent. As Richard McCormick points out, "*The*

Challenge of Peace did not condemn *any* use of nuclear weapons. It came close, but it did not do so. And it was precisely this tiny opening that allowed its provisional and strictly conditioned tolerance of nuclear deterrence" (1984:200–201). Despite grave skepticism about the possibility of controlling any nuclear exchange (pars. 157–61), the bishops do not find it inconceivable that a legitimate and limited retaliatory nuclear strike may be undertaken in response to an initial crossing of the threshold.

The first thing to say is that, by their own lights, the bishops are justified in retaining current, provisional, deterrent capability. This is so principally because of the stance taken toward the natural law and a methodological break between consistency and prudence. The bishops' "tiny opening" depends upon finding no formal inconsistency between the principles of natural law and particular findings of fact as to the possession of nuclear weapons. Had they judged there to be no conceivable morally tolerable use, then there would be no acceptable possession, which would have led them in the direction of Markus et al., namely unilateral nuclear disarmament. (Cf. Stein 1961:83–88.) But unlike their British coreligionists, the bishops, it would seem, maintain that conscience is only bound at this outer edge, where there is clear inconsistency with principle. The contrast with Anthony Kenny, for example, is instructive. Having restated the argument up to the point of targeting, Kenny admits that a person of conscience can tolerate deterrence, but "only if he has good reason to believe that his government has no intention of using its deterrent weapons in murderous fashion." Conscience compells him to ask whether this is the case and, based on the available evidence, Kenny concludes that present deterrent policy continues to incorporate direct attacks on noncombatants. Thus, he maintains that deterrence "demands that Western military men shall be ready to commit murder if ordered to do so," and holds that renouncing deterrence now and unequivocally is "a moral imperative. We must give up our nuclear deterrent not because by so doing we shall achieve some desirable aim, but because to retain it is wicked" (Stein 1961:164–65). Conscience issues an immediate "No!" because prudence recognizes the situation for what it is, and what it might be is at best a matter of hope. Despite their grave skepticism, the bishops excuse conscience, not on the basis of a prudent assessment of the facts but because an interpretation of the situation is conceivable that does not render the particulars of policy formally inconsistent with principle.

There are, no doubt, responses to be made on behalf of the bishops' consciences,[7] but it is plain that even their provisional acceptance of deterrence weighs heavy. And it should. For the only acceptable form of deterrence is achieved with weapons that are inherently wicked. Weapons sufficiently discriminatory to be usable in tactical situations make "deterrence unstable in a crisis and war more likely" (1983:par. 184), leading to the claim (par. 189) that those weapons which are not inherently wicked are expressly forbidden while the unusable strategic weapons currently held may, for the interim, be retained. This last is part of the bishops' general opposition to "proposals which have the effect of lowering the nuclear threshold and blurring the difference between nuclear and conventional weapons" (par. 190). Nonetheless, when a simple substitution (terrorism) is made, the strangeness of the reasoning emerges:

1. Terrorism, since it involves a direct attack on noncombatants, is wicked.
2. Threatening just reprisal may deter terrorist acts, but it may equally provoke preemptive terrorism.
3. In order to avoid any acts of terrorism, we should threaten forms of reprisal that cannot conceivably be just.
4. To adopt a policy of unjust threat is to deter terrorism with terrorism, whatever the end envisioned.
5. Once a policy of unjust threat is in place, alternatives that eliminate threats of terrorism with threats of just reprisal must be rejected as destabilizing.

Proposition 2 the natural law reasoner invokes to justify deterrence, admitting the risk but accepting it as part of the pursuit of justice. Terrorism is wicked because it refuses to distinguish between belligerents and noncombatants, and if we wish to deter terrorism then we should pursue only just reprisals whatever the perpetrators may threaten in return. The move from 2 to 3 rests on an as yet unestablished question of fact. Perhaps the terrorist will strike before the deterrent threat can be put into place, although this assumes that terror is the primary goal rather than a means to some further end. Otherwise we would have to weigh the terrorist's commitment to that end against the loss of this particular strategy. In any event, the risk acknowledged in 2 should not affect our commitment to the pursuit of justice, and it surely doesn't license the move to 4. That proposition is clearly repugnant to justice, for it admits the plausibility of 3 and then forsakes justice in favor of deterrence alone. It will not do to claim that the threat facilitates negotiating an end to all such threats. That, after all, is what the terrorist wants, and the moral dilemma is only compounded if we assume that the desired end is formally compatible with justice. The terrorist with a just cause foresakes justice on its own behalf, affirming thereby "a world that is morally self-contradictory, a world that obliges one to morally evil acts." This, as Stein goes on to remark, "ensures that one's choices will actually be evil choices" (Stein 1961:38). And so with nuclear deterrence. If the weapon is unjust, then the threat is unjust, and if the threat is serious—a situation required by creditable deterrence—then it evinces a willingness to engage in terrorism. The move from 4 to 5 only exacerbates the wickedness since it registers the refusal to give up this willingness. It says, in short, that we would rather secure our ends than reform our means.

Clearly the bishops think that nuclear war is so terrifying and staving off this prospect a goal so compelling as to outweigh the implicit terrorism in their position. But to admit this is to admit that physical consequences can lead to abrogating the conditions of natural law. To the extent that the just war tradition rests on the natural law, the bishops can scarcely cloak their policy in the mantle of that tradition. Rather, they approach the position of Michael Walzer, for whom the advent of nuclear weapons creates a perpetual state of "supreme emergency" in which the constraints imposed by the legalistic paradigm are suspended. Such weapons "explode the theory of just war. They are the first of mankind's technological innovations that are simply not encompassable within the familiar moral world" (1977:282). Rather than attempting to find justice in a suspect policy, Walzer acknowledges "that deterrence itself, for all its criminality, falls or may fall for the moment under the standard of necessity." The consequences, he believes, are simply so terrifying that they overpower our moral resolve. Our criminal intent may be mitigated, however, by admiting that "the readiness to murder is balanced, or should be, by the readiness not to murder, not to threaten murder, as soon as alternative ways to peace can be found" (1977:283). At the point of supreme emergency, the gravity of the consequences overrides principles of justice and law.[8]

To be identified with Walzer, if the charge can be made to stick, must be a serious embarrassment to the bishops. Their commitment to the just war tradition precludes, at least in theory, allowing consequences to override the demands of justice. Nonetheless, steps toward this end are discernible at various points. Note the remark early on that "just war teaching has evolved, however, as an effort to prevent war" (National Conference of Catholic Bishops 1983:par. 83). This seems to me importantly wrong. Perhaps *politics* evolved as an effort to prevent war, but just war teaching attempts to prevent injustice in going to and prosecuting war. Justice may, although the bishops nowhere note this, be invoked to urge a nation to war, and this may be less infrequent than imagined. Isolationism, after all, can be as much an affront against justice as other forms of nationalism. Failure to recognize this stems almost certainly from the sort of confusion noted by Anscombe. Murder is wicked, a species of injustice; but peace, violence, injury, killing and war—while there may be an escalating presumption against them—are generically neither just nor unjust. "Peace," Thomas Aquinas rightly notes, "is not a virtue, but the fruit of virtue" (*S. Theo.*:2a2ae, 29, 3 ad 3). The person of virtue desires a just peace, maintained through temperance and courage by prudent persons, whereas an unjust peace is odious. When the responsibility to protect ourselves and others from injustice leads to war, we can be sure that killing and destruction will follow. This is tragic, but it is not unjust. To place avoiding war above securing justice risks subverting virtue and sacrificing the very goods, not to mention the people, who make life worthy.

The bishops take a second step down Walzer's path when they introduce "comparative justice" as a condition of *ius ad bellum*:

The category of comparative justice is designed to emphasize the presumption against war which stands at the beginning of just war teaching. In a world of sovereign states recognizing neither a common moral authority nor a central political authority, comparative justice stresses that no states should act on the basis that it has "absolute justice" on its side. (1983:par. 93)

This is puzzlingly ambiguous. Although there might be degrees of wickedness—it is, after all, more wicked to seduce your own daughter than your best friend's daughter, and his daughter than a competent adult—there are no degrees of justice. Doing justice may take more or less courage, and we praise the agent accordingly, or it may involve tragic consequences and elicit our pity. Those noble souls who exceed the demands of justice perform acts of supererogation, and this is another matter altogether. But the magnanimous or supererogatory is not "more just" nor the less wicked "comparatively" just. This is simply to misunderstand the concept.

If we look at it carefully, "comparative justice" is not a just war criterion but a metaethical constraint on any account of justice. It is, in short, a thesis about moral epistemology. Furthermore, it is a skeptical thesis that can be broken down as follows: In the absence of recognized authority or consensus it is difficult, if not impossible, to justify claims about moral "facts." Furthermore, "given techniques of propaganda and the ease with which nations and individuals either assume or delude themselves into believing that God or right is clearly on their side" (1983:par. 94), we should not be satisfied with any but the most stringent demands on justification. With failure a possibility, we should limit our willingness to engage in conflict, asking instead, "are the values at stake critical enough to override the presumption against war? . . . Do the rights and values involved justify killing?" (1983:par. 92). Can we, in short, be sufficiently sure of ourselves and our cause to risk the consequences of undertaking war?

It is important to distinguish this last point from proportionality, a criterion that also has a place in the bishops' list. In the context of *ius ad bellum*, proportionality is closely bound up with the traditional requirements of last resort and possibility of success. It is taken for granted that war expands the prospects for destruction; thus, right reason directs that we try all available means before resorting to war. Not only this; if there is no reasonable prospect of success, then the destruction attendant on war is purposeless and wanton. There are difficulties here that should not be minimalized. Last resort, for example, presupposes the work of prudence in the sense of distinguishing what must be done and when. Consequently, the appeasement of Chamberlain at Munich was not dictated by the criterion of last resort; it was imprudence, which is a defect of virtue. Chance of success, in turn, is conditioned by the nature of the threat as well as the relative strength of forces. If the alternative to war is genocide, then risking everything is not unreasonable. Risking everything, that is, but justice itself.[9]

The criterion of comparative justice is another matter entirely. Acts and states of affairs, as far as they involve rational agents, are either just or unjust, in accord with or contrary to right reason. Introducing the modifier "absolute" does not accomplish anything because justice is a moral species. Acts no more straddle the boundaries of a species than do apples and oranges. Here again it is important to remember Anscombe's injunction that generic acts, such as killing, become specific in commission, where they are modified by context and the character of the agent. Perhaps the bishops are confusing a question of fact with an epistemological one. A sound fallibilism is committed to the revisability of beliefs and to the further view that even the most transparent of our justified true beliefs possess no self-warranting property which can be discovered by inspection. But admitting either point offers no good grounds for giving up the belief that many, perhaps most, of our beliefs are true. Nor does the epistemic point call into question our further belief that many, and perhaps most, of our beliefs about justice are true. If justice is a condition for achieving rational human goals, then any community which is doing that is operating at some level of justice, even if, parallel to the general epistemic argument, we must allow that some of those beliefs about justice are false. Admitting epistemic fallibilism does not mean embracing the view that there is no truth, in science or ethics.

If the bishops intend to do no more than endorse fallibilism in the epistemology of ethics, then well and good. But if they are suggesting that we do not have justified true beliefs about justice, then what they are saying is both false and dangerous. I've already explained why I think such is a view false; it is dangerous because it suggests not that we give up actions which are contrary to principle but that we give up principles in the face of consequences. It risks precisely what critics of "proportionalism" such as Ramsey feared, namely, denying the incommensurability of justice and injustice in favor of a policy based on the calculation of consequences (McCormick and Ramsey 1978). And whatever else this betokens, it marks an even more serious departure from the just war tradition than the bishops' position on deterrence. In fact, it is the precondition for that position. The reasoning involved in the move from 2 to 3 rested on the fear that undertaking what was clearly just increased the risk of tragedy. Fear of tragedy, disguised as "comparative justice," inclines us to settle for injustice, if it is not too odious, and blocks our pursuit, however risky and fallible, of the good. This is different from the prudent exercise of temperance and courage. It is, as Yoder might say, a step down the slope that strips the tradition of its credibility.

I don't deny the bishops make this move out of compassion; surely they do. But when compassion clouds justice, the good of the whole is lost. The bishops, as ministers of God, have a vocation of their own, which is to guide the community in accord with God's will for all. Given that they acknowledge "the weakness and sinfulness of human communities," it is wishful thinking at best to believe that states and their citizens will be helped toward the good if only we don't demand too much. To claim that "comparative justice is designed to relativize absolute claims and to restrain the use of force even in 'justified' conflict" (1983:par. 94), even if it were true, would amount in fact to the willingness to make concessions in order to secure peace. But to give up justice is no way to protect it, and this, by way of metaethical innovation, is what the bishops risk.

There is, finally, a particularly theological failure adding impetus to the bishops' inchoate consequentialism, and it is best brought out in the contrast with Aristotle. For the Aristotelian, justice is inextricably bound to the other cardinal virtues. To be habituated into justice, in the sense of seeing and being disposed to do what justice requires, cannot be adequately explicated apart from an understanding of prudence, temperance, and courage. Justice requires that we recognize which among the possible courses of action open at a given moment contribute to achieving and maintaining the good for our community, and it further requires that we be inclined, through precept and habit, to undertake a good course of action. Justice, in other words, cannot function without prudence. But at the same time, it cannot function without courage. Merely to say to ourselves that such and such would be a good course on a particular occasion does not ensure that we will do it. We may be weak, in the sense of being unable to accept the risk or unwilling to undertake the exertion necessary to complete the task. Cowardice takes many forms: failing to face up to an attacker; tempting someone else to protect you at her peril; neglecting to advise an employer of nefarious deeds. All are failures of courage and subvert the doing of justice. Since they are at the same time ways of avoiding the truth, these acts undermine prudence. And then there is temperance. It is obvious how failure in temperance can undermine courage, but the converse is true as well. If I do not have the courage to say "no" to my peers for fear of being derided or cast out, then I may be carried along with them into an act I know to be imprudent or unjust. And virtue being susceptible to deformation, as we will see in the next chapter, I risk losing what prudence I have as my habits are reshaped. I may, in other words, acquire new habits which make it difficult for me to discern and to contain my actions within the boundaries conducive to my welfare and that of the people around me. The unaided Aristotelian, thus, must hope that members of the community remain fully established in this web of virtue, for those virtues alone make possible and sustain the goods they all pursue.

The Christian, however, can call upon yet additional resources: those theological virtues of Faith, Hope, and Charity. Despite their differences on the particulars of Christian ethics, the Catholic natural law tradition and John Yoder's Mennonite pacifism share the belief that God is Lord, that as Lord his providential will determines the good for his creation, and that he revealed his will for people and the means for doing that will in the incarnation, crucifixion, and resurrection of Jesus. These are taken, by both traditions, to be facts about the world, with exactly the same status and considerably more importance than facts about tables, chairs, and Neptune. We should suspect, given these beliefs, the importance of God to manifest itself in the structure of the virtues, and this clearly is the case with Yoder.

From the perspective of natural law, the issue is somewhat more complicated. Thomas Aquinas remarks that "wherever we find a good human act, it must correspond to some human virtue" (*S. Theo.*:2a2ae, 17, 1). Human acts properly are expressions of a person's character and that character is the general term for the virtues, vices, and other dispositions which make up a person's identity. Thus, to say of a human act that it is good, as opposed to fortunate, is to say that its proper description incorporates reference to the virtues of the agent, that its consequences and the way in which it was done reflect the character of the individual. But as a Christian theologian, Thomas cannot leave it at that, for "human acts have a twofold measure; one is proximate and homogeneous, that is to say the reason, while the other is remote and excelling, that is to say God" (*S. Theo.*:2a2ae, 17, 1). Because the other cardinal virtues cannot operate without prudence, which discerns what is to be done, they all take reason as their measure. But since reason discerns the way the world is, and God determines the nature of the world, human acts are also, as it were, measured against God.[10] This is true, ultimately, for believer and nonbeliever both, but the believer's conscience is reordered to the extent that the natural virtues are informed by the theological. Faith, Hope, and Charity are not optional but constitutive of what it means to be a Christian. A Christian without faith, after all, is at best a sentimental deist. The absence of hope is at least as puzzling, for to believe in God encompasses belief in His powers and promises, including His mercy and the offer of salvation. Given the components of faith, an absence of hope suggests either that the believer does not understand the nature of the Christian message or has fallen into despair, and despair is a pathological state as opposed to one that the common believer might inhabit.

Charity is a different matter. Some have thought Christian *agape* should exclude all thought of self, whereas others have held proper self-love to be a prerequisite for Christian ethics. (Cf. Outka 1972 and O'Donovan 1980.) On any interpretation, however, the Christian is called to go beyond the bounds of even the most virtuous nonbeliever in loving concern for the neighbor, even when that neighbor is an enemy. Taken together, the theological virtues transform the natural and may, in fact, lead to judgments at odds with the natural virtues. Faith, for example, may lead the believer to make claims that seem wildly implausible to the nonbeliever. Such claims needn't suggest Tertullian's "credo quia inanum est," but only that the believer claims both a source and authority for beliefs that his compatriot does not have. This may, in the context of war, be no more (though no less) than the belief that violations of justice are not merely wrong in themselves but run contrary to God's will for His creatures. Nonetheless, the resulting argument is different in substance from that of the nonbeliever, even if they reach the same conclusion.

Sometimes, however, they cannot, rationally, reach the same conclusion. "The object of hope," Aquinas remarks, "is a future good, difficult but possible to obtain" (*S.Theo.*:2a2ae, 17, 1). If hope is based on faith in God's providential care, then we can expect many occasions when the believer continues to hope for a positive outcome although the nonbeliever has given up. More than faith, hope leads to a conflict of action, for as long as he hopes, the believer may reasonably continue along a path. Not only that, but given that his hope is in God, he may elect a course of action which is beyond his unaided power and which looks to all the nonbelieving world futile, willful, or even mad. Nonetheless, if he hopes in God, then his action is as reasonable as that belief; and if his belief is true, the path he follows is that of right reason, whatever the nonbelieving world may think.

Just as the cardinal virtues must work each in conjunction with the others, so must the theological. Hope without faith is unreasonable; hope and faith without charity can become demonic. In the context of war, it produces the crusader. Thus, charity cannot be ignored; and when we introduce it into the structure of just war thinking, still further conflicts arise with those who do not believe. On even a modest account of the demands of charity, our national boundaries must be seen as artificial when compared to the solidarity Christians should feel with all people. Thus, Christians will be inclined to minimize the distinction between Ethiopian and American and go to the aid of the starving, even if it means expending resources that might be used to raise the standards of the poor at home. They feel a positive obligation to aid the starving and experience remorse at their failure or inability to do so. Non-believers, conversely, do not have the same directedness toward strangers and more distant neighbors. Should they go to the aid of others, they undertake acts of magnanimity, expending resources on which the Ethiopians have no claim. Should they be unable to help, or choose to devote their energies to their families and friends, there is no guilt and no reason for remorse. This doesn't betoken, I think, any lack of humanity on the pagan's part, much less baseness or injustice. But it points to the distinctive quality of charity when it enters into deliberations. Charity directs the believer toward positions that may be diametrically opposed to those of the responsible nonbeliever, but nonetheless compelling, *if only* what Christians believe is true.

Surely the bishops are committed, no less so than Ramsey and their British coreligionists, to the truth of Christianity. If I am right in believing that religious commitments are constitutive of character, then those beliefs must be functional in the bishops' application of just war thinking to the present situation. Otherwise, as Yoder suggests, their judgments and stated resolves will lack credibility. To be virtuous, after all, actions must not only be formally just but "proceed from a firm and unchangeable character" (Aristotle *Ethics*:1105a). *The Challenge of Peace* departs from the specifically Christian understanding of the relation between the natural law and the virtues, both natural and theological. By introducing the metaethical constraint of comparative justice limiting themselves to formal consistency, the bishops drive a wedge between prudence and conscience that makes it possible to envision compromising justice here and now. But we do not, as Yoder would have it, need to admit that the just war tradition is no longer credible. Instead, we should admit that it requires support from a tradition of the virtues, whether this be limited to the natural virtues adumbrated by Aristotle or augmented by the specifically Christian tradition of the three theological virtues. The latter alternative is not mine, and I will leave it for others. But to sustain a coherent interpretation of justice in war, I need to bring together my desultory gestures toward the tradition of virtue in a sustained Aristotelian account of character enduring the stress of conflict.

Notes

1. Here as elsewhere in the ethics of war, the literature is extensive, but there is no single treatment known to me that is both comprehensive and reliable. The historical studies of James Johnson (1975, 1981) and Frederick Russell (1975) combine historical discussion with moral analysis. Both provide an extensive bibliography. James Childress's "Just War Criteria", in Childress (1980) has been very influential, and will be discussed in part later on. In mounting his critique of the tradition, the classical criteria are laid out clearly in Yoder (1984). Walzer (1977) and the discussions in Ramsey (1961, 1968) are subtle but difficult. The cumulative argument in Stein (1961) is brilliant and has been restated in great detail in Finnis et al. (1987), although it must be extracted from the context of their criticism of deterrence. For clarity of argument it is still best to go to the source, St. Thomas's *Summa Theologiae*, particularly 2a2ae, 34–42, 57–66, although Thomas does not present "the just war theory" as a unified whole. A major desideratum in the scholarship is an up-to-date, book-length discussion of de Vitoria's *Reflections on the Indians and the Right of War* (1944; see also Skinner 1978, 2:chap. 5). Johnson provides an introduction, but de Vitoria's detailed scholastic analyses of the case of the indigenous population against the Spanish invaders, with its juxtaposition and resolution of cases through competing arguments should be more widely recognized as a model for just war analysis in the natural-law tradition.

2. This point applies to any military, as opposed to mob, action and not simply to the complex tactics of the contemporary military. Sun Tzu (1963) insists on it, and it is indispensable to ancient, medieval, and renaissance ways of waging war, despite their own notable differences. See, for example, Hanson (1989), Contamine (1984), and Hale (1985).

3. The debate over nuclear deterrence suffers from a sharp divide between those interested in "workable" strategic analyses that incorporate the complexities of current international relations and those interested in the the moral questions as setting the limits of any possible strategy. The background to the strategic issues is clearly and authoritatively presented in Lawrence Freedman's "The First Two Generations of Nuclear Strategists" (Paret 1986). Insider reflections of some interest are collected in Kennan (1983), and some of the key issues on the border between strategy and ethics are nicely addressed by Bryan Hehir and Richard Miller in their contributions to Whitmore (1989). General philosophical discussions outside the natural-law tradition have tended to revolve around explicitly consequentialist issues, as, for example, the exchange between Lackey and Kavka reprinted in Beitz et al. (1985) and the ethics symposium cited by Miller (Whitmore 1989:36). I suggest some of the limits of such approaches later in the discussion, and they have received extensive detailed criticism in Finnis et al. (1987).

4. For the steps on the way to this position, and the qualifications introduced in response to criticism, see the relevant chapters of Ramsey (1968) (as well as Ramsey and Hauerwas [1988:chap. 3] and the book's appendix, "A Political Ethics Context for Strategic Thinking," originally published in 1973).

See also Ramsey's amplifying remarks throughout his and Hauerwas's 1988 work that cite and respond to various of his critics. Of contemporary writers on the subject, the one who comes closest to carrying on Ramsey's argument in style, background, and direction is James T. Johnson (1984:chap. 3–6).

5. The letter in question was reprinted in a shorter version, as Ramsey notes, in *Newsweek*, 5 July 1982. It is Ramsey's response to a feature by Walter Goodman, "What is a 'Just War' Today?" which appeared in *Newsweek* for 14 June 1982.

6. The literature surrounding the bishops' pastoral and its drafting has become enormous. It has also prompted or at least played a role in provoking pastoral statements not only by the Catholic bishops of France and Germany but also those of other denominations, most notably the United Methodists. Richard McCormick (1984) provides a guide to the literature surrounding *The Challenge of Peace*, with very brief remarks on the European pastorals. Charles Curran (1988) adds to this, and adds a useful comparison with the German bishops in chapter 8. A lively and very partisan account of the Methodist bishops' deliberations, along with contrasting critiques, may be found in Ramsey and Hauerwas (1988).

7. Curran (1988) makes some moves in this direction in chapter 9, "Official Catholic Social Teaching and Conscience." Nonetheless, he recognizes that the quest for consistency with principle was central to the bishops' reluctant commitment to retaining deterrence and that "the history of the drafts indicates a continuing search for such a rationale" (1988:175). He recounts how, during the final voting, "a motion was made from the floor and passed by the body of bishops to condemn all use of nuclear weapons," but when it was pointed out that this would logically preclude deterrence, the bishops were persuaded to "change their mind on this amendment, and thus the document did not condemn all use of nuclear weapons" (1988:177). Although anecdotal, this evidence seems to clinch the view that the bishops allowed the end of retaining deterrence to guide their moral analysis, thus justifying my criticism to come. I believe that Curran continues to disagree with me on this, but this shouldn't obscure the great debt I own him and his work. In particular he was kind enough to read earlier versions of several chapters of this volume, although it is with regard to the bishops' pastoral that his trenchant criticism forced me to rethink the issues. Whatever its limits, the current version benefitted greatly.

8. A brief but cutting analysis of the consequentialist slide may be found in Yoder (1984:56–73). Walzer is mentioned as only one among many, but the challenge is clear. Walzer figures in the useful discussions of Hehir, Miller, and Hollenbach found in Whitmore (1989). The most extensive and devastating critique of deterrence and its philosophical underpinnings, in which Walzer comes in for extensive analysis, is Finnis et al. (1987). The harsh and frequently confrontational tone of this volume may be off-putting to some in the philosophical fraternity, but its natural-law analysis of consequentialist arguments and their application to deterrence is unmatched in the contemporary literature. Finnis (1983) is perhaps a more useful introduction to the general ethical position than his denser 1980 work. The flip side of just war and

natural-law critiques of Walzer emerges in the exchange between him and David Luban, reprinted in Beitz et al. (1985). Here, rather surprisingly, Walzer is cast in the role of conservative by critics who wish to move from what I consider the already shaky ground of the legal paradigm to the even more vague and ill-grounded realm of "human rights."

9. Proportionality as a condition of *ius in bello* requires that the military value of operations be weighed against the damage done to the noncombatant population. It is, as I've already indicated, subordinate to the requirement of discrimination; hence, we can assume, before the question of consequences is broached, that the operation is at least in principal just. On either the *ius ad bellum* or the *ius in bello* version of proportionality, there is no question of giving up principle; only after the general justice of the case has been established is the contemplated action modified by circumstance and consequences. I'll have more to say about threat and proportionality in discussing revolution.

10. Thomas explicates these issues in terms of the natural law's relation to the eternal. There is no fully satisfactory account of these topics, which remain, in fact, matters of considerable debate. A. P. d'Entreves (1951) provides a guide to the history of the tradition, although it is the adequacy of the traditional account that becomes the principal issue. That he grounds his discussion in a legal paradigm derived from stoicism ensures from the outset that his account will not be adequate for Aristotle and Aquinas. An alternative analysis, from which the current debate takes its start, is attempted by Germain Grisez in "The First Principle of Practical Reason," reprinted in Kenny (1969). Grisez's interpretation of Thomas and the natural law is elaborated with great depth by John Finnis (1980) and elegantly sketched in his 1983 work. Two very provocative, and frequently persuasive critiques of the Grisez-Finnis interpretation, are to be found in McInerny (1982) and Hittinger (1987). My interpretation has most in common with McInerny's, although I think my way of putting the issues would be somewhat different. Simplistically, Aquinas envisions the hierarchy of laws rather like a set of nested boxes. The eternal law refers to the systematic order of the created universe in toto and provides the answers to all questions of the form, "why did such and such happen just the way it did?" This includes questions of physical causality, but much more. The natural law is that part of the eternal law which applies to all persons simply as rational agents and should be construed as a theory of rational action rather than a code of conscience. Human law is the positive law enacted by particular communities in order to enable them to pursue the good. As such, it depends for its soundness on the natural law, but takes into account questions of ecology, circumstance, tradition, and material culture. Divine law, as distinct from eternal law, is positive legislation promulgated by God and has itself two divisions, the Old Law that God established for the Israelites and the New Law revealed in Jesus. When placed in the context of this vocabulary, the dilemma of Mario Cuomo, to use an earlier example, is whether his conscience as a public servant should be informed by the natural or the divine law. His confusion, however, stems from the failure to realize that abortion and justice in war are matters of the natural law already, and do not require his invoking anything which depends on positive religious teaching. The interesting question is

whether the eternal law remains the same if we deny the existence of God. If the way the world is can be fully discovered by what we have come to call the natural sciences, then Thomas's analysis of the eternal, the natural, and the positive human law remain the same for the Christian and the atheist Aristotelian, the latter refusing to admit that there is a divine law. To the extent, however, that there is supernatural purpose in the eternal law, such as the dedication of animals to human purposes, the subordination of female to male, or the establishment of sexual function exclusively or primarily for procreation, then the nonbeliever, denying that purpose, rejects these alleged relations. Given that these examples apply to human activity, this will mean a difference in the natural law. The ramifications of this are vast, but may be suggested by the consequences for homosexuality. If our sexual capacities are not informed by any superadded purpose, then how they are employed, all things being equal, is a matter of cultural sanction and personal preference, although judgments about particular exercises of sexuality will still be made in accord with the virtues. Differences over the eternal law, to put it another way, will change the findings but not the structure of virtue and right reason.

4.
Warcraft and the Fragility of Virtue

Where have we arrived? In the first chapter I advocated an Aristotelian approach to justice that was both realist and antifoundationalist. I began the second chapter insisting that we should not deny our prereflective "pacifist" feelings, but went on to argue that a consistent pacifism collides with the demands of justice when it comes to protecting the goods we rightfully hold most dear. Nonetheless, *pace* Jan Narveson, pacifism is not morally incoherent. In looking at John Yoder's work, I attempted to draw out the relations between truth, belief, and vocation, arguing that the believer, responding to the claims of Jesus, is committed to acting out the implications of those beliefs; and should there be a collision between what God asks and what justice seems to demand, the believer legitimately can, and indeed must, align himself with God. That Jesus is Lord is not a metaphor, or conceptual scheme, but an inescapable fact that determines the meaning of human life. This is the fundamental point of division between the Christian and the pagan. The nonbeliever, unable in conscience to believe the claims made for Jesus, can only view the self-sacrifice of Christian pacifists as a tragic loss. There is, however, a subsidiary dispute between the believer who would follow Yoder's interpretation of the Christian message and one who would understand that message differently. This is an important dispute for the ethics of war, because just war thinking, as embodied in the Catholic tradition of natural law, manifests a commitment to justice much closer to the Aristotelian than any of the secular, philosophical alternatives. But there was evidence that the Catholic tradition might be shaky as a practical institution. The locus of concern, it turned out, was not in the tradition criteria of *ius ad bellum* and *in bello* but in the failure of the bishops to be true to the tradition of virtue.

In turning to the classical Aristotelian account of virtue, I am asking what understanding of practical action might be necessary to sustain a community committed to justice but lacking a grounding in religious belief?[1] My goal is to show how discussion of the virtues makes a difference in moral philosophy and how that difference shows itself in discussing war. I'll call my account of the virtues "orthodox Aristotelianism" in order to distinguish it from the virtues appropriate to Yoder's Messianic community or Aquinas's account of the natural virtues informed by the theological.

A virtue for Aristotle is an excellence of character achieved through training and practice. It is a habit that enables a certain sort of activity to be chosen and to be carried to a successful completion. Habitual success is a necessary but not a sufficient condition for ascribing virtue, for we also insist that the agent know what he is doing, choose that action for its own sake, and be of such a character that he would normally choose that sort of act in those sorts of circumstances (Aristotle *Ethics*:1105a–5b). Possession of a virtue renders a person—or anything else, for that matter—not adventitiously good, but good after his kind. It renders the agent praiseworthy in the capacity as a mature practical actor, who has become a responsible contributing member of the community. In this sense, a virtue must be distinguished from "raw ability" much the way we distinguish athletic potential from competitive talent. The muscles come from nature and we deserve no particular praise for nature's gifts. But the individual who develops those gifts in the service of a particular sport rightly receives applause.

Sports, however engaging, are merely a facet of communal life; and if we applaud the talented athlete, all the more should we applaud those who have cultivated the virtues central to life together. This, after all, is what we mean by the "cardinal" virtues. Because of their centrality to all aspects of human life, those virtues are not limited to a single activity but extend across the spectrum. This, in turn, means that we must respond not to the rules of some artificial enterprise but to the nature of things in general. Thus, courage involves fearing "the right things and from the right motive, in the right way and at the right time" (Aristotle *Ethics*:1115b), where rightness means seeing things for what they are. We wouldn't, after all, call someone courageous who fought resolutely against a field mouse; that would just be comic. Nor should we call someone courageous who knowingly fought, however strongly, against justice. Such resoluteness should be attributed to stubbornness or overweening pride. Even someone who pursued the right things for the right reasons would forfeit the claim to justice should he or she resort to cheating or continue the battle after victory had been won. Aquinas puts this particularly well when he characterizes courage as the virtue which "removes any obstacle that withdraws the will from following the reason,... curbing fear and moderating daring" (*S.Theo.*:2a2ae, 123, 3). Consequently, when a person strays from reason the external act properly attributed to courage becomes a counterfeit of virtue. This would be the case should passion cast reason out, be it a passion "of sorrow that he wishes to cast off, or again of anger," but it may also happen "through choice, not indeed of a due end, but of some temporal advantage to be obtained... or of some disadvantage to be avoided" (123, 1 ad 2). Courage gives one the ability to bear the greatest threats because "it binds the will firmly to the good of reason in face of the greatest evils" (123, 4). If we believe, with Aristotle and Aquinas, that justice is among the greatest of goods, then any other passion, advantage, or disadvantage should reasonably be subordinated to it. And if we also believe that some acts are in themselves despicable, which "we cannot be forced to do, but ought rather to face death after the most fearful sufferings" (Aristotle *Ethics*:1110a), then courage is the virtue that allows us to face them well.

What is less frequently recognized is that the virtues of human character are, of their nature, fragile. This fragility is not an unfortunate happenstance but an essential aspect of what it means to be a virtue. For virtues are always being tested, and they frequently require reaffirming our resolve and reminding ourselves of where our true love lies. There is no rest in the past achievements of virtue, any more than there is for the competitive athlete or concert musician. Virtue, if it is to flourish, must be practiced, not merely possessed. Like any other skill or art, it will weaken and eventually vanish if not regularly employed. The most common enemies of virtue are indifference, self-indulgence, and despair, which persuade someone that something needn't be done, or not just now, or can't possibly be accomplished anyway—note the language of necessity, to which we will return—and thus might as well be dispensed with. Aristotle treats some aspects of this problem in book 7 of the *Ethics*, but there is an earlier, and much more vivid diagnosis that will repay a detailed analysis of the text.

Thucydides reports that, at the end of the first year of the Peloponnesian War, Pericles delivers a funeral oration for the Athenian dead. But, says Pericles, he will not praise the dead. Their sacrifice speaks more clearly and more eloquently than anything he could say. Pericles undertakes, rather, to give an account of what they died for and why.

And so Thucydides constructs for him the classic account of Athenian virtue. Why did these men die? For Athens. Why would somebody do such a thing? Because Athens, unlike Sparta, offers justice to stranger and friend alike. Athens is the center of wisdom and learning for the civilized world. Athens is the wellspring of culture. "This," he concludes,

is the kind of city for which these men, who could not bear the thought of losing her, fought nobly and nobly died.... You should fix your eyes every day on the greatness of Athens as she really is, and should fall in love with her. When you realize her greatness, then reflect that what made her great was men with a spirit of adventure, men who knew their duty, men who were ashamed to fall below a certain standard. (Thucydides 1954:bk. 2, par. 34–46)

Note the connection of Athens "as she really is" with a "certain standard." It is the reality of Athenian virtue that makes the polis lovable, and it is that reality for which men fight and die. The loss of Athenian virtue would mean the loss of that loveliness and render Athens itself unworthy of their deaths. Thus, Pericles' account of virtue presupposes the same sort of "truth" and "objectivity" required by Yoder's commitment to Jesus or the bishops' to the natural law.

It is also subject to the same strains and failures. While Pericles' funeral oration is well known to everyone, what follows immediately in Thucydides' account rarely receives the analysis it deserves. The plague: like an invisible enemy it lays waste the city with hideous, indiscriminate, and unpredictable disease.

Those with naturally strong constitutions were no better able than the weak to resist the disease, which carried away all alike.... The most terrible thing of all was the despair into which people fell.... no one expected to live long enough to be brought to trial and punished: instead everyone felt that already a far heavier sentence had been passed on him and was hanging over him, and that before the time for its execution arrived it was only natural to get some pleasure out of life.

The citizens of Athens ceased caring, and gave themselves up to all sorts of bestiality and vice. The uncertainty of the hour and the expectation of future misery conspired to crush Athenian virtue:

People now began openly to venture on acts of self-indulgence which before then they used to keep dark.... As for what is called honour, no one showed himself willing to abide by its laws, so doubtful was it whether one would sur-

vive to enjoy the name for it. It was generally agreed that what was both hon-
ourable and valuable was the pleasure of the moment. . . . No fear of god or
law of man had a restraining influence. As for the gods, it seemed to be the
same thing whether one worshipped them or not, when one saw the good and
the bad dying indiscriminately. (bk. 2, par. 47–55)

Thucydides concludes that "Athens owed to the plague the beginnings of a state of unprecedented lawlessness." This lawlessness does
not extend simply through the duration of the plague. Once virtue is
lost, it is hard to recover, and the continuing war perpetuates the inclination to self-seeking. There is, in Thucydides' account, a close connection between the lawlessness of the plague and the reduction of
justice to self-interest in the Mytilenian debate. Given this trajectory of
decline, the rejection of all values in the Melian dialogue and the ultimate destruction of Athenian culture come as no surprise.

In fact, war is much better captured by the metaphor of plague than
that of hell, for in hell everything is final and accomplished, whereas
plague, with its constant and unanticipated variations on horror,
breeds despair, self-indulgence, and indifference to the way I shape
my life. It leads to accepting the bestial and the vile as something we
have to live with—note again the language of necessity—and perhaps
even undertake ourselves. It is, in short, the ultimate laboratory in
which to test the strength, or fragility, of virtue. An example may
help.

Discussing obedience to superior orders, Walzer tells the story of a
German soldier who refused to serve in a squad executing noncombatant civilians. The soldier was summarily court-martialed, placed with
the civilians, and shot. Walzer comments:

Here is a man of extraordinary nobility, but what are we to say of his (former)
comrades? That they are committing murder when they fire their guns, and
that they are not responsible for the murder they commit. . . . Responsibility
passes over the heads of the members of the firing squad . . . because of the direct threat that drives them to act as they do. (1977:314)

These are not their acts, it would seem. The soldiers are but parts,
screwed inescapably into the machine, which is manipulated by their
superior. But that this is false is shown by the one soldier who refuses.
Walzer's language blinds him to the fact that this is a man of "extraordinary nobility" only when viewed from a perspective so fully debased
as to believe that persons could fail to be responsible for the murders

they commit. In order not to be responsible for my actions, I must truthfully be able to say that I did not know what I was doing or that I was unescapably constrained in my actions. But this is not the case. If one soldier can act courageously that is an indictment of the rest. For, as Aristotle notes, "there are some things we cannot be compelled to do, and rather than do them we should suffer the most terrible consequences and accept death" (*Ethics*:1110a). The need for discipline in an army requires individual soldiers to delegate the work of conscience to their superiors, but, when confronted with clear wickedness, conscience reasserts itself. Surely this happened in the case of the courageous soldier, and even if his comrades did not grasp the evil in executing noncombatants, they still must have recognized that their comrade was refusing to participate as a matter of conscience and this itself should have been enough to stay their hands. That they did not give up participation must, then, be considered either a breach of justice or courage or more likely both. It is a failure of virtue and as such is blameworthy.

To think it extraordinary that someone refrain from murdering reflects poorly not only on Walzer, but on our own self-understanding as well. For we are tempted to say that the soldier's refusal is heroic. And we're tempted because we worry that we could not do the same. If this situation seems familiar it should; it is the individual version of the Catholic bishops' fear. The most brutal irony of war is that conducting it justly demands, on the one hand, the firmest and most self-disciplined exercise of the virtues and, on the other, war does everything in its power to shatter the very virtues it demands. Even if we do not wish to call the individual soldiers "murderers," reserving this perhaps for their superior officer, we're still inclined to think that a world made up of such men would not, unlike Pericles' Athens, be worth living in, much less dying for.

To be ready to die for a community requires loving it. To love a community, as Pericles suggests, is to have a clear perception of its virtues, to judge them worthy, and in some degree to participate in them. The last qualification is intended to take care of cases where an outsider recognizes the excellence of a particular community without being a member. Surgery, for example, is typically a closed community. If my friend David waxes poetic about the exhilaration of practicing his discipline and the immediate sense of achievement in a difficult procedure well executed, this is something I accept on his say-so. Lay spectators are not welcome in the operating room. Nonetheless, there are activities we share that are connected with the virtues of a good surgeon. And after I witness major surgery firsthand, say as a husband watching a cesarean, I approach still closer an appreciation of his field. I also become aware of the magnitude of the risks and the enormous commitment involved in maintaining the virtues of a surgeon. The more I know, the more I am impressed by the fragility of things—Vergil's *lacrimae rerum*.

The fragility of the virtues is no different from that of any skill or craft. Ascribing virtue is rather like calling someone a craftsman in that his products must not merely be of an acceptable standard, they must achieve it through the systematic practice of the craft. If someone were to produce one good pot and never duplicate the feat we would not call him a "potter." If he were to set himself up in business and produce pots of an inferior sort we might, charitably, call him an inferior potter, but if every time he attempted to fire one it crumbled to bits or if every pot he sold disintegrated as soon as it was used, we'd say he is no potter, but a fraud.

Not all failures are met with censure, however. At the learning stages, for example, we give the apprentice much greater leeway and room for failure. This is how people learn. We might refer to a student as a potter, but this is really a sort of shorthand for saying that she is on her way. As yet, she needs external guidance and instruction, correction, and discipline, but when she can succeed on her own, choosing the steps because she sees that they are the right steps toward creating an acceptable product, we say she has mastered her craft. And we say, by and large, the same thing about children as they mature and become responsible members of the community. Fully mature human acts are those the individual initiates, carries out, and acknowledges. Aristotle is right, I think, to claim that a child cannot, properly speaking, be called happy, "for he is not yet capable of such acts, owing to his age; and boys who are called happy are being congratulated by reason of the hopes we have for them" (*Ethics*:1100a). Happiness requires the exercise of well-developed virtue over the course of a lifetime. The child has the status of my potter's apprentice; the skills needed are what we call the virtues.

The virtues are skills for crafting a life, which must be assessed in its fullness (*Ethics*:1098a). Some virtues, such as prudence, justice, temperance, and courage, will have to be brought into play repeatedly by any independent, responsible adult. Other virtues may only emerge under more narrowly specified situations. Magnanimity, to use one of

Aristotle's examples, requires a surfeit of resources and a community setting that makes it appropriate to distribute them publicly. War, as Aristotle also notes, is the natural arena for the expression of courage (*Ethics*:1115a). This doesn't mean that courage proper only exists in war or that the other virtues make themselves scarce in battle, but only that war is typically the theater in which the highest demands are made on courage and with the highest risks. But I'm getting ahead of myself. I need to look more closely at crafting and its relation to character.

When an accomplished potter throws her clay, what is she doing? She is not simply tossing about mud, but is beginning a pot, which will have a particular size and shape, serve a particular end, and be representative of her craftsmanship. It is a product of that craftsmanship, and one to which no one else can lay claim. In fact, she will allow no one else to claim the products of her craft. This, in large part, is the difference between craftsmanship and the assembly line. In an assembly line the individuals are merely parts of a machine. That they are made of flesh and blood and go home at five is incidental to the product of that machine. If they can be replaced efficiently by individuals made of steel and circuit boards, so much the better.

Let me pause to guard against a possible misunderstanding. I am not saying that assembly workers cannot be craftsmen, and often superb ones. My point is that their craftsmanship is incidental to the work of the machine, and this may be made clear in three ways. The assembly worker cannot lay claim to the product of the machine, but only to some aspect of that whole; the car, for example, is trash, but those are damned fine welds. Further, the assembly worker is answerable to a standard he does not set, but which is set for him by the nature and requirements of the machine. What is required of the worker is that he meet this standard, and if he does not he is replaced, like any other faulty part. But most telling is that the standard may not measure up to the worker's own, so that his craftsmanship may well conflict with the workings of the machine in such a way that he is forced to sacrifice his craftsmanship in order to remain a part. He must content himself with the set standard rather than the best of which he is capable. It is here that he has most clearly begun to function as a part.

One consequence is that he can no longer take pride in his product, for pride is the prerogative of craftsmanship. In order to take pride in something, it has to be, one way or another, mine. And properly to take pride in something requires that it be of my doing. I must have chosen it, known what I was choosing, and succeeded in producing it as a consequence of my craftsmanship. This way of putting the point should sound familiar. Indeed, I intend to draw a close connection between virtue, craft, and pride. A good craftsman takes pride in his work, and this is part of what it means to be a craftsman as opposed to a cog in the machine. For to take pride in something is to put it forward as worthy and to claim the credit for its praiseworthiness. In so doing, the craftsman also exposes himself to risk, for he must acknowledge and accept responsibility for failure. More than this, pride that is honest allows no one else to accept that responsibility, no matter the magnitude of the failure. Only his craftsmanship enables him to negotiate this risk, but how should this be understood?

A good craftsman masters the skills necessary to his craft, but it is important to remember that this mastery is not simply learning the rules. For rules of a craft can only be rules of thumb, starting points for responding to the demands of a particular project or situation. This is so because the rules are only generalizations derived from studying the creations and methods of the great practioners of the past. By following the rules I can, I suppose, be confident of regularly producing an acceptable product, something at least "minimally decent." (Cf. Thomson 1971.) But I could not really claim to be a leading member of the guild, much less *set* the standard. If I wish to excel, what is required is not action in accord with the rules for beginners but the continual practice and discipline that make my craftsmanship second nature and enable me to meet a situation with something worthy and uniquely mine.

Consider the following story.[2] An emperor of China was presented with a most exquisite piece of jade. He sent it to an old and famous jade carver with instructions to make a lion, as fitting the stature of an emperor. Some time passed, and the old man arrived at court with two exquisite fish and a box containing the remnants of the original jade. The emperor asked how the old man dared flout his orders in such a fashion. The old man simply answered that there was no lion in the stone. Less than pleased, the emperor asked what he meant by this, whereupon the old man opened the box, revealing only enough jade dust to cover the nail of his little finger. This, I take it, is pride in craftsmanship. But the story illustrates several other points as well. The jade carver responds to the task in no preordained way. Rather, he perceives the nature of his material and what its possibilities are. He does this on the basis of skills developed and perfected through

time. These skills, in other words, have what we might call an epistemic component that enables the craftsman to perceive the world, or at
least that part relating directly to his craft, with a fineness and specific-
ity inaccessible to the uninitiated. This is not to say that such perceptions are some mystical realm of experience closed to all others; with
enough application anybody can learn the basics of the art or craft.
But when it comes to applying skills to a particular task, where "it is
not possible either to take away or to add anything" without compromising the product, the direction to be chosen "is perceived by the
senses; such things depend on particular facts, and the decision rests
with perception" (Aristotle *Ethics*:1106b–1109b). Although Aristotle
clearly distinguishes the skills of the craftsman from the work of the
virtues, he does so to acknowledge the difference between making and
doing. Epistemically, the distinction is not relevant: both the skilled
craftsman and the virtuous agent have their perceptions, along with
their desires, shaped by the process of becoming the kind of persons
they are. They see the world better than those whose education has
been deficient, and it is for this reason that the accomplished craftsman and the individual of practical wisdom are the standards to which
the community looks.[3]

Hand in hand with the epistemic analogy goes the analogy of responsibility. The jade carver desires and executes the best that he sees,
and he presents it as his own, come what may. If he fails to carve the
fish, it is because he holds his craft in too little esteem. Perhaps he pre-
fers fortune, or fears the wrath of the emperor. But from the perspective of *our* jade carver, subordinating his craft to any of these concerns
would be to prostitute himself and the craft to which he has dedicated
his life. Simply to do the emperor's bidding would be contemptible,
and while he might excuse another, he cannot excuse himself. This
isn't to say that there might not be some circumstances under which
craft should be subordinated to other values, but this isn't one of
them. To put yourself forward as an artist is to claim certain insights
and the prerogatives that go with them. It is also to accept a level of
risk should your vision clash with others. The same is true for the mature moral agent. The willingness to adjust your understanding of virtue and the good is a sign of persistent childishness. This is not to reverse myself on moral fallibilism, but an attempt to place fallibility
where it belongs: at the limits of practical wisdom. Just as it would be
scientifically irresponsible in this day and age to entertain the plausibility of a flat earth or creationism, it would be morally irresponsible to

suggest that murder, rape, or slavery might be acceptable undertakings. This, after all, was the danger of "comparative justice."

This brings me to a another point that emerges from the analogy of craft and virtue. The craftsman insists on taking responsibility for his acts, with its attendent risks. But when he is successful, he's entitled to the pride that goes with it. He is, after all, seeking the best, trying to set the standard of excellence. A corollary to this reasonable pride is a robust ability for contempt. This isn't the place to elaborate on the virtue of contempt, but the ability to recognize an inferior product and the inclination to hold it and its maker in disdain are part of what it means to have developed a particular skill or virtue. Pride impells the craftsman to accept, and even desire, the risks present in the pursuit of excellence; he would shame himself, become an object of contempt, were he to do less than his best.

Here, I'll guard against another possible misunderstanding. My emphasis on pride and contempt may sound as though I were endorsing a haughty and elitist perfectionism, refusing to accept anything that doesn't measure up. But this would be a mistake. The contempt by my craftsman stems from his perception of pretense and sham. He does not expect perfection; there is no such thing. But he does expect a member of his guild to strive honestly to produce a quality artifact. Part of being a member lies in sharing standards of quality and recognizing whether a particular product measures up to the level of its maker. Thus, what my potter disdains from the hand of her equal she praises as the early assays of the apprentice. And, of course, what she would frown on if offered her by the apprentice, she accepts lovingly from her five-year-old. To have contempt for shoddy workmanship should not suggest pridefulness or arrogance in general, and there is no good reason to think it does. She just goes on about her business, and the expression of pride in her work is that work.

As an orthodox Aristotelian, the work of life is the crafting of a product in which I can take pride, which I wish to claim for my own, and offer as praiseworthy. The cardinal virtues are the basic skills for crafting a life and make it possible for me to acquire, hone, and protect whatever other skills I choose to pursue. They allow me, in short, to perceive the way the world is, recognize what is in accord with human flourishing, choose that, and pursue it to a successful completion. All I am claiming is that among the key animating aspects of this moral psychology are pride and contempt.

Two important points emerge from these considerations. First, as

I've already noted, rules are for beginners. Not only do I achieve but I also recognize the good as a result of habits and perceptions that are in accord with virtue and right reason. Once I have acquired the virtue in question, rules become superfluous. Second, there is little purchase here for the language of obligation. It has no epistemic import, so such language does not help me see what virtue requires. To invoke an obligation can be to do one of two things. If my potter says to herself, "I have an obligation to deliver that commission by the third," she is reminding herself not to be distracted, reminding herself what the situation at hand requires if both she and the customer are to be satisfied. It expresses a desire to produce something in which she can take pride, which she can offer up without embarrassment. But there is another use to which the invocation of obligation might be put. It might be used not by the potter, but by her client, and here again there are two ways to take it. It may be an insult, indicative of the low estimation this person has of her. To think, after all, that she is so low as to neglect what she has said or to avoid the consequences of what she has said is a vulgar affront. Also, if the averring to obligation does in fact have any weight, that itself is a symptom of the contemptible. It indicates that pride in one's craft has decayed to such an extent that the ability to count on even the adequate, the minimally decent, is lost. Such a situation is not worth preserving, much less cultivating. It is not clear what, if anything, the genuine craftsman can or should do, but it is a sorry state of affairs. To invoke obligation calls into question the characters involved and the world in which they live. As with rules, obligations come into play to supplement or rectify a situation where the agents involved can't be counted on to see what is required and take steps to achieve it. This describes, however, the breakdown of virtue, a situation in which prudence and the other cardinal virtues are no longer thought to be operative. Even when they are found together, the language of the virtues and the language of obligation, law, and duty are in tension because the latter is irrelevant when the virtues are functioning and probably useless when they are not.

More troubling than these internecine philosophical battles, however, is the prospect suggested by Alasdair MacIntyre that talk of "the just" and "the good" has lost credibility in the contemporary social world, being replaced by "the effective." When brought to bear on the ethics of war, an emphasis on effectiveness, coupled with the appeal to "expertise," can generate what Richard Wasserstrom calls "moral nihilism," the often inarticulate feeling that to invoke considerations of moral conduct is simply beside the point. Ethics, from this perspective, is a luxury in which the realistic, hard-nosed statesman or office holder cannot indulge. Wasserstrom cites, as an example, Dean Acheson on the cold war and the threat of nuclear destruction:

A respected colleague advised me that it would be better that our nation and people should perish rather than be party to a course so evil as producing that weapon. I told him that on the Day of Judgement his view might be confirmed and that he was free to go forth and preach the necessity for salvation. It was not, however, a view which I would entertain as a public servant. (1970:78–79)

Here, we have an important and by no means isolated example of the tendency of policy makers and holders of the public trust, in Mac-Intyre's words, to "justify themselves and their claims to authority, power and money by invoking their own competence as scientific managers of social change" (1981:82). First, Acheson defines himself primarily as a public servant, and in so doing limits his responsible actions to those which his station requires. Then, in that public capacity, he abstracts himself from all but technical questions of provocation and response, "the appraisal of dangers and risks, the weighing of the need for decisive and effective action against considerations of prudence," which leads him to conclude that "moral talk did not bear on the problem" (Wasserstrom 1970:79). "Moral talk" here is one form of discourse among many; and although it may have its place, such talk should not be allowed to enter into deliberations about the welfare, indeed the survival, of the nation. Questions of ethics have their place not in the day-to-day deliberations of practical public agents but in the hopes for salvation that individuals may adopt. If those hopes turn out to have some basis in the cosmos, then so be it. He, however, has been charged with seeing that *our* side wins, and win it shall.

Acheson makes a compelling example here because he is in no way more inhuman or depraved than any other contemporary statesman. His stance reflects the received political wisdom we have already seen at work exerting pressure on the Catholic bishops to accept less than conscience might wish when it is a matter of national security. Politicians, statesmen, and generals are expected to put national interest and political ascendancy before, we might say, the temptations of conscience. They are enjoined to be clearheaded, objective, and scientific. For many, the paradigm example of the modern, scientific attitude to warcraft is Carl Von Clausewitz, member of the Prussian general staff,

director of the War College, and author of *On War*. Clausewitz, as Peter Paret aptly notes, "stands at the beginning of the nonprescriptive,
nonjudgemental study of war as a total phenomenon.... But the detached interpretation of organized violence continues to pose the
greatest difficulties to the modern world" (Paret 1986:213). In the
century and a half since his death, Clausewitz has been studied by
strategists throughout the world, been embraced by Engels and Hitler, among others, and alternately praised and damned by critics for
his refusal to let ethics enter into his analysis of war as a professional
enterprise. To look in some detail at his account of war will help to
bring out what is at stake in viewing war as something to be managed
as opposed to part of the life crafted by its participants.

As Clausewitz understands it, war is "a clash of forces freely operating and obedient to no law but their own," a political act undertaken
between nations or city-states manifesting three aspects: "The *armed
forces*, the *country*, and the *enemy's will*" (Clausewitz 1976:78). Two (or
more) powers enter into war when they engage armed forces against
each other in "an act of force which compels our enemy to do our will"
(1976:75). In the formal sense, war is indifferent to the content of
that, its internal logic being "*always* and *solely* ... to overcome the enemy and disarm him" (1976:90). Insofar as we are dealing with war
proper any other goals or motives of the adversaries do not figure in.
It begins as a clash of wills and "cannot be considered to have ended so
long as the enemy's *will* has not been broken" (1976:78). Clausewitz
assumes that the natural result of deploying forces will be battle,
hence we should expect war to be violent when compared to times of
peace. But violence is a comparative term, a fact unfortunately
masked by nominalization. Acts can be violent without being warlike,
and wars can be more or less violent in their prosecution. If the force
of one adversary is sufficient to break the will of the other, then the
war is over; but so long as force is countered by force the conflict goes
on. And as long as the desire to impose one's will on another persists,
the magnitude of the force employed will increase, with reciprocal escalation on the other side. As Clausewitz puts it, "there is no logical
limit to the application of that force. Each side, therefore, compels its
opponent to follow suit; a reciprocal action is started which must lead,
in theory, to extremes" (1976:77). The end of war is reached only in
the extinction of the adversary's will, and there is no internal check on
the intensity of the conflict. This is the essence of war. All war, in theory, is absolute.

Clausewitz has received considerable criticism for his account of the logic of war, on both the moral and the technical level. Walzer, for example, notes that as "soon as we focus on some concrete case of military and moral decision-making, we enter a world that is governed not by abstract tendencies but by human choice. . . . No one has ever experienced 'absolute war' " (Walzer 1977:24). W. B. Gallie reconstructs Clausewitz's argument, only to claim that it is formally inadequate, a point he then uses to support the further claim that Clausewitz jettisons, in his later thought, the concept of absolute war (Gallie 1978:49–58). Both criticisms miss the mark. Gallie, for example, takes the central failure of Clausewitz's argument to reside in the premise that

(3) The prospect or fear of [destruction] may induce our opponent to stop fighting long before the result itself is reached; but this possibility cannot affect the way—the only logical way—in which we should conduct the fight (or war): viz. by applying from the outset and for as long as necessary all the force that we can command. (1978:56)

He claims that this premise incorporates a logical blunder, affirming the "cannot" of the second clause, when all Clausewitz is entitled to claim is that "'this possibility *need* not affect the way'" (1978:57). What Gallie seems at pains to avoid is the conclusion that the only "logical" way to fight a war is to prosecute it as a war of total destruction, what he calls a "knock-out" war, but in doing so he fails to see what Clausewitz is up to. In a conflict that has become war there is, Clausewitz notes, an instinct toward the destruction of the enemy, and to deny this is self-deception. But hostile feelings and hostile intentions must be distinguished, with the intentions given analytic primacy. Hostile intention determines the nature of the conflict if only because it is the conflict of proposed courses of action that marks the occasion for war. Should our intentions coincide we could act with a single will. By the same token, once the will to resist has been broken, the war comes to an end, whether or not the enemy has been destroyed or our hostile feelings dissipated. Of course, an implacably hostile victor may wreak destruction on his enemy after the successful prosecution of a war, but that's genocide and not Clausewitz's topic.

Perhaps an example will help. Suppose that we have undertaken war against an adversary similar in strength, resources, and resolve. *Ex hypothesi*, our opponent has the will to resist us, intending to coerce us into giving up our own hostile intentions. After several inconclusive engagements, no new initiatives are undertaken, although armies are left in the field, suspended on wary alert. How should we describe this impasse? It might be the case that both sides have expended their war-fighting resources—no more bullets, bombs, or what have you. This is nothing more than an external check on the inner workings of war, and we may assume that the war would continue *if only* one or both had the present means. What if only one of the protagonists has run out of bullets? Its adversary, assuming that the hostile intention persisted, would be expected to pursue the advantage, but, given the example, it does not. This is puzzling. Is there some taboo against pursuing an enemy who has run out of resources? Do these protagonists share a view that such ruthless prosecution of a contingent advantage isn't sporting? Both are possible, and both give evidence for the truth that wars are never pursued in a vacuum, free from other interests and intentions. Among the Meru of Kenya, for example, "ripening crops were protected by warriors on both sides. Raiders passing through their opponents' banana groves were permitted to snatch what they required at the moment, but were forbidden to cut down or otherwise harm the trees" (Fadiman 1982:41). Such constraints are linked to the total ecology of the Meru and their neighbors and hedged round with various forms of human and supernatural censure. They are no doubt similar in origin and import to Yahweh's injunction to the Israelites not to destroy the fruit trees of their beseiged enemies, for "the trees of the field are not men that you should besiege them" (Deut. 20:19). But none of this reflects anything of the inner workings of war, and this is Clausewitz's point. In this sense, war resembles a game; the point is winning. But it might be better to say that war is the general condition of any competitive game, the difference being that victory in a game is specified by the rules, regardless of the will of the contestants. Once the conditions for victory have been satisfied the persistence of conflict usually manifests itself in playing again. Going outside the rules to impose your will isn't victory, it's cheating.

Here we should pause. As Clausewitz describes the inner workings of war, it is impossible to cheat. You can blunder, or get lucky, be reckless or cunning, but questions of "fair play" don't gain a foothold. At least not yet. When Clausewitz proposes that we analyze the pure concept of war without regard to its political context, he is not claiming that we undertake war in a political vacuum. As we shall see, he insists on just the opposite. Again, the Meru provide interesting data. Traditionally, they acquired and augmented their herds through raiding. In the education of their youth, it was important to foster martial virtues, and the display of these virtues required conflict. Consequently, groups of aspiring warriors "were encouraged by taunts from the appropriate adult observers to band together and then to seek out similar groups . . . in order to provoke them into conflict" (Fadiman 1982:58). Such conflicts, nonetheless, were carefully orchestrated and controlled. Certain kinds of weapon were forbidden; and before serious damage could be done, their elders "intervened to stop the conflict and inspect each boy's body for evidence of injury. Those who emerged unscathed would be rewarded with songs of praise" (1982:61). Here, conflict can only be judged and understood from within the larger order of the culture as a whole. Such war games promote character considered worthy and appropriate to the common good. This sense of the common good defines the meaningfulness of these activities, and it is crucial for understanding their character to relate them to other of the community's enterprises.

On the face of it, no greater contrast to the Meru could be imagined than Clausewitz's bracketing the question of the larger good in discussing war. Indeed, a certain indifference to the good is assumed by both Walzer and Gallie, and would no doubt be applauded by Acheson. But how secure is this reading? The remarkable chapter "Military Genius" suggests an interpretation quite different. Here, at the very beginning of his work, Clausewitz insists that the ability to envision and execute military operations rests squarely on the character, virtue, and imagination of the commander. The climate of war is one pervaded by danger and exertion. Not unlike Thucydides' plague, the uncertainty and prevalence of chance work to sap the army of its strength. "The machine itself," Clausewitz writes, "begins to resist, and the commander needs tremendous willpower to overcome this resistence. . . . As each man's strength gives out, as it no longer responds to his will, the inertia of the whole gradually comes to rest on the commander's will alone" (1976:104). In this context, "courage" is of two kinds. There is the indifference to personal danger that has become habitual and there is the impetus toward achievment derived from some positive, and perhaps fleeting, motive. "The first," in Clausewitz's estimate, "is the more dependable; having become second nature, it will never fail. . . . The second tends to stimulate, but it can also blind. *The highest kind of courage is a compound of both*" (1976:101). In the prosecution of war, such courage must be incorporated into a stable character. Even when the misery, fear, and sheer exhaustion of the campaign provoke extremes of emotion, "judgement and principle must still function like a ship's compass.... Only those general principles and attitudes that result from clear and deep understanding can provide a *comprehensive* guide to action" (1976:107–8). Emerging here is a complex analysis of character as a prerequisite for the soldier. Courage incorporates habit and belief about the good, unified in the man of character, whose understanding is informed by a reasoned reflection on the nature of things and a willingness to adjust attitudes to ever clearer perceptions of reality. Failure to be guided by the nature of things is obstinacy, "*a fault of temperment* . . . a special kind of *egotism* which elevates above everything else *the pleasure of its autonomous intellect, to which others must bow*" (1976:108). The opposite of obstinacy, to give it its Aristotelian name, is prudence, the virtue of seeing what is and what ought to be done. In the person of character, self-control "assures the dominance of the intellect" and liberates "the noblest pride and deepest need of all: the urge *to act rationally at all times*" (1976:106).

War is a destructive and terrifying undertaking, not to be entered into lightly. Chance and uncertainty are augmented by the particularities of space, and the commander must be a man of prudence, surveying the immediate situation with the ability to bring the details together in a clear, coherent picture. The commander is driven by the ambition for honor and renown, but this is inextricably linked to the responsibilities of command. The goal of *On War* is to lay the foundations for warcraft, the special skills that will help the commander carry out his responsibilities and display the imagination and insight that merit applause. As with any other craftsman, "the commander's superior intellect and strength of character . . . express themselves in the final success of his work" (1976:112). In short, Clausewitz is not indifferent to character, but assumes a robust and fully operative foundation in the virtues.

The depth of this commitment emerges forcefully in Clausewitz's reflections on his dictum that war is the "continuation of political intercourse, with the addition of other means," insisting that it "cannot be divorced from political life; and whenever this occurs in our thinking about war . . . we are left with something pointless and devoid of sense" (1976:605). War is made possible because groups and nations compete for power and resources. It is a rational, human activity because these competitions are directed toward the good of the groups involved. Because humans are fallible in their judgments, differences emerge as to where the good lies. Consequently, "nothing is more important in life than finding the right standpoint for seeing and judging events. . . . One point and *one only* yields an integrated view of all phenomena." The soldier is not charged with finding this point, however; that's the job of the makers of policy, whose charge "is to unify and reconcile all aspects of internal administration as well as of spiritual values, and whatever else the moral philosopher may care to add" (1976:606). The makers of policy must attempt to discover how best to secure the good of their constituency; and if war is a reasonable possibility, then they should incorporate someone knowledgeable in warcraft as party to their deliberations, but the military perspective must remain subordinate to the political. The very notion of "purely military advice" is an illusion, and a dangerous one, for to contemplate war without a clear political vision, grounded in the search for the good, is to risk losing the good that war is intended to protect (1976:609–10).

Just as soldiers defer the work of conscience to their commander, the general defers policy determinations to those who have the responsibility for the common good. But at no level are the demands of conscience simply dismissed; thus, at no point do questions of ethics cease to be germane. There is no little irony in the realization that Clausewitz feels free not to discuss ethics *because* he thinks it impossible to investigate any aspect of human activity without coming up against moral and political issues. Like the Aristotelian he thinks of justice as the rational management of social practices that are worthy in themselves and whose standards are generally recognized and maintained by the community at large. There can be disagreement and malfeasance, policy "can err, subserve the ambitions, private interests, and vanity of those in power," but at the level of analysis that "is neither here nor there" (1976:606–7). Like Aristotle and Aquinas, Clausewitz recognizes that all facets of human life depend on the character of individuals and community.

We have, then, two contrasting readings of Clausewitz's *On War.* Walzer and Gallie read him as the apostle of total war, the servant of national interest, indifferent to questions of justice and morality. Gallie in particular views him as ruthlessly pursuing his analysis to a merciless conclusion in total and unbridled destruction. On this reading, the "logic" of war compels the rational strategist to reject as superficial and incoherent any so-called ethical constraints, and this is why

Clausewitz's analysis must be resisted. Put in MacIntyre's terms, Clausewitz, on this reading, is the quintessential manager, sacrificing everything for effectiveness.

Closer attention to the text, however, reveals an argument that presupposes a fully developed moral tradition in which the work of the cardinal virtues is essential to the successful practice of warcraft. Intellect and imagination combine to enable the officer to cut through the welter of conflicting information and perspectives to see things for what they are and elaborate an appropriate response. Courage and temperance allow him to transform insight into action. And the army as a whole works together because its members, tried in battle, "think of themselves as members of a kind of guild, in whose regulations, laws, and customs the spirit of war is given pride of place" (Clausewitz 1976:187). Justice operates here in a typically Aristotelian way, by which I mean that it is not a universal standard against which soldierly conduct is measured but a disposition emerging out of the division of labor, working for a common good, in which individuals are accorded their due, as determined by their place in and contribution to the work at hand. This pretheoretical disposition to work for the good, as understood by the group, Clausewitz captures nicely when he suggests that the soldiers think of themselves as members of a guild, who have taken on the responsibility of exemplifying and protecting the standards of excellence passed down through a tradition of military service and solidified by fears and privations faced and overcome.

For all his extolling "the military spirit," Clausewitz immediately acknowledges its fragility. "Even the highest morale in the world," he insists, "can, at the first upset, change all too easily into despondency, an almost boastful fear; the French would call it *sauve qui peut*" (1976:189). It is for this reason that training in peacetime, a mere knowing the procedures and principles, is no substitute for the arduous practice which incorporates that knowing into the character of general and footsoldier alike. Further, if war is to be an extension of politics and if the military is to be the instrument of political action, then the soldiers who surrender the exercise of conscience to their leaders must assume that those leaders share these qualities of character. For coherent political action, this must hold all the way up the ladder of command. The consequences of failure may be extreme, a point dramatically brought out by the growing dissatisfaction with Hitler's command that led to the conspiracy of July 1944 (Keegan 1987:258–310).

In war, as in the rest of life, action stems from character, and character cannot be understood or appraised apart from its virtues and defects. Some consequences of the failure to ground an understanding of *ius ad bellum* in the character of the agents emerge from a look at James Childress's influential essay "Just War Criteria." Discussing the traditional criterion of just intention in resorting to war Childress writes:

Some would hold that the dominance, if not the mere presence, of hatred vitiates the right to wage war even if there is a just cause.... Such a contention, however, is difficult to establish, for if all the conditions of a just and justified war were met, the presence of vicious motives would not obliterate the *ius ad bellum*, although they would lead to negative judgments about the agents. (1982:78)

The reasoning behind this relies heavily on the vocabulary of rights, duties, and obligations, and the steps of the argument go something like this: (1) There is a prima facie duty to refrain from injuring others; (2) this prima facie duty is overriden by a sufficiently severe violation of rights on the part of some other; (3) given this violation of rights, there no longer exists an obligation to refrain from injuring that particular other; (4) while acting hatefully would be nasty, it would not be in violation of any duty; (5) consequently, nasty motives do not render resort to war wicked if there is just cause.

The Aristotelian finds this way of proceeding very puzzling. While he might find (1) an awkward, although intelligible, variation of the definition of justice as rendering to each his due, (2) is very strange. Whence come these duties, and why should it be the case that the overriding of them licenses certain forms of behavior? It seems much clearer to avoid this vocabulary and say that when someone attacks me and mine I don't have any good reason not to resist, and all sorts of good reasons to do so. On this account (3) is superfluous, since there was never, strictly speaking, any such obligation. To injure someone is to detract from that person's well-being—that's what the word means—and so to do it without reason is unjust—that's what that word means. The person of virtue doesn't do that, any more than my potter gives her client a product she knows to be defective.

Step (4) deserves somewhat more detailed attention. What does it mean to hate someone? Hate is not anger. I can be angry for any number of reasons, and some of these reasons will justify my anger. If, for example, I have told my five-year-old son not to play with the computer in my study, and return to find he has done so, erasing my files, I will be angry. This anger is justified. Nor is hate the desire to inflict injury. Given what my child has done, I form the intention of punishing him and do so in a way that detracts from his immediate desires and well-being. A spanking, after all, is a spanking, and if you don't intend it to sting, you don't understand what you are doing. Perchance my son was courageously pursuing a colleague, who had broken in to erase my files, but I, not believing this, punish him anyway. This is unfortunate, and it may perhaps be unjust on my part. It is still not hatred.

What is hatred, then? In lieu of a detailed discussion by the Philosopher himself, I'll turn to his best commentator:

Now when a man turns naturally away from something it is because, by its nature, it ought to be avoided. Just as all creatures seek pleasure naturally, they avoid sorrow in the same way, as Aristotle says. And just as love comes from pleasure, so hatred comes from sorrow. We love what gives us pleasure because its pleasure-giving aspect is considered a good; so we hate what gives us sorrow because its sorrow-giving aspect is considered an evil. But envy is sorrow, i.e., over our neighbour's blessings, and sorrow is hateful to us. Thus out of envy comes hatred. (Thomas Aquinas *S. Theo*:2a2ae, 34, 6)

This passage from St. Thomas is useful for several reasons. In the first place, it displays the Aristotelian emphasis on moral psychology and the way the world is. Hatred is not some abstract notion, but tied up with feelings, habits, and responses to the world. Thomas undertakes his analysis free from the vocabulary of duties and obligations. Nonetheless, he provides a nuanced account that will help make clear why unjust intent renders a war wicked. Hatred stems from envy, and envy is sorrow over the flourishing of our neighbor. But this is not any sorrowing. If I am upset with the good life of a mafia capo, this may be an expression of my outrage over his unpunished wickedness. Envy is to want something another person has, regardless of the justice with which he acquired it. Hatred carries this a step further. When I hate someone I wish him injury, not to redress an injustice, but as a consequence of my envy. I move from wanting what is his to hoping he loses it, just so he doesn't have it. One of the impressive features of this Aristotelian account is that we can all, I trust, recognize firsthand the feeling under discussion.

How would the Aristotelian view a war undertaken out of hatred? What does someone who hates want, when he goes to war? He does not simply want to redress a wrong, although he might view this as a foreseen but unintended consequence. He wants to inflict injury for injury's sake. But this short-circuits the appeal to just cause. The person who hates, hates in the absence of *just* cause, and refrains from acting on his hate out of fear, or weakness, or what have you. He *wants* to inflict injury, whether or not it is due, and this desire is contrary to justice. Just because I don't like you doesn't entitle me to injure you, any more than it would entitle me to cheat you or otherwise take from you what you legitimately hold. Talk about obligation and duty obscures the deeper relations of action to character. Since justice is not simply a matter of meeting a generic standard but a function of character, acts carried out in hate cannot be just.

Childress's understanding of intention, and his account of just war criteria, is enfeebled by a poor moral psychology, which portrays acts as somehow to be understood apart from the agents who perform them. This is not only implausible but also perverse, as though we were looking at generic brands and judging them without considering how adopting them shapes our lives. But we don't commit generic acts. An act committed is specific, mine, in just the same way as the pots of my potter or the jade of my carver. Returning to the contrast between the craftsman and the assembly line, it's as though I were to say that the limits of responsibility for my creations simply were the limits of the warranty. You can't, I suppose, seek redress under law if I have fulfilled the obligations of the warranty, but if the product was inferior, then my craftsmanship was inferior. And if I don't insist on taking the responsibility for this, then I render myself contemptible, not merely in your eyes, but in my own.

In pondering the worthiness of war I am already asking how it might fit into and alter the life I am making. This leads me to another difference with Childress, for there is no and, in fact, can be no neutral ground for assessing war per se. Consequently, it will not do to think of just war criteria as "a formal framework within which different substantive interpretations of justice and morality as applied to war can be debated" (Childress 1982:90).[4] This is the moral of Clausewitz. Unlike some situations, where it is up to me to accept or decline the endeavor, war, and the circumstances in which war is a possibility vigorously impose themselves on me, circumscribing my movements, limiting my resources, hurting people, places, and things that I care for and, although we needn't think this is the most important point, putting me in jeopardy of life and limb. Some response is required. To ignore the issue is either gross stupidity or wishful thinking. At issue, however, are the resources I bring to my response and the character of what I achieve. The concrete and specific acts that I undertake, and which go to make up my life, are not carried out *in vacuo* but essentially involve a substantive understanding of justice. Even were I to grant that "there is no single substantive theory of just war," it would not follow that just war criteria can serve only as a "framework for debates" (Childress 1982:91). They must, on the contrary, be the sort of considerations that can help me discover how to shape a product that I can take pride in. Before surrendering his conscience to the judgment of his superiors, the responsible citizen must ask, "can I make this war mine?" and this question can only be answered by bringing to bear a concrete sense of the good.

Part of the point of exploring the metaphor of craftsmanship was to free our thinking from the notion that justice, or practical reasoning in general, can ever be merely formal. Reasoning about action, even imaginatively, involves asking whether or not it's the sort of thing I could do, now, as I am. This is different from asking whether I could do it *if I were a Dogon*, or *if I were depraved*, or *if I were ignorant of its nature*. These are perhaps the questions sparked by our encounters with anthropologists like Griaule or poets like Sophocles, but they are a step removed from the concerns of the craftsman. He has only a particular set of tools and skills and will be judged by a concrete set of standards operative here and now. In our practical deliberations we are all, for the most part, in the position of the craftsman. I can only make a course of action mine if I deem it worthy of pursuit, and I can only determine this on the basis of the substantive values that shape the whole of my life. I must know what I am doing because I am risking that life, and my ability to negotiate this risk depends on the strength of my virtues. And having virtues means having acted in ways that reflect concrete beliefs about what in this world is genuinely worthy and what is to be disdained. My orthodox Aristotelian occupies this position unaided by God or the theological virtue of hope; he alone is charged with making something out of life, with the help of whatever skills he has gleaned from the community around him. That his life and the goods he pursues are fragile and constantly in jeopardy is a fact made all the more compelling under stress. When subjected to the extreme test of war, when strength and virtue are most at risk, it is helpful to fall back on the just war criteria to clarify conscience.

This would not be possible in Childress's thin account. By treating just war criteria as "a formal framework" for debate, he only muddies the waters. The same is true, as I've already suggested, of Michael Walzer's treatment in *Just and Unjust Wars*. We looked briefly at his position on deterrence in the previous chapter, and at his remarks on heroic courage earlier in this. In both instances I claimed that his willingness to relax the demands of justice were incompatible with a tradition that values character and quality over mere survival. In turning now to his account of necessity, I'll argue that here, too, his attempt to secure a hearing for justice slides over into capitulating to evil.

It is often claimed that some acts are necessities of war, but Walzer rightly insists that "necessity" too often means "expediency," which degenerates into calculating acceptable and unacceptable risks in response to a threat. He suggests that

the mere recognition of such a threat is not itself coercive; it neither compels nor permits attacks on the innocent, so long as other means of fighting are available. Danger makes only half the argument; imminence makes the other half. (1977:255)

When both conditions are met we may be excused methods that would ordinarily be condemned. It is worth noting that this is very much a specialized use of "necessity," conditioned by the tacit refusal to accept the failure of a particular enterprise. An imminent threat "compels" me to attack the innocent *if* I am unwilling to accept defeat. But in any human endeavor it is possible to accept failure or admit defeat. I may not want to give it up. I may be afraid to give it up. But that is a different matter. The language of necessity, even carefully circumscribed, leads to neglecting this point, and this would be to neglect what the Aristotelian holds most important. For it fosters the false belief that difficult choices aren't choices, that at the extremes I cease to have control over my actions. But this is very rarely true. It was in no way necessary for the German soldiers to murder their comrade along with the other victims, though if they had refused they would have risked their own lives. Nor was it necessary for the citizens of Athens to give in to the despair of the plague, although their virtue was too fragile to see them through it. Walzer's use of legal paradigm makes it difficult to open a space for questions of character and virtue and thus makes it difficult to see what, beyond survival and self-interest, would motivate the just war criteria. For him, they are rules rather like those governing contractual relations in law. Once there has been a breach of rules, what is allowed is up in the air. Thus, "necessity," as Walzer uses it, is whatever we take to be sufficient to abrogate the rules, whatever we might think about the goodness of the actions that follow.

The dangers of employing this language emerge with particular vividness in Walzer's account of the disgracing of Arthur Harris. Harris was responsible for the saturation bombing of the German interior during World War II. The policy was a matter of debate at the time, but the British commanders, Churchill above all, considered it necessary for victory. Nevertheless, the neglect of Harris after the war, Walzer writes, amounted to public disgrace:

> Harris and his men have a legitimate complaint: They did what they were told to do and what their leaders thought was necessary and right, but they are dishonoured for doing it, and it is suddenly suggested that what was necessary and right was also wrong. (1977:324)

Walzer argues that the pursuit of the policy in the later years of the war was wrong, but at the same time allowing that the imminence of the threat might have made it necessary and thus excusable. He suggests that Churchill should have found a better way of responding than dishonoring Harris, perhaps by praising the bomber pilots:

> Even while insisting that it was not possible to take pride in what they had done... he never admitted that the bombing constituted a wrong. In the absence of such an admission, the refusal to honor Harris at least went some small distance toward re-establishing a commitment to the rules of war and the rights they protect. (1977:325)

This, I think, is a remarkable statement. It suggests at one and the same time that we needn't take responsibility for the wrongs we commit, that it is better to blame somebody else than nobody at all, and that in blaming somebody else we are affirming our commitment to decency. If he's willing to say that, I'm tempted to exclaim, he might say anything. Failure to accept responsibility, blaming others, is transparently base, and anything gained from it ill-gotten. The soldier entrusts his conscience to his superiors, and it is wicked and shameful for them to betray that trust. The wickedness is compounded if they then deflect responsibility from themselves and use the soldier to effect their escape. The act is cowardly and unfair.

Nor can it reestablish "a commitment to the rules of war and the rights they protect." A commitment reflects the resolve to pursue a particular good, subordinating and perhaps forsaking others. In this it is distinct from mere preferences, which may have no ordering at all. The commitment registers a willingness to continue pursuing the appropriate good even when you might prefer to be doing something else. It is only as stable as the virtues that underlie it, and those virtues cannot be maintained by refusing responsibility or foisting the blame for your failures on others. To advocate a policy that undermines virtue is to ensure that no commitments are reliable, and this strikes at the very possibility of coming together in a community worth defending. For it now becomes a serious question what our leaders *won't* do and then try to excuse themselves. And then to wonder about my co-workers and neighbors and erstwhile friends.

As with the bishops, so with Childress and Walzer. It is not so much the particular positions they defend that my orthodox Aristotelian finds suspect but the method and vocabulary they bring to discussions of war. Virtue as craft, understood in the Aristotelian sense, has no place, in its mature exercise, for appeal to rules and obligations, formal frameworks, and value choices. I can shape a life in which I die, protecting my wife and children, or one in which I hike over the mountains, leaving them before the rush of the approaching tanks. Which can I choose with pride? Which is contemptible? There is no getting around these questions, certainly not by invoking a spurious necessity. Talk of necessity, coercion, imminent threat, and formal theories fosters the view that shaping our lives is either arbitrary or out of our control, and this opens up the gates of indifference, indulgence, and despair. When this happens we lose the ability to take pride in ourselves, and we admit the contemptible as the norm. Virtue, being fragile, cannot thrive in such a community, as Thucydides shows us, for these are the conditions of plague.

Notes

1. In the prologue I alluded to a minority undercurrent of Aristotelian moral thought in recent and contemporary philosophical ethics. Much of the current debate, however, responds to MacIntyre's provocative 1981 work. Without minimizing its importance, I am going to decline to enter the lists here. Responses to MacIntyre are legion, and he deals with representative critics in the "Postscript" added to his 1984 work. A useful bibliography is compiled in Yearley (1990), but the most incisive analysis of MacIntyre, both his virtues and faults, is provided by Stout (1988).

2. I read this story many years ago, I think, in a book on jade by Richard Gump. I no longer have the book and can't find a copy, and so am unable to verify details or give proper citations, for which I apologize.

3. This is not an uncontroverted claim about the interpretation of Aristotle, although I think it is a correct reading. In any event, my goal is to present an Aristotelian account of moral epistemology, not provide a detailed exegesis of the master. Nonetheless, I should acknowledge that my reading here follows lines laid down in M. F. Burnyeat's "Aristotle on Learning to Be Good" and L. A. Kosman's "Being Properly Affected: Virtues and Feelings in Aristotle's Ethics," both in Rorty (1980). An exhaustive recent discussion of these matters and others, with an extensive bibliography, may be found in Irwin (1988).

4. I have a problem here that is not worth including in the body of the paper, but one I want to mention nonetheless. The language that Childress and Walzer use, despite differences between them, is so much at odds with the vocabulary I want to use that I am not comfortable with my own exposition. I've made this point with respect to "obligation," and I should also make it with regard to "value." Childress's remarks about formal frameworks, competing values, and "theories" of justice make it seem that we are presented a range of alternatives and then asked to adopt some set of them. Having done so, we say we have *these* values, from which follow our judgments about right and wrong, good and bad. My own inclination is simply to say of something, or person, or act that it is (or is not) good. If asked why, I want to respond that it is a fine exemplar of its kind. If asked what this means, there is no recourse other than pointing out other examples, making connections, and explaining that's the way the world is, that's the kind of critter we are. This way of proceeding betrays the fact that I not only consider myself an orthodox Aristotelian but also an orthodox Wittgensteinian as well. The impetus for providing this footnote came from Mr. Chris Iosso, who recently brought to my attention in seminar Stanley Hauerwas's essay "How Christian Universities Contribute to the Corruption of Youth: Church and University in a Confused Age," *Katallagete* (Summer 1986): 21–28. My remarks on value in the analysis of Childress should not obscure my agreement with Hauerwas's attack on teaching as presenting alternative theories of value.

5.
Friendship, Justice, and Military Service

"*It* is possible to imagine a solitary state which is happy in itself and in isolation," Aristotle remarks, and "the scheme of its constitution will have no regard to war, or to the conquest of enemies, who, upon our hypothesis, will not exist" (*Pol.*:1325a). But such a situation is not ours. The account of virtue begun in chapter 4 is not sufficient. My preliminary discussion of justice, in fact, ensures that no ethics based solely on the virtues can possibly be adequate. For while I have sketched how virtue can provide the epistemic capacity necessary to a serious moral realism, I have not as yet provided much of an account of how and why people are motivated to come together in the corporate bodies required to sustain more complex practices or what holds those bodies together. One way to focus the issue is to ask about the status of the armed forces. At no point in history have communities been completely free from the prospect of attack. Should we rely on our own abilities to rise to threats or should we establish an army? And if we feel the need for an army, should we rely on our fellows to staff it at reasonable levels or should we compel some segment of the populace to serve? The way these questions are answered says a great deal about how we understand our relation to others and to the community as a whole. Given that we do have to make some allowances for defense, we need to ask how they should be managed. But this itself, and here Aristotle anticipates Clausewitz, cannot be divorced from larger political questions, because the makeup of the armed forces will either reflect or undermine the form of government we possess. Geography that favors cavalry will be likely to breed oligarchy, for "it is only men of large means who can afford to breed and keep horses"; whereas heavy infantry, although still expensive, conduces to a broader form of oligarchy, and a light infantry and navy, drawn principally from the lower and middle classes, will be "wholly on the side of democracy" (*Pol.*:1321a). In military affairs, as in all aspects of human life, the attempt to create and sustain a community is shot through with the contingent and unpredictable.

There are, however, several preliminary traps to avoid. The thrust of the preceding two chapters has been to elevate justice over survival, or, to put it another way, to establish a preference for character over mere continuity. This position is neither novel nor radical. That defeat is better than committing injustice and that we must have the resolve to accept defeat is central to Anscombe, Ramsey, and the just war tradition in general. It is also manifest in the resolve of Walzer's heroic soldier. Thus, I will feel free to ignore, by and large, questions of feasability. A more dangerous pitfall, however, is the unargued assumption that "military necessity" allows the suspension of constraints otherwise operative in the quest for justice. Eliot Cohen, for example, remarks almost casually that the "dimension of external necessity is always present, and plays a particularly important role in wartime, when many objections based on principle and ideology must give way to the demands of survival" (1985:32). Central to my argument, however, is the role of virtue in empowering us to stand firm against such "necessity," so I shall feel free to slide over this sort of objection.

Nonetheless, both the urge to find a workable political order and the willingness to make concessions to ensure the survival of that order ground themselves in the notion that the state is worthy per se and can legitimately demand that the citizenry take up the burden of its defense should it come under attack. Is there a general obligation to defend the state and, if so, what is its basis? If no grounds can be found for a general obligation of this sort, is the Aristotelian perspective sufficiently powerful to account for the particular obligations we might have to the political order, their extent, and their limits?

James Johnson has recently argued that the volunteer army, at least as currently constituted, reflects a failure of moral vision. A look at this argument will provide a useful entry into the issues. Johnson draws his conclusion from three "general principles" taken from Helmut Thielicke:

(1) The state may demand military service; (2) the citizen must accept the state's demand, though the peculiar character of his acceptance may involve him in suffering; (3) the state should seek to minimize the suffering of its citizens. (Johnson 1984:159)

Logically prior, however, is the claim that the "safety of the community is every citizen's responsibility" (154). The argument goes something like this. Military readiness is necessary to ensure the ability of the state to preserve itself in a world of conflict. In order to achieve this readiness, the state may call upon its citizenry to serve in that military. Given their responsibility to preserve the state, individuals must accept the reasonable burdens such service puts on them. Nonetheless, the state should strive for equity in distributing those burdens.

For each individual who fails or refuses to take up military service there is an increase in the burden distributed over the remainder. Here, Johnson rightly sees that the issue "may not be narrowly reduced to one of an individual's decision to refuse military service; rather, it is a question involving the community as a whole" (1984:155). We cannot, as a community, pretend to be a collection of windowless monads, whose actions do not alter the possibilities and prospects for others. To do *nothing* by way of providing for our own defense would be irresponsible, both to ourselves and the rest of the people sharing our social space. On the one hand, to demand absolute and indiscriminate compliance with the state does not seem a worthy approach, for it cuts off the exercise of conscience and moral reflection which we should prize in others and which makes us the sort of agents who can rationally enter into political cooperation. On the other, the purely volunteer army seems to encourage an indifference to political responsibility that places an unfair burden on those who think most seriously about their role in the community. At the same time, it risks depleting the resources necessary for the proper functioning of the state. Since unreflective compliance and the volunteer army both undermine the integrity of the individual and community, the just response must be some form of conscription. Johnson concludes that on these principles we should establish "a law somewhere in the spectrum between recent draft law and the establishment of a service corps composed of military, various kinds of paramilitary organzizations . . . and civilians" (159).

Although he invokes no premises of a uniquely Christian sort, Johnson has reproduced an account of moral agency that traces it roots to St. Augustine. This is, of course, not surprising given the role of Augustine in the just war tradition. Still, it is important to be clear on the bases of Augustine's ethics. He synthesizes a number of strands in late antiquity, although they center on acknowledging and serving a stern, albeit loving, God. On this account the virtues are a manifestation of that service, reflecting, in Augustine's interpretation, the various requirements of love. In the social world, love of God manifests itself in love of neighbor, not merely instrumentally as a means of serving God but as part of understanding God's work, both in creation and in the death and resurrection of Christ. Without some understanding of the divine work, however shakey it be, no political order can actively cooperate in securing the highest good, for that good essentially involves reference to God. (Cf. G. S. Davis 1986.) Left to their own devices, people are not, for Augustine, misguided, they are positively fratricidal. He argues in *City of God* that the founding of the earthly community stems directly from the murder of Abel by Cain and that this bloodshed colors all corporate and individual behavior which fails to acknowledge God and which continues to be guided by earthly loves. At the same time, all states must establish a modicum of order if conflicts among individuals are not to thwart achieving any good at all. Thus, for Augustine, there is a constant tension between individuals and states, so that the potentially destructive inclinations of each are checked by the need to cooperate in seeking the goods which are the objects of their love.

It was Ramsey who most clearly articulated the just war tradition in Augustinian terms, and *if* we maintain, as he does, that "fratricidal love and brotherly love based on love of God are always commingled in human history" (Ramsey 1961:30), we will be inclined to allot considerable authority to the state as the principal earthly agent of restraint. The obedience owed the state on this account is not the total devotion appropriate only to God but the filial obedience due the father, who molds and corrects you until your majority. Of course, for Augustine that obedience is due the state throughout your earthly life, since the freedom of full maturity comes only in heaven. These presuppositions continue at work in Johnson, although stripped, here, of their theological context. But the loss of a theological backdrop has greater consequences than Johnson imagines, for the claim that it is only through participation in the life of the political community that we are trained into the imperfect justice of earthly life must now find justification in the thicket of philosophical argument. Without divine warrant this is easier said than done. John Dunn, for example, has emphasized the historicity of modern liberal theories of political obligation and their relations to complex assumptions about rationality and legitimacy. After assaying the complexities involved in untangling the distinct streams of political thought that come together in the contemporary intellectual world, Dunn concludes that the "types of theory of political obligation which have been constructed in the past can only be credited today (at least as theories about obligations which real persons may today *possess*) by an exercise in superstition" (1980:297). Coming at the matter from a more traditionally analytic direction, John Simmons argues than none of the principal strategies for grounding the liberal contractarian position on political obligation is compelling and "that citizens generally have no special political bonds which require that they obey and support the governments of their countries of residence" (Simmons 1979:192). It seems to me that the best way to read Simmons' argument is as a *reductio* of the liberal tradition. But to say this is not to go all the way in embracing Johnson's premises. For we may move to establish armed forces as an institution while rejecting the claim, central to Johnson's position, that membership in a community establishes an obligation to serve. Without thinking that it will yield a theory of "obligation" it remains for us to see whether and in what ways the Aristotelian tradition may provide insight where the heirs of Locke and Rousseau have failed.

We might as well take our cue from David Copperfield and begin at the beginning. As social animals we naturally discover goods in a communal context. Aristotle, in fact, goes further than this, claiming that we discover ourselves in interaction with others. But while we remain inescapably social, we are not wedded to any particular social order. The middle books of the *Politics* turn on the contingent and ultimately transitory nature of all embodied political systems. Shifts in demography, economic makeup, and political interaction will deform previously sound constitutional structures and create a demand for new forms of political organization. This is as true of the methods we adopt for protection as it is for any other area of our social life. As it happens, conscription is a fairly recent notion. The tradition in Greece and early Rome tended toward a citizen militia supplemented by mercenaries. This suggests rather a different relation to the community from the one presupposed by Johnson's Augustinian state, something more like a limited partnership, with two distinct functions. The citizen of appropriate rank defends his or her home and status within the community. Failure in doing so results in shame, loss of standing, and exclusion. Such a position is distinct from duty to the state as a superior authority. The analogy to business, or becoming a member of a team, is a point reinforced by the use of mercenaries. When the ranking members of the community cannot, for whatever reason, raise an appropriate force, they contract out to professionals. Protecting their homes and positions is the principal concern, not protecting the state in the abstract.

The gradual settling of western Europe led to the establishment of feudal relations as the basis for military obligation. Duby's *William Marshall* provides an intriguing glimpse of the life of the medieval soldier and leader. Loyalties are personal, volatile, and directly related to material achievement, individual reputation, and family loyalty. Rivalry and discord were the order of the day, but "warfare itself never went on for long. . . . It was always waged on the surface and unlikely to damage the network of relations that formed the armature of knightly society" (Duby 1985:115). Renaissance armies were a complex matter of militias, permanent garrisons, and mercenaries. "Without effective conscription, and with but scant anticipations of the jingoism that was eventually to be the chief assistant of the recruiter of volunteers," Hale writes of military preparedness in the fifteenth century, "there were seldom enough men effectively to bridge the gap between permanent nuclei, where they existed, and the required combat strength: in the case of large-scale campaigns, never" (Hale 1985:69). Despite flirting with conscription for the next three centuries, the institution only took hold with the *levée en masse* of France's revolutionary army.

What justification such a *levée* has comes from the contractarian tradition, most notably that found in Rousseau, who writes that "all citizens . . . should the need arise, have to fight for their country. . . . He who would preserve his own life at another's cost is under an obligation to give his own for him should the necessity arise" (Barker 1947:282–83). More than Hobbes, Rousseau, in his account of the sovereign and the "general will," secularizes the Augustinian notion of a benevolent father to whom the members of the community owe obedience. The state now becomes a super-person to whom we owe all the goods we might amass. We have, in other words, the apotheosis not of the emperor but of the fatherland. This no doubt accounts for Rousseau's vehemence in replacing Christianity with "the religion of man." In any event, universal conscription was retained by Napoleon, who had little practical use for the social contract, and the emergent modern armies of Europe were forced to respond. Even after Napoleon's defeat, however, important voices were raised against an army of conscripts and a professional officers corps. Like many of his contemporaries, Wellington worried that a large standing army, even if it were a more efficient fighting force, might ultimately prove a threat to the stability of the nation it was designed to protect. Wellington noted that the purchase of commissions "brings into the services men of fortune and character, who have some connection with the interests and fortunes of the country," and he resisted the sort of reforms designed to transform the army from "a midden fit only for outcasts," as Michael Howard puts it, "made up of long-serving volunteers who had said goodbye virtually forever to civil life" (Howard 1971:51–55). Reform of the British army was successfully resisted until the mid-nineteenth century, when its weaknesses proved detrimental to the establishment of empire. Empire won out.[1]

This brief sketch of the ways in which communities have defended themselves does not constitute an argument against Johnson's position, but it should suggest that compulsory universal service has rarely been thought the best way to maintain a politically healthy citizenry. The army has most frequently reflected either the assumption that citizens will take it upon themselves to defend their homes or that soldiering is a profession like any other. In fact, the revolutionary origins of the universal draft are disconcerting. They betoken a situation in which the citizenry does not identify with the state in a way that would make a militia effective, and this suggests that the people are not sure the state is worth preserving. They are asked, nonetheless, to risk livelihood and person, to defend not home, family, or liege lord, but a corporate entity that may be indifferent to their own welfare. Conscription would appear to be a recent experiment that has manifested no greater commitment to justice than have previous ways of assembling an army. It seems to have gone hand in hand with the development of states so large that they could not, on their merits, command the loyalty of the citizens. Thielicke's assumptions, central to Johnson's argument, are perhaps themselves a last-ditch effort to convince ourselves that the modern political order is worth saving.

Two avenues of response suggest themselves. On the one hand, Johnson may counter, it would be disingenuous to deny that I receive countless goods from the state. The contractarian tradition is sound at least in the notion that the citizen is obliged to contribute to the political system from which he receives protection, the chance for advancement, and the stability which allows him to pursue the goods he chooses. This is a matter of simple fairness, but determining a contribution commensurate with the services provided is no easy matter. What, for example, should a citizen contribute in exchange for paved roads or adequate schools? The most straightforward answer has been to levy taxes, since the burden, at least in theory, involves commensurable goods. We may quibble about the quality of the service or the allotment of shares, but this is rather different from being forced to sacrifice time and effort at a labor I would otherwise not choose. So clearly am I aware of the goods I receive that I put up with disgraceful levels of incompetence, wastrelsy, and neglect. This is more than I would do for a local merchant and reflects the difficulty of changing such a large mechanism as well as my disinclination to pick up and start a new life and career elsewhere. But it does not signal my willingness to accept any and every burden the state might attempt to impose. Nor does it establish an obligation to protect the state. If the argument is to be based on goods received, then the appropriate analogy should be my relation to other providers of goods, and the principle guiding those relations is fair return. What I do not do is contract to place in jeopardy that which nobody can replace, namely life and limb.

On the other hand, a more subtle line might be to reassert the Augustinian position and argue that I have failed to grasp the larger human need for political authority. I treat the state as an optional, voluntary association in a way that makes no sense, given human propensities for self-interest, injustice, and brutality. Here, Johnson can make one with Gilbert Meilaender's critique of civic friendship as unstable, utopian, and ultimately incoherent. The Aristotelian ideal of community based on civic friendship, Meilaender argues, is "belied by the history of the polis" (1981:70). Athens, the very paradigm of the polis, was eventually ripped apart by the factionalism of groups of erstwhile friends, vying with each other for command of the city. It was the rigid discipline of Sparta that came closest to creating the community of like-minded individuals suggested by Aristotle, and "to see that," Meilaender remarks, "is to begin to appreciate the political costs of civic friendship" (72). Not only does the ideal of civic friendship totter between instability and authoritarianism but it is also fundamentally utopian. The Aristotelian ideal credits the natural virtues with too much power for good. Aristotle himself acknowledges an unbridgeable gap between the life of the gods and the limited resources and achievements of humans. The *phronimos*, Aristotle's standard of practical reason in action, is not perfect and remains to no small extent subject to the contingencies and limitations of his character and surroundings. Only the fortuitous coming together of a group of exceptionally virtuous individuals could approximate the sort of community I am suggesting. The likelihood of such a rare confluence of good fortune is scant, and to predicate political action on such an unrealizable ideal partakes more of romantic wistfulness than deliberation in accord with right reason. And Meilaender goes on to argue that, contrary to appearances, such a community would be at odds with the demands of fairness in our communal intercourse. As soon as we admit the need for some mechanisms of justice we will have to allow an *impersonal* authority to justice as an impartial means of arbitrating between competing preferential claims of individuals and groups on behalf of their friends. This sets friendship at odds with the rule of law.

The Augustinian tends to think that there are only two states of human existence, that in extended political society and that in the chaos of nature. Johnson and Meilaender, I suspect, share with Ramsey the sense that failure to respect political authority risks undermining the possibility of any and every human good in this life. In arguing the justice of bluffing, for example, Ramsey would be only too happy to accept a deterrent policy that did not countenance the threat of massive nuclear attack "if I could forget the men in positions of political responsibility for all the order there is in the world. . . . Have I, as a moralist, the right (if I could) to *require* this shift, this denial, of *them*?" (1968:362). Here, Ramsey envisions a world teetering on the brink of self-destruction, threatened with a collapse into brutal and murderous chaos. If the political leaders were truly responsible for "all the order there is in the world" it would be difficult, to say the least, to maintain the level of distance I claim for the Aristotelian. But they aren't responsible for all that order. Once again the Myth of the Garden, and our ancestral loss, intrudes to set up an untenable dualism: Private Willfulness vs. Public Good. But this does not exhaust the spectrum, nor does it sufficiently credit the contingent and organic nature of political development. In an age where political boundaries reflect not so much the local ecology as the vicissitudes of conquest and empire, we cannot assume the coincidence of state and community. Political boundaries shift in ways that frequently have little to do with the communities they encompass. The lives of most peoples of the Indian subcontinent, to mention but one example, were scarcely touched by the periodic change of nominal ruler, be it Raja, Mogul, or the British Crown. Almost two hundred years ago the Abbé Dubois cataloged the nomadic peoples of the subcontinent, noting that "each forms a small and perfectly independent republic of its own, governed by such rules and regulations as seem best to them" (Dubois 1906:72). This is, perhaps, the extreme, but it is not without contemporary analogs. The Amish of Lancaster County form a community tolerated, and even appreciated by the surrounding communities despite their theological commitment to the rejection of the modern nation-state. The forest peoples of Brazil, Malaysia, and New Guinea are watching their own ecosystems being exploited and destroyed in the name of third-world development; and even when that is not a mask for amassing wealth on the part of the nation's ruling class and its clients, it would be difficult to claim that these peoples have an *obligation* to defend their states. Nations rise and fall; people, like Faulkner's Dilsey, endure. That we are inescapably social beings makes it pointless to fear overmuch some decline into the state of nature: community is our nature. But particular communities may be tested. Loyalties have to be earned, and they are always subject to rational revision.

This doesn't mean that I can be completely indifferent to the state. In a sense, Ramsey correctly observes that "a citizen may be required to serve in the armed forces and to be willing to lay down his life for his country" (1968:92). But it remains to be considered whether the requirement is one of justice or merely one of law. Despite his general commitment to an Augustinian view of politics, Aquinas, for one, insists on the distinction between positive human law and the dictates of justice. If a law violates the just expectations of all or part of the community, it "does not bind in conscience, except perhaps in order to avoid scandal or disturbance, for which cause a man should even yield his right" (*S.Theo.*:1a2ae, 96, 4). This passage deserves some detailed consideration. Thomas insists, as can the Aristotelian, that positive law is, generally speaking, binding on the citizen's conscience. After all, when properly understood, the point of law is to stabilize the community and provide the order necessary for the pursuit of goods both common and individual. These positive laws create both obligations and expectations for the members of the community, but those particular statutes cannot override conscience. Conscience is the perception in the particular case of what justice and right reason demand; and if there were no hierarchy relating it to the demands of the law, then the agent would be caught in a paradox, and this would paralyze action. In order to resolve the impasse, we must acknowledge some heirarchy, and St. Thomas affirms that what we recognize to be a truth as a matter of nature cannot be made false by human fiat. Here, as elsewhere, Thomas shares Aristotle's moral realism.

At the same time, every reasonable person acknowledges his own fallibility, and there is no guarantee that the individual's judgment will prove sounder than that of the community. "To avoid scandal and disturbance," Aquinas concedes, I should give up the right of exercising my conscience and defer to the community. Ramsey would seem to be echoing a similar point in writing that "no political society can be founded on a principle according *absolute* rights to possibly errant individual conscience," although he displays his deeper Augustinian commitment when he continues that "it is the aggregate-individualism of such a view, and not true conscientiousness, that makes such an account of political obligation a radically non-political and an ultimately inhumane viewpoint" (1968:93). But here again we confront an overly simple dualism. The community of moral reflection that informs my conscience may well be much larger than the state and its laws; and whereas an untutored individual conscience may be subordinate to the law, a conscience nurtured in the tradition of moral and political reflection may be in a better position to assess the quality of the law than those who, despite a lack of training, become legislators. This is why the sketch of the history of conscription is of more than academic interest. To someone cognizant only of recent law it might appear as though the draft were a natural and evidently sound way of raising an army. But the more we know about political thought and history the less evident such a claim seems. The Aristotelian, ironically, can make one with John Yoder's critique of modern political developments as themselves fostering the decay of community virtue. Yoder's remark that "democracy seems rather to have increased the space for demagoguery" (1984:38) echoes a repeated theme of Aristotle's *Politics*.

When viewed from the larger perspective of political thought and history, the role of the individual and the community is reversed. It is the political system which undertakes innovation that finds itself in the role of individual, subject to the judgment of the tradition. Thus, to the extent that the individual's conscience reflects the judgment of the tradition, it may legitimately claim priority. It is still subject to the constraint of proportionality, and this is the meaning of St. Thomas' injunction that we forgo insisting on the freedom of conscience in case of scandal or disturbance. But when the stakes rise beyond scandal, as we will see in the next chapter, such restraint is no longer appropriate. When the demands of the state threaten the exercise of conscience or when they would involve the individual in active support of injustice, the fear of scandal risks becoming an excuse for vicious indifference.

On three counts, then, I've argued that there are strong constraints on the demands that the political order can make on the individual. First, the recompense for goods accepted cannot, without argument, be extended to incommensurables; thus, the burden of proof lies with the state to show that risking my person and life can justly be demanded for the goods provided. Second, it does not follow from our inherently social nature that we owe even a qualified loyalty to a particular political order. As the example of the Amish should remind us, my true community may be nomadic, pulling up stakes when the intrusions of the political order become intolerable and maintaining its own integrity even to the point of martyrdom. And finally, even the citizen who acknowledges the claims of the positive law need not adopt an unquestioned obedience. To the extent that my moral tradition is more ancient and well grounded than a recently constituted polity, I can justly, as a representative of that tradition, judge and reject innovations. But these limits on what the political order may demand needn't suggest that loyalty to that community is necessarily misplaced. The questions are how such loyalty might arise, where can it be located, and what are its limits? What I propose is to look more closely at Aristotle's account of friendship and see if it can't provide some account of political community not subject the Meilaender's criticisms.

"When fraternity fades," writes Michael Sandel, "more justice may be done, but even more may be required to restore the moral status quo. . . . The breakdown of certain personal and civic attachments may represent a moral loss that even a full measure of justice cannot redeem" (1982:32–33). Although he does not cite Aristotle here, Sandel's remark invites comparison with the Philosopher's claim that "friendship seems too to hold states together . . . and when men are friends they have no need of justice, while when they are just they need friendship as well, and the truest form of justice is thought to be a friendly quality" (*Ethics*:1155a). Friendship establishes a primary motive for action, and one which seeks the common good of friends as its immediate goal. It renders the appeal to justice unnecessary. When I act out of friendship I seek as my end the good of my friends because this is a good that presents itself as intrinsically worthy. My friends and I constitute a society that I hold worthy on the basis of shared perceptions of the good. In fact, these perceptions incorporate our own goodness, real and perceived.

I need to qualify, then, my earlier claim that justice is a presupposition of any community that can sustain itself over time. If a community, whatever the specifics of its institutions and practices, were working smoothly and harmoniously, there would be no impetus to develop the concept, much less a theory, of "justice." But given that people of good will can disagree about the propriety and consequences of actions, disputes will arise about how the community should conduct its business. And given that we sometimes suspect the good will of others, there will also be situations where a person or group feels that it has not been treated fairly. And given that people all too frequently fail to act with good will, sometimes those feelings will be correct. It is at this point that the community experiences pressure toward formulating some account of justice. In a sense the contractarian tradition is right: justice reflects agreements about a fair social order. But the contract results from the decay of the inherited agreements and dispositions that would normally incline people to work together. Sandel, on my account, does not go far enough, for he imagines that in some circumstances the emergence of justice can be perceived as a purely positive event. This would only be the case if reasonable standards of practice were suddenly to be imposed upon a situation of human chaos in which no practical sense could be made of individual activity. But a situation in which the best account of social activity was analogous to the instinctual swarming of ants and bees—a situation already several steps removed from chaos—would not describe a human practice. It would be impossible to elicit from the erstwhile agents any reasoned justification of their activities. Thus, any change in a recognizably human situation where the agents place themselves under the constraints of justice must be one where a previous order has become an admitted failure. Invoking justice, as I suggested in the previous chapter, is an admission of moral defeat. Justice reflects the lapse, if not the end, of friendship. Unlike less developed species, humans deliberate about the goods they pursue, and in doing so weigh the merits of the goods themselves as well as the pleasures they bring. Such deliberation does not take place in a vacuum, but reflects a complex negotiation with the social world in which individuals act independently and as members of various groups at one and the same time. Implementing these negotiations means putting into action various plans, some of which we pursue over the long-term and others we come to abandon. Thus, at one and the same time, I plan activities that reflect my role as father, professor, baseball fan, and whatnot. I attempt to balance these activities so that life is harmonious and satisfying for myself, my family, and my colleagues. Even as professor I balance and plan around distinct aspects of that role. I don't want to teach the same course over and over, but I don't want to increase my preparations. I want to create a positive classroom atmosphere, but I don't want to neglect my writing. In all this planning the successful completion of a task is pleasurable, but I sometimes forsake one, at a particular time, for another. This is not something I can reasonably bemoan, however. Only the gods—a point Aristotle also makes—can have it all.

If the natural arena of human life is community, it is unlikely, in the extreme, that the pleasures attendent upon the happy life will have no connection with that community. Not only that; since communal activities require fairness and cooperation their successful undertaking will require mutual acknowledgment of one another as the rightful recipients of goods. These are no more than the ordinary demands of virtue. Persons of virtue see the world as it is and their senses and desires are attuned to those things that are good with respect to human life. Their beliefs cohere because they are not misled by vice or unbridled desire. The pleasures they achieve result from activity in accord with right reason. This doesn't mean that everything they do is perfect, because both the intellect and the body are limited by natural and historical circumstance. But the good person, Aristotle's *phronimos*, is the standard in which the community recognizes itself. And such people recognize the good in themselves, as well as acknowledging it in others. They love themselves because they are genuinely good, and they love others for exactly the same reason. Those they both love and associate with are their true friends.

It is in the relation of friendship that Aristotle's account of practical motivation is clearest. All practical agency pursues its ends under the aspect of the good if it is intelligible at all. But the pursuit of goods must be informed by the virtues if it is to be integrated into a rational plan for living. Pleasure, for example, is a good, but it is epiphenomenal in the sense that pleasures arise as the consequence of pursuing various, not necessarily commensurable, activities. There are pleasures of the body, of the intellect, of the spectator and performer, pleasures of the senses taken singularly or together. There are pleasures available exclusively to the person of virtue and there are vicious pleasures, hurtful to oneself and others. That pleasure comes in so many incommensurable forms should have kept anyone from seriously proposing it as *the* object of human pursuit. The person of virtue desires appropriate goods *and* correctly perceives them. But the practice of virtue is not the end of life. We become happy by bringing the virtues into play as part of the pursuit of a great many human goods.

Through engaging in the activities that make up a life, relationships develop, some closer than others, that individuals come to value for themselves. It's part and parcel of living in a community.

My friends, however, are more than individuals thrown in my path by the vicissitudes of life. They matter to me because I find them lovable and worthy. We share our hopes, accomplishments, and sadnesses, and in doing so open up new possibilities for ourselves. I might never notice my flaws were I not acquainted with their virtues; I might never have realized my most precious goals without their encouragement. My sense of self is expanded through my friendships. A friend becomes part of me, in Aristotle's phrase, "another self."[2] I am motivated to pursue a friend's good in just the same way I am to pursue my own. A true friend, Aristotle writes, "does many acts for the sake of his friends and his country, and if necessary dies for them . . . since he would prefer . . . one great and noble action to many trivial ones" (*Ethics*:1169a). The great and noble action is to save that which you love as you love yourself. The only thing that could keep me from so doing would be cowardice. Notice also that Aristotle expects a similar relation to obtain between virtuous individuals and their country. Here, he reflects at least the remnants of Pericles' vision of the Athenian ideal, the polis as a positive force encouraging all who come under her influence to cultivate in themselves knowledge, virtue, and an appreciation for human possibility. We love such a country because it, like our best friends, is truly good and helps us achieve goods we might never have dared to dream.

But it would be foolish to pretend that we live exclusively among our friends. Even in a moderate-sized family, there are distinctions of interest, authority, and obligation not captured by the notion of friendship. And, in general, our closest friendships depend upon a larger social order in which we function with many people we wouldn't call "friends." Even if the friendship of *phronimos* with *phronimos* renders appeals to justice unnecessary, it remains to connect that friendship with our obligations to the social order—that is to say, the "common good." By the "common good," I intend something more concrete and mundane than the collective good of the state, recently popular with the advocates of "civic virtue." What I have in mind is closer to Aristotle's lowest form of friendship, the friend for the sake of benefit. "Now those who love each other for their utility," he writes, "do not love each other for themselves but in virtue of some good which they get from each other" (*Ethics*:1156a). There are several mistaken readings to guard against here. The passage betrays to some readers an unworthy callousness. Love for the sake of gain is scarcely love at all. It seems to be the opposite. But this invests "love" with too much of our modern sentimental affection. Aristotle has already indicated that for two individuals to be friends "they must be mutually recognized as bearing goodwill and wishing well to each other" (*Ethics*:1156a). Crucial to the relationship is the reciprocal desire that the other flourish and receive all that is properly due him. In other words, even the friend for benefit acknowledges the character of the other as a constituent of the social fabric and seeks to fulfill the responsibilities and generate the goods appropriate to interaction between such characters.

Nonetheless, as John Cooper argues, there is a distinction between the paradigm case of friendship based on virtue and the derivative forms based on benefit and pleasure. In friendship based on virtue it is the character of the other as a person that is central (1980:301–8). The good qualities of that sort of friend are ideally those that everyone would and should recognize. In wishing good for the person of virtue, we endorse the good in an unqualified way. In friendship for benefit, however, it is the other in a particular role that we acknowledge. Thus, such friendships are subordinate in two distinct ways. Playing a role requires that I have sufficient virtues in general to recognize and perform in accordance with the standards of the practice, whereas acknowledging a role requires that I be able to distinguish persons from occupations. Take, for example, Koji, chef and proprietor of a neighborhood sushi bar. I patronize his establishment because he offers something that I want. There are certain standards of quality and service that we both acknowledge, and in his role as restaurateur he strives to present me with a quality product and naturally desires that I enjoy it. Because I like raw fish and think his cafe nice and inviting, I try to stop by once every other week, and I like to see that business is good. He, in turn, likes my patronage and is inclined to make suggestions, offer a taste, and sometimes add an extra flourish. Neither of us is required to do any of these things; they are just part of our relationship. If the restaurant failed, I would deeply regret it, not just because I'd have to go elsewhere but because something good had been lost. But Cooper rightly warns against pressing the business example too far. "A businessman," he writes, "is no friend of *all* his regular customers, and when a personal relationship is more or less purely exploitative, it would be taken for irony to describe the persons in questions as friends" (1980:316). This is a sound qualification, but it does not undermine the usefulness of the example. A stable community environment requires that even in the most exploitative relation the parties involved acknowledge and respect the positions being occupied and the goods expected. We do not always, in this era of fast-food and chain bookstores, regard local merchants as friends of Aristotle's useful sort, but we do need to be convinced that they acknowledge our entitlement to a fair exchange.

It is here that we should expect the entry of positive law. A small community is more likely to be one where friendship predominates. The healthy family is the obvious example, and it is Aristotle's. (Cf. *Pol*:Bk. 1.) But even in very traditional cultures, the stability of the community requires interaction among families, and the possibilities for conflict are many. At least one of the functions of rules of kinship and their cosmological warrants is to clarify the chains of authority and loyalty in the extended families that became distinguishable peoples.[3] As peoples interact and personal relations become more complicated, it is natural to augment the rules of social order by positive legislation that ensures at least the semblance of good will among the citizens; and so we arrive at the contemporary situation. The attendant at the corner gas station may actively bear me ill will, but state and local regulations keep him honest, I hope, in his role as provider of gasoline. It is too bad; I wish we didn't have to rely on the law. If only it were like the old days, when life was simpler and neighbors were friends.

What emerges is a heirarchy of practical motivation within the social order. The community that provides my principle happiness is that of my friends, with whom I share the active pursuit of recognized goods. Pace Meilaender, friendship is both the ideal social relation and the paradigm of virtuous motivation. But this ideal is not irredeemably utopian. When I move beyond the sphere of my friends, a different set of considerations come to the fore. In the larger community, I treat others as friends with respect to the roles we are playing in the social fabric. When they reciprocate, as in the case of Koji, we have a genuine friendship of utility. My own disposition to render each her due expresses itself in the pride I take in performing my role well, even if the other does not reciprocate. Lacking that pride, others may be constrained by appeals to "duty" or "obligation"; but if these appeals lack force, we would be better off disassociating ourselves from such a contemptible lot. In those cases where we must interact, the positive law provides some level of assurance that we can expect our due. Finally, the criminal code may come into play where malice results in injury. That's the sorry fact of life in a community where baseness and vice cannot be excluded.

Friendship, then, accounts for the good we do those others closest to us in our community and provides the measure for fairness and ultimately for the justice of the positive laws we enact to secure the stability of the social order. Here, it is best to think of moving down the Aristotelian spectrum from friends for the sake of pleasure, to those for the sake of benefit, to those whom I should treat as friends for the sake of benefit, to those with whom I have no positive connection beyond a shared humanity. As we move down the spectrum, the strength of my tie to another individual or community diminishes, ultimately to the point where I have no good reason for considering them in my deliberations at all. Not that I can abuse, cheat, or ignore the claims of others; they simply don't count for much until some particular endeavor brings us into contact. In the absence of some specific relationship, what good I do those outside my community is strictly supererogatory.

Between true friends very little is supererogatory, between strangers almost all, but we typically live solely among neither. What about the state and my fellow citizens? There is no general answer to this question because there is no single character manifested by states, any more than there is a single character shared by our fellow citizens. The relationships that go into making up our lives exist at different times between persons who have lesser and greater claims on our affection and concern, and this means that there will be no *a priori* way of determining what obligations will obtain at a given time and how they should be fulfilled. Aristotle notes, for example, that "we must for the most part return benefits rather than oblige friends, as we must pay back a loan to a creditor rather than make one to a friend" (*Ethics*:1165a). This is true, "for the most part," because the creditor was under no obligation to afford us a loan, but we took it nonetheless. Consequently, he has every reason to expect us to meet the terms established and none to release us from this contract. But should the stakes rise, the balance may change. Rather than my abiding by the established deadline, for example, it would be proper to meet some emergency—Aristotle instances ransoming one's father—and risk the consequences. If the creditor is a person of virtue, some alternative arrangements will be made; he, if in my position, would admittedly have done the same. It's important, however, to insist that this is not a license for fraud or theft. It is just that the relations we have in society are not of equal weight, and what is due in one may take precedence over another. This is not unjust, but is a consequence of living in a complex society. We try, in framing our laws, to take this into account, although every circumstance cannot be foreseen.

The same holds true for our relations with the state itself. Our relation to the political order will be different depending on the character of that state. In general, it will carry less weight than our relations with family and close friends, but this is not absolute. Friends who become "incurable in their wickedness" (*Ethics*:1165b) lose their claim on us; and if they act against the best interests of the community, we should, even if regretfully, side with the common good against our lost friend. At the extreme, the same holds for family. Otherwise, we perpetuate the vice of our friend, subvert our own virtue, and detract from the common good. This is more obvious still in the case of mere acquaintances and faceless fellow citizens. The state supplies the stability and material upkeep necessary to the welfare of myself, my family, and my friends. In an attenuated sense, the state acts as a friend by acknowledging my place in the social fabric and doing its part to secure such goods as I might justly strive to achieve.

This claim, however, is conditioned by the assumption that the institutions and policies of the political system continue to foster situations in which virtue flourishes. If they do not, then my commitment diminishes accordingly. In the extreme case, when corruption reigns, I may have to reject the political order altogether and perhaps work for its destruction. But the topic of revolution I'll reserve for the next chapter. The question of the moment is how best to keep corruption from getting a foothold, and this brings me back to Johnson and the volunteer army. Johnson argued that the volunteer army undermined social integrity by failing to insist that the individual shoulder a fair share of responsibility. But I think this misplaces the issue. It won't do to cite Aristotle and Aquinas on the pedagogical role of law and the state because both envision communities where it may be assumed that there is a shared grasp of the common good. That we now live in states that encompass communities with incommensurable visions of the good renders this assumption unworkable. Virtue and responsibility are learned as parts of practices and role playing, whether in the home, on the field, or in the classroom. Internalizing such a practice requires acknowledging an authority who can demonstrate a personal mastery in a way that clarifies the standards involved, enlists my admiration, and creates a desire to achieve a similar standard. Assuming I have the required mental or physical abilities, from there it's practice and a little bit of luck. The state at large cannot undertake this role because it is not sufficiently personal to constitute a partner in the education of the citizenry. Instead, it needs to see that the institutions in which citizens develop are structured so as to maximize the quality of education.

As an institution central to the workings of the nation, the armed forces demand particular attention in this respect. Thus, the force of Johnson's argument can be assessed only if it is possible to answer the following: which is more conducive to a responsible citizenry, a volunteer army or an army of conscripts? Having put the question, I am not sure how to answer it. The variables are too many to allow any simple sociological analysis. Not all agree on what makes a good soldier, and it is more difficult still to trace the relation between a good soldier and a good citizen. A draftee may become either, unexpectedly awakened to a new role in the social fabric. At the same time, not all volunteers fully understand what they are choosing. It is perfectly possible that once they see the workings of the army they will rue their decision. Certainly the "pals," who volunteered en masse to make up battalions of clerks and workers from the same town and business, could not have imagined what awaited them at the Somme (Keegan 1976:207–29). Paul Fussell's classic 1975 study of World War I memoirs discusses the steps by which many an idealist became disillusioned, not only with war but also with the entire fabric of western culture, and at the same time how the experience of solidarity in the trenches shaped the remainder of a life. It would seem there is no way to predict, for any given individual, whether service in the armed forces—as draftee or volunteer—will create a better citizen.

Nonetheless, the volunteer chooses to serve, and that constitutes a significant point. Part of what it means to be responsible is to acknowledge the role that your own choices play in developing events. Draftees, unlike volunteers, have someone else to blame for the state they are in, and in a literal sense they are doing someone else's work. For to institute a draft is, at one and the same time, to claim that the state is worthy and in need of protection and to admit that not enough people are willing to take up the job. Among those other people are the draftees. Either they think that the community is not sufficiently attuned to their needs or they think their needs will be better met pursuing something else. Even though they are paid, the services they perform are involuntary and rest on the premise that a corporate body may rightfully force other responsible agents to take jobs they find repugnant. The point of Johnson's requirement that all citizens serve is supposed to be securing a just distribution of resources, but it exceeds the limits of justice, demanding what is arguably not its due. It is not enough that those in charge of the political system fear for the survival of the state. The burden lies with them to convince the citizenry to join them.

There is an unsuspected connection here to Aristotle's account of slavery. The natural slave is defective precisely in his ability to recognize and deliberate about ways of securing the good. Thus, he is in need of a master to undertake those deliberations and help him achieve goods that would otherwise elude him. To institutionalize procedures that alienate deliberation from the agent is to treat that person as though he were defective, a slave in Aristotle's sense. But this is contrary to the intent of the draft. Rather than enabling the volunteer to defer the workings of conscience to a political representative, it coopts the conscience. But if properly human acts are those undertaken with deliberation and intent, directed toward securing an arguably sound goal, then such a coopting represents the subversion of what is most human in the individual. Under no circumstances, for the Aristotelian, should such a law be incorporated into our institutions if our goal is to create a moral climate where the virtues may flourish.

Like the Catholic bishops, Johnson is liable to the charge that his reading of justice is skewed by the quest for security. But the advocate of conscription is in a worse situation than the advocates of deterrence because the judicial treatment of conscience, at least in the United States, is clearly at odds with the demands of justice. There is in American law a tradition of exempting from military service members of the traditional "peace churches" such as the Quakers and Mennonites, who universally object to participation in war. Challenges in the 1960s and 1970s led to extending this exemption to secular pacifists, but it remains the case that selective conscientious objection is not grounds for exemption. Thus, the Supreme Court, ruling in Gillette v. U.S., held that the difficulties attendant upon determining administering the exemption made it "supportable for Congress to have decided that the objector to all war—to all killing in war—has a claim that is distinct enough and intense enough to justify special status, whereas the objector to a particular war does not" (cited in Childress 1982:206). The court, of course, is ruling on the constitutionality of the law, but that's not relevant. If they are correct in interpreting the *Constitution*, this shows that our fundamental law is inimical to the exercise of conscience and hence to virtue in general. For conscience, as opposed to prudence, is a first-person exercise of judgment about a specific act that I can undertake or refuse. I argued in chapter 2 that prudence does not find war in general inherently wicked, thus allowing for the possibility that I can in conscience take part in some wars. But not necessarily all. The cumulative argument of chapters 3 and 4 indicated how the just war criteria, guided by virtue, might lead to the judgment that a particular war was one I could make my own. Participation and objection both, from the perspective of virtue, are always particular; and unless it is overridden by a sufficiently powerful vocation, conscience is binding. Despite crediting the state with more authority than I have argued is appropriate, Childress himself concludes that "the government should bear the burden of proof that the class of COs should not be exempted from military service" (1982:215). Johnson goes further, admitting that "even the most recent versions of American draft law appear immoral" (1984:157) for essentially the reasons I have adduced. Neither Childress nor Johnson puts the point in a way that could satisfy the Aristotelian, however, for if we are attempting to create institutions conducive to virtue, then we should actually prefer the selective conscientious objector. That the law fails to acknowledge this calls into question the probity of the political order and makes it even more imperative that we maintain a volunteer army. Universal objectors do not need to take into account the character of a particular war; they have already assumed a position that makes distinguishing between just and unjust wars irrelevant. Selective objectors, to the extent that they are conscientious, examine both the character of the political order and the policies undertaken by the authorities and, on the basis of such investigations, determine whether the government has acted in accord with justice and right reason. Failure brings censure, and habitual failure indicates a turn to vice. When the political order turns to vice, it has no more claim on my loyalty than a friend who has done the same. If selective objectors insist on holding the state to the standard they set for themselves and their friends, this is a minimal condition, given the much greater responsibility for maintaining the common good. After all, when my friend falls into wickedness, he endangers, as a private person, only himself and comparatively few others. When the state strays, the good of all its members becomes unstable. Thus, it is only fitting that when there is a question as to its character and policies the burden of proof falls upon the state. The selective, as opposed to the universal, conscientious objector calls our political order to account. A legal system that does not recognize selective conscientious objection refuses to accept a legitimate check on its power, and the responsible citizen can at least impose an alternative limit to state power by refusing to countenance any move beyond a volunteer army.

Having argued this point, however, I have opened myself to the following objection. I have as yet provided no criterion for distinguishing the 'conscientious' from the ill-considered or positively self-serving objection. This objection gives the Augustinian position a different twist. Initially, the Augustinian argued from a theological anthropology for which human sinfulness makes it necessary to accord the political authorities a very powerful position in constraining sin and establishing what minimal justice might be possible in this world. It would surely be foolish to deny the ample evidence for human wickedness, even depravity. As Augustine reiterates throughout *City of God*, history provides example after example of nations torn apart by the wickedness of their rulers, entire peoples decimated by the urge for dominion, and the innocent slaughtered as others accumulate wealth and power. And Augustine didn't live to see the Crusades, the coming of the Mongols, and the destruction of the indigenous peoples of the Americas, not to mention those nineteenth- and twentieth-century horrors so familiar to most of us. Nor need the Augustinian emphasize the global. Greed and self-serving indifference to others have always been part and parcel of daily life. If the Aristotelian is going to proclaim himself a "naturalist," he should admit the weight of the evidence.

The Aristotelian counters by pointing out the persistence of stable human communities over millennia, noting that the Augustinian focuses on the horrors perpetrated by the few and rejecting the notion that we should judge actual communities against a philosophical ideal. People are not gods, and to judge them as if they were is unfair. Nonetheless, it remains open for the Augustinian to grant that the anthropological point is up for grabs and to shift to an epistemological argument. The Aristotelian asks us to risk too much by being overly optimistic in asking the community to give the individual the benefit of the doubt. And if he is wrong, it is the entire community that bears the consequences. In a community where the level of Aristotelian virtue is low or under pressure from forces, such as the threat of war, that work against virtue, the authorities have a positive duty to impose upon the citizenry a discipline under which it may well chafe. Later, perhaps, after the safety of the community has been secured, they may internalize that discipline in ways that foster the growth of genuine virtue. It is not, in other words, that virtue should be ignored but that the exercise of an imperfect or threatened virtue may be deferred until we reach a stage where it can flourish. In any event, the absence of a criterion for genuinely conscientious objection justifies both Meilaender and Johnson, on prudential grounds alone, in reasserting the claims of community against the unbridled exercise of individual choice.

But I think I have already laid the foundations for a response here. It is not sufficient for the objector to assert a position without argument. Unless the community has degenerated into tyranny or chaos, assuming this were possible, the laws we pass carry authority in the absence of argument against them. Law, as Aquinas pointed out, is binding unless it would lead to injustice; and injustice can't simply be asserted, it needs to be demonstrated. But the Aristotelian is in a position to do this, for the tradition he represents incorporates a well-established set of criteria concerning justice in war. The cumulative weight of the just war tradition, despite its internal disputes, is more compelling than the claims of the state; and to the extent that I can bring into play criteria for *ius ad bellum* and *ius in bello*, I can explicate my objections to the state and its policies. Not only this; it is also possible to array the just war criteria so as to create a scale of conscience, if you will. A political authority may be in a better position than private citizens to determine matters of fact, and this means that the criteria *ad bellum* may be satisfied without their knowing it. Suppose, for example, that political negotiations have broken down—a fact known only at upper diplomatic levels—and military intelligence determines that the potential adversary has begun to deploy troops along lines betokening an attack. To launch a pre-emptive assault does not seem, here, to violate *ius ad bellum*. If this is the case, then it is the responsibility of the authorities to make the facts known, as events permit; and until then, the potential objector may justifiably be asked to suspend judgment. If, however, at any time the available information suggests that there has been a failure of *ius in bello*, the person of conscience must put the authorities to the test, and if they condone the breach of justice then that person must cease to cooperate with the government and its policies. This has to be a two step judgment, because a simple breach of justice in war may not be the responsibility of the authorities. As Walzer points out in his discussion of the My Lai massacre, orders may be ambiguous and the officer in charge, like Lt. Calley, may order a massacre on his own initiative (1977:310). If this is the case, then the malice rests with individuals who committed the massacre. We need, nonetheless, to see what happens next. If justice is swift and appropriate, then we can affirm our commitment to the state. If, however, the massacre is brushed aside, or we discover that it reflects the policy, albeit tacit, of the general staff, we must assume that the very character of the war is vicious as well as those who prosecute it. At this point, not only does it become necessary to withdraw all support from the authorities but we should also either work against the authorities who persist in the wickedness or remove ourselves from the community. To do otherwise is to reap the benefits of a known evil, and this is no better than joining the gang. This is not, moreover, a standard of responsible citizenship applicable only to membership in the armed forces. If a teenager contemplates joining an urban gang, we hold him responsible for his involvement. It is not an excuse for him later to claim that his friends were joining, or that gang members pressured him into going along. That he didn't pull the trigger does not make him innocent. The same holds true for someone joining the Ku Klux Klan or the Aryan Brotherhood. If an institution or organization is clearly wicked, there is no member untainted. Except in the case of very young children, the community expects that its members hold themselves responsible for a minimal level of reflection about the groups they join, even if they are not professionally trained in the details of philosophical ethics.[4]

At one end of the spectrum, then, conscientious application of the just war criteria may give the government the benefit of the doubt, but at the other it should lead to active dissent. There will, of course, be innumerable shades and complications in between. But this doesn't render the traditional criteria inapplicable; it only points up the difficulty of judgment under difficult circumstances. All of our attempts to do justice are subject to that sort of difficulty. So the epistemological argument doesn't strike home. The traditional just war criteria do make it possible to recognize the relevant evidence and articulate specific grounds for objecting to or removing a previously granted support for a particular war.

Ramsey writes that "in the forum of conscience there is duty to a moral power higher than the state. But the Congress is not *legally or constitutionally* bound to do this," and that "under the proposed system of selective objection I see no reason why conscientious objection to certain modes of warfare ... might not be allowable grounds," giving the impression that conscience must convince the state before it may operate (1968:93, 135). My argument has been to reverse this relation. Whatever loyalty I owe the state is conditioned by the character of that system, as I respond to it in concrete, practical situations. Because we are inescapably communal animals, there is no Hobbesian state of nature, but instead a constantly shifting set of loyalties to multiple communities which may only partially overlap with the political powers that be. Should we refuse this pressure we may risk our selves and our livelihood, but we have committed an affront against justice only if the state can show a fair and reasonable obligation on our part.

In a just and ideally balanced global order we might make do with a local militia, which could respond as needed to threats and disturbances that exceeded the capacities of the police. But this is an option open to few communities in the contemporary scheme of things, and some provision should be made for a standing army. I have not argued against this, but only insisted that a volunteer army best reflects our commitment to a virtuous political order because it is made up of people who have freely chosen their profession. If we want, as we should, to encourage as many people as possible to enter the army, we should make it an institution as honorable, choice-worthy, and rewarding as possible. But this said, it remains to be shown that conscience binds us to obligatory service. Thus, any draft, other than that which establishes an order of induction among volunteers, oversteps the bounds of justice, and my first recommendation is to avoid establishing such immoral burdens. But should it be beyond the virtue of the political order to accustom itself to the risks involved, we should at least attempt to limit the government to attaching only those citizens who have no objection to such service. Maybe a stint in the army will give direction to a life that is otherwise unfocused. After all, nothing I have argued here suggests that being a professional soldier is any less worthy than being a lawyer, doctor, or university professor. If, however, the moral fiber of our community is so weak that our legislators feel compelled to introduce a "blind" draft, such as that which obtained in the last years of the Vietnam War, then we should make provisions for an appeal on the basis of selective concientious objection, and I've suggested that we key the weight we grant the objection to the applicability of the traditional just war criteria. I want to make it clear that this is a concession to political weakness. The citizen who, having otherwise contributed to the maintenance of the state, rejects military service has nothing to answer for, whereas the state which would penalize the conscientious objector does.

Perhaps the most radical aspect of my argument, in this chapter and throughout, is the systematic devaluation of political community in the sense of the modern nation-state. This move, however, follows naturally from the account of craftsmanship in chapter 4. We identify with the practices and institutions that have the greatest impact on our day-to-day lives, and this means that we are potters, or poets, or farmers first, and other loyalties may be up for grabs. Family and friends take natural precedence, and the intensity of our commitment decreases as we move from the neighborhood to the city and from there to more remote political structures. But this is how it should be. What we know we can judge, and only what we judge worthy should we incorporate into the fabric of our lives. We take on what obligations we have as part and parcel of the lives we live, and these are inescapably part of a very particular history, in which the players, individual and corporate, must be tested over and over again. Thus, there can be no general, nontrivial account of "political obligation," as opposed to the political obligations of people in some time and place. John Dunn rightly notes that the "hope that political duty can be rendered cut-and-dried, simple, dominant, and perspicuous is in essence the hope that historical contingency can be conclusively eluded" (1980:292), and such hope will not be fulfilled this side of paradise. Better then that, we should be wary of the simple and the cut-and-dried; it is a sad path too well trodden. As a grade-schooler I memorized poems and famous phrases, and one that is still familiar saw the light of day as a toast: "My country, may she always be in the right. But my country right or wrong." This disturbed me when I was twelve. A quarter of a century later, I am sure it reflects a sentiment that even an Aristotelian naturalist can scarcely keep from calling demonic.

Notes

1. The most comprehensive introduction to the literature on conscription is Anderson (1976), although for all its bulk it is surprisingly spotty. Cohen (1985) provides additional material, particularly on philosophical matters. I have yet to discover an up to date history of conscription, although many suggestive comments are to be found throughout the essays in Paret (1986). The extensive bibliographies also provide clues for investigating these matters. For obvious reasons, the end of the military draft in the United States meant a considerable decline in the number of discussions of conscientious objection. Childress reviews the most important literature (1982:165–219). A related discussion is that of Finnis et al. (1987:pts. 4–5), where the authors elaborate a detailed moral realism grounded in the natural-law tradition and go on to argue the necessity for informed dissent, up to and including civil disobedience, on the part of citizens who judge policies of nuclear deterrence morally unacceptable.

2. Hauerwas (1990) lays out some of the points I am trying to make very nicely. Despite our obvious differences about Jesus, Hauerwas and I make one in our uneasiness with both the foundations and consequences of Augustinian and Kantian moral theory. That I have chosen not to make a long essay even longer with a discussion of Hauerwas should not obscure my respect and gratitude for his work.

3. Any introductory anthropology text will give some account of the variety and workings of kinship systems. The close interrelation between kinship and cosmology, and its ties to the organization of everyday life, comes out in Griaule (1965), but this shouldn't make us think that such matters are foreign to the traditions of European society and law. Any student of the Talmud knows how important women, sexuality, and family are in the Hebrew Bible and the *Mishnah*, and the reading of the bans prior to a medieval betrothal reflects continued concern with these matters.

4. The argument here reproduces, in compressed form, that of R. A. Markus (Stein 1961:79–88). Finnis et al. (1987:342–57) elaborate the argument but do not improve on its general power, which is very great and which finds ever new application in the contemporary urban context.

6.

Revolution and Regret

"*I* hold it," wrote Jefferson from Paris, in January of 1787, "that a little rebellion, now and then, is a good thing, and as necessary in the political world as storms in the physical" (1944:413). He evidently liked the thought, for he wrote Madison again in December of the same year, "that one rebellion in thirteen States in the course of eleven years, is but one for each State in a century and a half. No country should be so long without one." He was repeating almost word for word what he had written the previous month to yet another correspondent, William Smith, concluding famously that "the tree of liberty must be refreshed from time to time, with the blood of patriots and tyrants. It is its natural manure" (1944:436–40). To exist without the need for government, "as among our Indians," would doubtless be the best social order. "But," he writes Madison, "I believe it to be inconsistent with any great degree of population," and consequently any large body should be one "wherein the will of every one has a just influence; as is the case in England, in a slight degree, and in our States, in a great one" (1944:413). This republican constitution may, nonetheless, occasionally trample upon justice and when that happens it is not surprising that rebellion follows. It is, as it were, a form of pruning necessary to keeping the state vigorous, and "an observation of this truth should render honest republican governors so mild in their punishments of rebellions, as not to discourage them too much" (1944:413). But Jefferson is no friend of revolution in the sense we associate with France and Russia. He contrasts the relative stability of the United States with the yearly revolts he witnesses in France, and almost three decades later writes his old friend LaFayette that the French failure to secure a reasonable constitution led "to the destruction of order; and, in the end, the limited monarchy they had secured was exchanged for the unprincipled and bloody tyranny of Robespierre, and the equally unprincipled and maniac tyranny of Bonaparte" (1944:655). Thus, rebellion per se is as likely to lead to tragedy as to promote the health of the body politic. Nonetheless, Jefferson's remarks are more than epistolary rhetoric. Like his contemporary, Clausewitz, Jefferson presupposes a stable tradition of virtue underlying discussions of political change, discussions of what Aristotle calls *stasis* and Thomas Aquinas, *seditio*.[1]

As Aristotle uses the notion, *stasis* is the forming of parties to bring about constitutional change. Such change is a natural aspect of political life for the simple reason that innovation and circumstances admit of minimal prediction. A constitution sufficiently general to cover all the possibilities would be devoid of content. Historically situated societies are perpetually trying to fine-tune their political structure in the face of unanticipated changes and competing forces. In the process, the citizens can themselves become persuaded that the political order has lost touch with its reason for being. We saw in the last chapter the difficulty of balancing justice and security in the military draft. Whether the constitution be democratic or oligarchic, "either side turns to sedition if it does not enjoy the share of constitutional rights which accords with the conception of justice it happens to entertain" (Aristotle *Pol.*:1301a). That Aristotle acknowledges competing conceptions of justice here shouldn't lead to charges of relativism. It merely signals the distinction between that which is just in the sense of pertaining to the character of fair and reasonable agents, just according to the law, and equitable in a particular case (*Ethics*:1134a–37b). Even just persons can disagree about the propriety of a law, its application in a particular case, and how failure of law can be made good. It is a mark of good character and political wisdom when a person, as Aristotle puts it, "is no stickler for his rights in a bad sense but tends to take less than his share though he has the law on his side. . . . And this state of character is equity" (*Ethics*:1137b). The limits of character and intellect, coupled with the unpredictability of events, make dispute certain, contributing thereby to the fragility of all communal order. But, as in other cases, our uncertainty about where justice lies reflects our fallibility, not the relativity of justice.

Disagreement about equity and the fair distribution of goods can escalate into factioning and party politics. Repeated failures to address the situation provoke calls for change and clashes of will. At this point we have sedition. One of the benefits of Aristotle's approach to politics is the absence of any modern distinction between the "subjective" and "objective" or the "scientific" and the "humane." Consequently, he can include among the causal factors leading to sedition "insolence and profit-making," "fear," the "disproportionate increase of a part of the state," and "accident" (*Pol.*:1302b–3a). All of these can play a role in the best account of how change happens, and there is no prima facie reason to believe that any one of them can be eliminated or that there is a single explanatory model to which all human phenomena can be reduced. For any given instance of pressure toward constitutional change, it will be necessary, as Aristotle does at several points, to provide some narrative that accounts for the factors, predictable and unpredictable, at work in a particular case. The benefits of this procedure, if we are seeking clarity in political understanding, are borne out, as John Dunn (1972) makes clear, in the causal dissimilarity of the most notable modern revolutions.

Dunn's articulation of the differences between revolutions has more than methodological interest. The more we grasp about the complexity of revolutions and their consequences the more wary we should be of oversimplified claims about the justice or injustice of a particular situation and what we should do about it. In terms of the just war criteria, we should expect that satisfying the *ad bellum* demand that the good to be achieved outweigh the miseries of war will be very hard to do. If we wish to avoid, as any reasonable person should, the horrors of the French Revolution and Pol Pot's killing fields, we should build into our political structures as many constraints on abuse and possibilities for redress as are compatible with a functioning state. This was Jefferson's point, and it is no surprise that his remarks on revolution are tied to his arguments for political accountability, freedom of press and religion, and the need for a bill of rights in the new constitution. He is, in other words, committed to revolution in the sense of challenging and reforming the political order. When, as sometimes it must, reform necessitates force, then that underlying tradition of virtue must come into play more profoundly in order to ensure that we do not end up with Robespierre, Bonaparte, or something worse.

We can pursue the Aristotelian analysis of these matters in the work of Thomas Aquinas. As is also the case with war, Thomas treats sedition not under the general heading of justice, but under charity. This is less surprising than it might at first seem when we consider that charity plays a role in Thomas's ethics analogous to that of friendship in Aristotle's. Charity is the optimal relation between people. It is, as it were, friendship transformed by the knowledge of ourselves and others as creatures of a benevolent God. War, as we saw in chapter 3 is acceptable only when directed to the good of the whole and only then if constrained by the demands of justice. It is a tragic undertaking forced upon us as a last resort in protecting the good of others. But whereas Aristotle's *stasis* may be neutral with respect to justice, Aquinas condemns *seditio* as contrary to the "unity of law and common good" (*S.Theo.*:2a2ae, 43, 1). Since sedition encourages discord, it runs counter to the charity that should be the norm of community. The contrast, however, is merely apparent. When a government becomes tyrannical it has ceased to be directed to the common good, "being conducive to the private good of the ruler, and to the injury of the multitude" (43, 1 ad 3). Discord, and even violence directed toward a tyrant, does not take as its object the common good, but the private person who would usurp that good. "Consequently," Thomas concludes, "there is no sedition in disturbing a government of this kind, unless indeed the tyrant's rule be disturbed so inordinately, that his subjects suffer greater harm from the consequent disturbance than from the tyrant's government" (43, 1 ad 3). This last point is crucial. Revolt against injustice is consonant with virtue. It may, as in the case of war, be required by charity. Nonetheless, there is a standing presumption against rebellion because it deprives those abiding by the law of what they can reasonably expect. For instance, some group within the community may have a genuine grievance against the state. Let's say that the state supports one religion while taxing others. Members of the unsupported religions can either convert, which puts a grievous burden on their conscience, or they can pay the tax, which cuts into their ability to compete on an equal footing with their fellows for other goods. A case can be made against the justice of this arrangement, but the argument is not clear-cut. We are frequently called upon to sacrifice one good in the pursuit of another. How onerous is the tax? How is it implemented? Are there other, more injurious forms of discrimination supported by the government against dissenters? To lobby for a change in the constitution is reasonable; rebellion may be out of proportion to the grievance. Despite the admitted burden, there are other goods I partake in as a member of the community and which I share with the rest of the citizenry. Rebellion disrupts the life of the entire community, sacrificing the general run of things. There is also the possibility that the original community will not survive and that the breakdown of that society will be so extensive that a new and more equitable order cannot easily emerge. Something of these uncertainties can be gathered from John Reed's classic account of the November Revolution. Reed resembles Thucydides rather more than the eyewitness he portrays himself to be, and he captures the sense of confusion and loss that earlier plagued Athens. His own sudden vision, "that the devout Russian people no longer needed priests to pray them into heaven. On earth they were building a kingdom more bright than any heaven had to offer," finds its check in the bombarding of the Kremlin, "pounding to dust the sanctuary of the Russian nation," and in Commissar of Education Lunacharsky, who "broke into tears at the session of the Council of People's Commissars, and rushed from the room, crying, 'I cannot stand it! I cannot bear the monstrous destruction of beauty and tradition'" (Reed 1977:230, 220). Whatever the justice of tearing down the czarist system, it is not at all clear that the subsequent history of the Soviet Union can be described as that kingdom more bright or that it has made good the destruction.

This presumption against revolt constitutes a check, but not an absolute barrier. What it does is force a reinterpretation of the just war criteria as they apply to my own community. First, the government must be actively wicked, as opposed to mistaken, incompetent, or unfair. Take, for example, our system of taxation. By granting benefits to investors, it may turn out that very wealthy people pay a smaller percentage of their gross income in taxes than does a middle-class family of three. This seems unfair. But the familiar response claims that the investor, by reinvesting, contributes to the overall health of the economy in a way that the simple middle-class family cannot, although that family will ultimately reap the benefits of the growth through investment. This argument is controversial and may be based on faulty economics, but that it can be made in good faith indicates that the government is not actively engaged in wickedness, at least not with regard to taxes. The same holds for the case where the government is mistaken or a policy ill-conceived. Even if the unfortunate judgment leads to severe misery, up to and including loss of life, we do not have the conditions for revolution. Consider the United States' Panama invasion of December 1989. Morally, every aspect of this operation is questionable. Prosecution of a single individual, however corrupt, can scarcely justify a massive violation of national sovereignty, even if some part of the populace welcomes it. A domestic operation of this size, with substantial fatalities, would never be tolerated to apprehend a single suspect. When combined with the level of destruction visited on the civilian population—hundreds dead, thousands injured, and uncounted homeless and displaced—the invasion fails every just war criterion. It should provide occasion for international outrage. But it does not justify rebellion. For while the act is irresponsible, malicious, and culpable, it does not manifest active wickedness directed against its own citizens. The proper response is condemnation and subsequent rejection of the officials responsible.

A second condition involves our own common good. Suppose that we were convinced that the government was involved in actively wicked endeavors, like, say, using the FBI and the IRS to suppress environmental activists so that political cronies might profit from unrestricted clear-cutting in the national forests. Here we have four distinct forms of wickedness. Injustice is being perpetrated against the environmentalists themselves as well as the common good, which has an important stake in the long-term health of natural resources. At the same time, business interests are unjustly reaping profits through the subversion of the rule of law. Finally, when public agencies become instruments of private manipulation and gain, no segment of the community can trust that it will not become the victim of its own elected officials. The continuing repercussions of shady dealings in the fight for water, for example, are never far from the thoughts of Californians. Nonetheless, the evil being perpetrated is less than the misery likely to result from revolution. Popular opinion, the media, and the courts provide avenues for exposing the situation and bringing down the criminals. But the stage has been set for a situation where rebellion would be justified. By perverting the instruments of government, those in power have driven a wedge between the community and the political order. Once corruption extends into the fabric of the bureaucracy, revolution becomes a serious possibility because the instruments designed to foster the common good have been turned against it, and the common citizen no longer has any compelling reason to support the system.

A third condition: active wickedness and injury to the common good are necessary but not sufficient grounds for undertaking revolution. It remains to ask whether there is a reasonable hope that the evils being perpetrated can be curtailed through rebellion. Continuing with our example above: if corruption has spread through the entire system, then the ability to bring force to bear will rest overwhelmingly with the officials, allowing them to counter the revolutionary moves we take. Unless we are sufficiently strong and well supplied, the attempt at revolution will have little chance of success. Under the circumstances, to push forward would be to risk ourselves with no reasonable expectation *and* to disrupt the existing order to the detriment of our noncombatant fellow citizens. Predictably, the results will be worse for our fellows because the corrupt regime, uncertain where popular support for the rebellion lies, will be likely to step up oppressive measures. The Argentine and Central American examples come readily to mind. Thus, even if the wickedness being perpetrated on the community justifies the initial disruption, it is not consonant with justice unless we can argue a reasonable hope of success.

There is a qualification, however. As the level and extent of the injury escalates, there is a related shift in what counts as reasonable hope. A relatively small injury is tolerable in an otherwise undisrupted cycle of life. Looking the other way while a policeman cadges a piece of fruit is a minor aggravation, unjust and destructive, but tolerable if I wish to avoid further harassment. As the depredations increase, however, the freedom from harassment comes to be worth less; and when my life and livelihood become the object of threat, success is measured in terms of avoiding destruction. Thus, although the criterion is always operative in general, as the stakes increase, the demands on reasonable hope of success go down. We reach the outer limit when a government institutionalizes the murder of its own citizens; for if we are all potential victims, then anything that works against this state of affairs is to be preferred.

There remains a fourth condition. Dunn remarks that "there is a wide gap between the skills needed to exercise governmental power and the skills needed to gain it. . . . The only revolutionary achievement is the creation of a new order" (1972:18). Revolution is not an end in itself, but a regrettable, indeed a horrible, need in order to recapture a lost good or establish a new one. It encompasses pain, destruction, and the killing of neighbors. Except for the genocidal situation, the overthrow of a predecessor regime is only the beginning. Those who would undertake revolution may be reasonably expected to have given thought to what new political order will emerge. If there is no end envisioned or if there is no reasonable hope that a better order can be established and maintained, then the entire enterprise is irresponsibly defective.

These constraints clarify, they do not replace the just war criteria. The same holds for the following test of just intent. Merely by virtue of her role in overthrowing the previous regime, the revolutionary is not entitled to special consideration in the reconstituted community. I don't mean that she is not worthy of the respect and gratitude due a hero, but that being a revolutionary does not give her a special voice or greater authority in determining the shape of the new political order. The point of revolution is restoring the integrity of the community, not molding one in your own, unchallenged vision of the political ideal. For the just revolutionary this means, among other things, that if she fights in behalf of a new and innovative political order it must be one which can ultimately be made both intelligible and acceptable to the bulk of the community.

The most notable, and frustrating, consequence is the nagging feeling that the community could be a much better place if only people could be made to see what's truly good. Perhaps. But societies are radically contingent, in the sense of being constantly threatened by internal tensions, external conflicts, and the general unpredictability of the economic, political, and technological future. Even if our community might be better, it would not be perfect and it would certainly not be eternal. Where is the justice in sacrificing the freedom and conscience of others for the chance of bettering a society that will no doubt pass away in time? Just as we should not tolerate wishful thinking by our leaders, we should not accept it from the revolutionary.

I have taken it for granted that recognizing injustice is tantamount to rejecting it, but what if the "recognition" of injustice is itself nothing more than a product of oppressive forces? Engels suggested, against Dühring, that "morality has always been class morality" (Tucker 1972:667). In the context of modern capitalism, our moral vocabulary reflects the interests of those in power; and internalizing the virtues taught through that vocabulary trains those who are not in power to accept their lot. Picking up on this notion, Lenin concludes that bourgeois rights and justice must be eliminated through revolution because "in capitalist society, we have a democracy that is curtailed, poor, false.... The period of transition to Communism, will, for the first time, produce democracy for the people, for the majority" (Lenin 1932:74). The oppressive, and ultimately self-destructive nature of capitalism stunts genuine moral development in favor of a system of brutal exploitation. To the extent that capitalist morality inhibits the movement toward revolution it must be overcome and eliminated.

This argument reflects a recurrent theme in much Marxist thought: revolution as vocation.[2] The parallel to Yoder's pacifism is intended, for I want to argue that the revolutionary of Lenin's sort shares with Yoder a willingness to give up what would normally be thought of as basic goods—family, friends, the pursuit of private goods—in the name of a calling perceived as transcendent. Both Yoder and Lenin see the tradition of justice as merely a moment in the development of human community, and both argue that allegiance is better placed in the source of revolutionary change than in a contingent human tradition. For Lenin, the end is to attain genuine freedom by liberation from class oppression. Violent revolution is unavoidable in attaining that end, and should not be hindered by caring about norms and practices on their way out. The traditional moral norms, where they serve the oppressors, should be rejected, for the true revolutionary is dedicated to the ultimate good of liberation even though the first phase of the transition to a classless society will not produce a new justice and equality. However, "the suppression of the minority of exploiters, by the majority of the wage slaves *of yesterday*. . . will cost far less bloodshed than the suppression of the risings of slaves, serfs or wage labourers, and will cost mankind far less" (Lenin 1932:74). If it is not to suffer the fate of the Paris Commune, the new revolutionary order must "suppress the bourgeoisie and crush its resistence" (1932:37), replacing it with "an iron discipline" (1932:43) dedicated to bringing about the final phase in the withering away of the state. Like Yoder, Lenin places action in support of the revolution above any allegiance to traditional standards of moral conduct. He is willing for the revolutionary to bear the burden of moral denunciation and the sacrifice of life itself if the revolution should require it. In this sense, he advocates a form of revolutionary martyrdom.

More than a few people have committed themselves body and soul to some version of this vocation. There is, nevertheless, a notable tension between economic analysis and moral fervor, traceable to Marx's very early writings. In the preface to the manuscripts of 1844, Marx insists that his position has been reached "by means of a wholly empirical analysis based on a conscientious critical study of political economy" (Marx 1971:63). At the same time, there is throughout the manuscripts an intense awareness of the dehumanizing and morally destructive power of capitalist society. Money itself frequently takes on a demonically independent personality, as when Marx writes that "it transforms fidelity into infidelity, love into hate. . . . It is the general *confounding* and *compounding* of all things—the world upside-down—the confounding and compounding of all natural and human qualities" (1971:169). In passages like this he displays a level of moral outrage sometimes suppressed in his later writings. But this makes even more important the question of how we should interpret revolutionary rhetoric based on Marxist theory.

If we accord a certain primacy to Marx's early moral impetus, the inclination would be to see him as a young Hegelian impressed with the brutality of the Prussian state and the inequities through which a wealthy upper-class sustained itself on the backs of the poor. In the intellectual climate of Berlin, Marx's desire became to see the material transformation of an oppressive society into one of genuine liberation, and this, as Isaiah Berlin characterizes it, meant shouldering "the plain duty of the philosopher . . . to promote revolution by the special technical skill which he alone commands, that is by intellectual warfare" (Berlin 1963:54). On this reading, the manuscripts of 1844 are diagnostic. Marx traces alienation and the loss of genuine human values to the workings of a capital-driven economy, and he traces the general torpor of philosophy back to the overly abstract analyses of Hegel. Revolution is both justified and appropriate, but on grounds of justice not despite it. This he elaborates in *The German Ideology*, where he describes the proletarian as "sacrificed from youth upwards and, within his own class, has no chance of arriving at the conditions which would place him in the other class"; and since this oppressive system is unjustly secured by the apparatus of the state, "the proletarians, if they are to assert themselves as individuals, will have to abolish the very condition of their existence hitherto. . . . They must overthrow the State" (Tucker 1972:164). Here, Marx pays more attention to the means by which alienation is overcome and freedom secured, but it is still viewed from the perspective of genuine human goods. From this perspective, there is no clear justification for exceeding the bounds of justice in carrying out the revolution. In fact, it would be odd to argue for suspending the conditions of justice in the pursuit of human good.

It is also possible to read the later work of Marx and Engels as analytic and predictive. Such a reading needn't attribute to them a reductive determinism; Engels, in a letter of 1890, disowns such a reading entirely (Tucker 1972:640). An understanding closer to the spirit of Marx's *Capital* would emphasize the dynamic structuralism of economic development. It would point to the details of Marx's historical research to justify the developmental claims for particular forms and patterns of the relationship of work to material culture. From this might emerge a moral relativism to form the background of Marx's caustic remarks on "equal right" and "fair distribution" in the *Critique of the Gotha Program*, a critique designed "to show what a crime it is to attempt, on the one hand, to force on our Party again, as dogmas, ideas which in a certain period had some meaning but have now become obsolete verbal rubbish, while again perverting, on the other, the realistic outlook" (Tucker 1972:388). Here, we have Marx eschewing the obsolete moral notions of the past in favor of scientific realism. Such a reading takes seriously the analogy Marx draws with the physicist, who "either observes physical phenomena where they occur in their most typical form and most free from disturbing influence, or wherever possible, he makes experiments under conditions that assure the occurrence of the phenomenon in its normality" (Tucker 1972:192). A passage like this, from the preface to *Capital*, reflects the scientific spirit of Darwin, the book's initial dedicatee.

But the more emphasis is placed on the "scientific," as opposed to the "moral" Marx, the less coherent becomes any revolutionary rhetoric based on the theory. A comparison with Darwin is instructive. In putting forward the theory of natural selection, Darwin argued that the fossil record and the observable relations between species and their environments suggested a competition for local resources in which those individuals endowed with some competitive edge, and those species in which that edge was preserved and developed, would replace the less fortunately endowed. There is no attempt to predict the nonbiological events that shape and reshape the parameters of the competition, nor is there any hint that some species *should* triumph over others for the good of the animal kingdom. If an asteroid collision changed the climate of the earth and if smaller reptiles were thereby rendered better off vis à vis their dinosaur relatives, then the situation would have favored the smaller beasts and the larger might well die out. Had there been no such change, naturally occurring variants in the dinosaurs themselves would have favored one species over others. That's the way nature works.

But the comparison with Darwin has another lesson to teach. The theory of evolution is one of the great achievements in thought because it accounts for a substantial part of the evidence, does so with clarity and an explanatory economy appropriate to the topic, and invokes powers and forces that cohere with our understanding of the rest of our world. But it remains a theory about the nature of things, and should it be found explanatorily wanting, we will justifiably demand revision. A theory about the nature of things, in other words, lets itself be led by things rather than attempting to shape them. That is a job for engineers.

Not only is a scientific theory revisable in principal but also the certainty with which we hold it should be roughly inverse to the complexity and importance of the investigation. The heart, for example, is a very complex organ, and understanding the functions and interrelations of the components takes considerable time and effort. But the physiologist who has mastered the internal organization of the heart has gone only part way in learning the makeup of a single body, the behavioral characteristics of the species, and the relation of the species to its ecosystem. At each stage, the complexity of the system increases and the importance of being clear on a particular subsystem increases as well. Misunderstanding the relation of the panda to a certain species of bamboo, for example, would threaten the existence of the species, even if the zoologist had a sound grasp of panda physiology. Explaining the workings of a system becomes even more difficult when a key part can revise previous forms of behavior. This introduces a new and unpredictable factor that may alter the outcome of a previously well-understood course of action. Consequently, the riskiness of any single prediction rises and the likelihood of needing to revise the theory increases. As the likelihood of revision increases, the viability of any engineering projects based on the theory decreases. This is a point illustrated, ironically, by Reed, who reports Lenin addressing the Congress of Soviets in almost visionary terms, proclaiming that "the revolution of 6 and 7 November has opened the era of Social Revolution. . . . The labour movement, in the name of peace and Socialism, shall win, and fulfill its destiny" (Reed 1977:132), whereas the details of the narrative portray a situation of unpredictability bordering on chaos.

It is at this point that the reasonableness of revolutionary activism becomes suspect. Lenin might best be thought of as a brilliant engineer, appropriating and modifying Marx's thought in order to carry out and establish a new regime that will, ultimately, be of substantial benefit to the community. The benefit extends, by the way, to the capitalist as well as the proletarian, since the new order does not suffer from the structural incoherences that constantly place the superficial well-being of the successful capitalist in jeopardy. Not only that, but the capitalist will also be relieved of the alienation that effects him as it does the worker, and he will be further relieved of the necessity to mask his alienation in consumption and oppression. But, in order to achieve this transformation Lenin asks the community to forsake both justice and their own freedom of conscience. The forsaking of justice comes not in the destruction of the capitalist system. If it is truly a system of oppression, then it would be just to destroy it. And if the capitalists have unjustly employed the system, then it is appropriate to take punitive action against them. On this much the advocate of justice can agree with the Marxist. But Lenin clearly wants to go further. A successful revolution must eschew any constraints of capitalist justice in the prosecution of the war and in implementing the new political order once it wrests control from the current rulers. Even those capitalists who have benefited without being themselves unjust are subject to the suppression necessary for the transition to communism and the withering away of the state. At least this means that Aristotle's *stasis* and Jefferson's sense of revolution cannot be tolerated, for not unless "all members of society, or even only the overwhelming majority . . . have 'established' control over the insignificant minority of capitalists" (Lenin 1932:84) will the withering away envisioned by Marx and Engels come about. A situation that envisions regular opposition and occasional constitutional change impairs the completion of the revolution.

Lenin sees this period of revolutionary oppression as necessary to cleansing the new order, a necessary purgative on the way to establishing a truly liberating society. Nonetheless, this aspect of his revolutionary theory presents a challenge to practical reasonableness. If we allow that questions of justice have no place in revolutionary motivation, it becomes appropriate to ask what does. Allen Buchanan suggests that the argument from rational self-interest founders on the problem of public goods. Public goods are those available to each member of the community, regardless of his role in creating them. The security achieved by a standing army, for example, extends to all members of the state, whether they serve or not. But to the extent that there are public goods, there is the problem of the "free rider," who benefits without contributing to the overall good. Leaving aside questions of fairness, the presence in the community of free riders creates a dilemma for all reasonable agents. Whatever good they seek, be it their own or the common good, will be thwarted if others don't contribute. Public goods are typically such that they cannot be secured by a single individual. But my contribution is lost to me, and benefits no one, if it is swamped by a sea of indifference. Thus, I might as well see whether others will contribute; but then if they do, that will suffice to bring about the good and I can continue to withold any contribution. "So," writes Buchanan, "rational self-interest requires that I not contribute and go for a 'free ride' on the efforts of others" (Cohen et al. 1980:269). The implications for the revolutionary are evident, even if we consider revolution the means to a great public good. Given the great risk involved, a reasonable person cannot act hastily; most revolutions fail, and the cost of failure is death. Buchanan canvasses four strategies for solving the problem: denying the existence of the problem; coercion; in-process benefits; and moral principles. He is none too sanguine about any of these strategies for the Marxist who wants to maintain continuity with the tradition, although he suggests how moral principles might play a part in revolutionary agitation (Cohen et al. 1980:286–7). Once Lenin allows the influence of moral concerns, however, he opens himself to those objections on behalf of justice that he wishes to rule out of court.

If there is a difficulty for the committed revolutionary it is even greater for the uncommitted proletarian. Consider what he is being asked to accept. Let's grant that he considers the capitalist system oppressive and views himself as victim. He might be willing to bring down the system and perhaps take punitive action against its immediate beneficiaries, but he must also agree to give up the exercise of political activism in the future should he decide that the new system is not working in his best interests. The grounds for this concession are found in a complex theory which is one among a number of equally complex accounts of economic activity. Suppose that advocates of one of those alternative theories, say that of Adam Smith, had asked him to make a similar concession. Had he done so, he would now not be in a position to join the Marxist. Thus, the proletarian would be giving up the very form of action which allowed him to recognize and act on his own behalf.

For those who do not perceive themselves the victims of oppression, the challenge to practical reasonableness is even greater. Given the complexity of human societies and the sheer contingencies that can impose themselves at any time, the degree of unpredictability of the details of human history is high. Our certainty in the predictions of any given theory should be appropriately low. They will, in any event, be lower than the certainty with which we hold many if not most basic moral judgments, such as the wickedness of murder, rape, infidelity, and torture. But the certainty, indeed the intelligibility, of these concepts is very closely bound up with the notions of fairness and equality Marx recommends we jettison as verbal rubbish. They are all reflections of the general agreement on justice necessary to any functioning society. Thus, for most people the choice between retaining the old vocabulary and tossing it on the trash heap of history is weighted heavily in favor of the status quo. To the extent that the community has not been alienated by the wickedness of its rulers, the exhortation *ad bellum* appears unreasonable. The revolutionary demands allegiance to the forces of history, but his certainty rests on an implausible, almost idolatrous view of economics as a science. Absent a grounding in justice, his threat of force against the political order is no different in kind from terrorism.

If justice is the goal, any relaxing of the just war criteria risks the worthiness of what we would protect. If anything, carrying out a revolution among your fellow citizens should mean strengthening the criteria. After all, these are not merely the faceless noncombatants of a distant enemy, they are your neighbors. Your revolution is, at least ostensibly, on their behalf. Consequently, even if the *ad bellum* conditions for revolution have been satisfied, the *in bello* demand for discrimination and proportion imposes itself with more force on the revolutionary than on the general in conventional circumstances. Failure means the destruction of those very neighbors who are already suffering oppression. The refusal to discriminate implicit in terrorism suggests, in Walzer's phrase, "a malign forgetfulness, erasing all moral distinctions along with the men and women who painfully worked them out" (1977:204). To forget all this is to make rational politics impossible.

It remains to ask how the *in bello* criteria, particularly discrimination, can be exercised in a revolutionary context. Who are the undoubted targets? Here, there will be a problem directly related to the makeup of the political system. In a one-person tyranny, it is fairly clear that the tyrant is an object of direct attack. He is, after all, the agent *ex hypothesi* of the injustice. But this opens up a class of target typically outside the limits of targetability in a conventional war. As Walzer notes, "Characteristically (and not foolishly) lawyers have frowned on assassination, and political officials have been assigned to the class of non-military persons, who are never the legitimate objects of attack" (1977:199).[3] If we grant that the tyrant can be targeted, we're loosening the reins of discrimination. Does this mean that anyone connected with the political system is now a legitimate target? Private individuals remain exempt, even if they contribute to the evil, because they are not part of the system of repression. At most they can be dealt with when the legal order is reestablished. To be a legitimate object of attack, it is necessary that the individual or class be part of the government, but the revolutionary also needs to isolate the class of officials that can legitimately be targeted. Office workers, having nothing to do with the flow of evil, are just going about their daily business, Xeroxing memos and processing forms the way they would under a perfectly upright government. To strike at them is not to strike at the source of the evil, nor does it deter those responsible for the evil. It is an act of terrorism whose only relevant result is to keep others from taking government clerical jobs. We can grant that this might disrupt the activities of the tyrant, but it achieves this only through a direct attack on the innocent. Discrimination requires that the innocent be protected, and this means that they cannot be used as a means, even to a good end. To do so would be to submit them to an injury they do not merit and this is unfair, the definition, as it were, of injustice.

Nor is it fair to target a particular service on the grounds that some of its members are directly involved in evil. FBI agents, for example, might present likely targets because of their role in the internal policing activities of the state. But it is perfectly easy to imagine them engaged in ordinary cases, pursuing criminals without being coopted into the machinery of tyranny. Political corruption, after all, is not the only injustice perpetrated against the common good. Suppose, however, that the president and his advisors recruited FBI agents for death squads, controlled directly from the White House. In this case it's not business as usual. Such squads clearly exceed any constitutional authority, and their wickedness is so evident that no agent can hide behind superior orders. Were I to wake to the sound of such a squad arriving at my door, there would be no question about my responding with force. That would be self-defense. And were I a member of a revolutionary cell, such death squads would be legitimate targets. But that wouldn't make all FBI agents targets, merely suspects.

This suggests a certain test for targetability. If the criteria for a just revolution have already been satisfied, then and only then individuals are legitimate targets who satisfy the following criteria:

1. They hold a legally constituted position within the executive branch (or its analogue for forms of government other than the American).
2. They are either the makers, advocates, or agents of the injurious policies cited as sufficient causes for revolution.
3. Their involvement in those injurious activities is such that any mature moral agent should recognize its wickedness.

The first criterion is required to ensure that only those persons are targeted who are part of the immediate machinery of oppression. Its analogue in the conventional just war criteria is joining up and donning a uniform. It is a necessary condition because targets must in principle have a public status, but it is not a sufficient condition for the reasons canvassed above. In a nation the size of the United States, there is bound to be a division of labor within the executive branch simply in order to get done the ordinary tasks of government. This isn't part of the problem; and insofar as government employees are simply carrying out day-to-day business, they are no more objects of attack than ordinary citizens in the conventional context of war. As we shrink the size of the political system, the division of labor will contract into fewer and fewer hands, and this will make it easier to determine where the agents of tyranny lie. The more day-to-day business rests in the control of a single individual, the more that individual is responsible for the consequences, so that the limiting case is the classical tyrant, who holds all the power himself. He is clearly an object of attack, as Aquinas explained. But tyranny in this sense is distinguished from monarchy by the injustice involved in expropriating the public good for private enjoyment. Hence the third criterion. A monarch whose policies are injurious to the common good may simply be inept; and that being the case, he may reasonably be removed. We would only call his removal a revolution were he to resist and employ the powers of his office in that resistence. In that case, his ineptitude would have crossed the line into the malice of tyranny, acting unreasonably against the common good. But the principle application of the third criterion is not in establishing the culpability of the single tyrant or the tyrannical oligarchy. The case of the FBI agent is the problematic one. Given the wickedness of the president and his advisors, the intelligence uncovered by the agent in the pursuit of his ordinary duties may well contribute to state oppression. The agent, however, may be unaware of this and may even be attempting to ensure that the letter of the law is followed, guaranteeing constitutional rights. He may, for example, be refusing to turn over classified material to other agents suspected of being involved with the death squads. So there is nothing in his capacity as agent that justifies targeting him. Given the level of uncertainty in the situation I might be justified, even if mistaken in fact, were I to respond with deadly force to the agent's approach, but that is a different question. The proper objects of attack are the death squads themselves, and the burden of proving membership lies with the revolutionary.

And so, who besides the corrupt president is a legitimate target according to *ius in seditione*? Up to this point there are relatively few members of the executive branch who can, merely by virtue of their position, be justly attacked. Elected officials and workers outside the policy-making circle are typically immune. Appointees examined and confirmed by the legislature are also immune *in their formal capacity*. Those appointed by and large without scrutiny from the confirmation process, however, would seem to be just targets. They are public figures, but their loyalty is primarily to the president. Security advisors, legal counsel, and others who consort directly with the head of state, both in making and putting policy into action can legitimately be considered limbs directly attached to the principle source of the injustice. To the extent that the tyrant may justly be attacked, so may they. It may also be justified, although the burden of proof is greater, to attack some of the cabinet members if, like our rogue FBI agents, they have ceased to carry out the legally mandated roles of their offices and have become the equivalent of presidential appointees *simpliciter*. But I do not think this assimilation to the tyrannical executive can be extended to even the most malevolent private advisor. As I argued above, a revolution can only be just if it is directed against a corrupt political order, or, in the case of a divided government such as the American, that part of the system directly responsible for the injury to the common good. The private citizen, no matter what his actual influence, does not satisfy this condition.

To the extent that this test is sound, it provides the revolutionary a means for meeting the *in bello* criterion of discrimination. Once this is done the demand for proportionality presents no greater difficulty here than in the conventional case. Perhaps it will be more useful to summarize the steps taken in interpreting all the just war criteria for the revolutionary situation. For obvious reasons, the traditional criterion of due authority must be modified in the revolutionary context. The regime in power holds the trappings of authority, whereas the revolutionary movement claims that authority null and void. For the revolutionary, authority has reverted to the members of the community, who may now take steps to rectify an unsatisfactory situation. What makes it unsatisfactory? If we want to maintain continuity with the just war tradition, the answer must be that injustices have been perpetrated and that these injustices were intended by the government in power. The regime, in other words, has committed acts of aggression against the community itself. The revolutionaries, then, have the same obligation as a conventional government to establish just cause, and what replaces the criterion of duly constituted authority is just intent in the revolutionary leaders.[4] Although just intent is necessary, it is not sufficient that there be injustices in the current political order. In most constitutional systems, there are built-in mechanisms for redress and change of policy. Some will require merely righting a particular wrong, while others will require systemic change. The forms of political activism that may be undertaken to bring about these changes fall under the general notion of *stasis*, as used by Aristotle, and reflect a reasonable expectation on the part of the citizenry that it will have a say in how the community regulates itself. Who else, after all, should have the last word here? In order for revolution to be justified, the situation must exceed the ability of the system to right itself, even over the long run. Revolution has to be a last resort. But the injustice that constitutes the cause must be proportionate to the evil brought about, and this means the disrupted lives, miseries, and deaths suffered by your neighbors. Revolutions are never impersonal, and a handy rule of thumb for measuring the justice of their leaders is the level of regret with which they enter into the task. The decrepit anarchists of Conrad's *Secret Agent*, a ragtag of aging outcasts, do not have the rich personal identification with the community necessary for the just revolutionary, a fact made clear by Verloc's indifference to the death of his retarded brother-in-law. His wife Winnie and her brother, his indifference shows, were never friends, much less family, but merely a cover for his revolutionary pretensions. His goal was to make revolution, not to right the wrongs suffered by those he had promised to care for. Without the appropriate level of concern for his erstwhile loved ones, he is not entitled to undertake revolution and under no circumstances to use them as means to his ends. Verloc is made all the more pathetically depraved by the total absence of any reasonable hope that a revolution could be created, not to mention won. In the absence of these considerations, revolutionary violence is a sham, "a brazen cheat . . . a blood-stained inanity" (Conrad 1942:340). Justice remains the arbitor of ideological reasonableness.

Taken together, as they must be, these are not criteria easily met. But that is as it should be. Revolution is not the equivalent of a communal career change, but a risky, destructive, and invariably tragic undertaking. It should not be entered into lightly. On the conditions I have outlined, most of the notable revolutions of the last century would not measure up. Nor would many of the ongoing conflicts of today. The terrorist activities preceding the founding of Israel, the indiscriminate bombings of the Irish Republican Army, the Munich massacre by the PLO, and the American-funded Contra insurgency are all, despite their distinctive ideological orientations, beyond the pale of justice and, whatever they may have accomplished, tainted with blood wickedly spilled. It follows from the argument of the past two chapters that no one committed to justice can in conscience join or support them as originally constituted.

Such pronouncements, aside from putting me in bad odor with various revolutionaries, expose me to one final argument, suggested by Jon Gunnemann's *The Moral Meaning of Revolution*.[5] Taking his start from Thomas Kuhn, Gunnemann suggests that revolution in politics, like its counterpart in science, begins with the break from ordinary procedures and justifications and the formulation of a new paradigm for talking about evil, the social world, and the possibility of political order. This new paradigm establishes both the vocabulary of the new vision and the parameters for acceptable justification of claims made within it. Thus, what counts as "justice" in the natural-law paradigm may not hook up with its twin in the Marxist. But the Marxist need not be any more troubled by this paradigmatic chasm than the contemporary particle physicist, whose use of "mass" has only a distant relation to the use of that term by eighteenth-century Newtonians. Specifically, for Gunnemann, "any attempt to apply the categories of the just war tradition would involve a fundamental distortion of what the Marxists mean by revolution" (1979:5). Gunnemann goes on to equate revolution with conversion, claiming that "the language of justification seems as unsuited to revolution as it does to conversion: it offends our sense of what is appropriate to ask whether a conversion is justified or unjustified" (1979:1–2). We have here a remarkable statement. Taking only the perspective of the history of religions, it is hard to imagine an era in which conversion would be undertaken without justification. Only very recently has religion been a matter of private preference and personal aesthetics. Even today, conversion out of an orthodox Jewish family is tantamount to suicide, complete with a funeral service. The apologetic tradition in early Christianity presupposes that conversion requires defense, if not formal justification. Among traditional cultures, to leave off the time-honored forms of worship and observance is to become an outcast; and for many families in contemporary America, entering an alternative religious tradition, be it ISKON or Islam, has provoked kidnapping and charges of brainwashing. Why? Because religion is not a set of beliefs, floating free in the intellectual atmosphere, but a complex of practices, commitments, and beliefs interwoven with the entire fabric of life and the goods deemed worthy of pursuit and protection. The most valuable things in life are not to be given up, or exchanged, without good reason, and those closest to us are most deserving of those reasons.

Nor does his claim hold for the scientific case from which it is derived. Advocates of rival scientific paradigms can and do demand justifications from each other, particularly if patronage and funding are involved. Kuhn's point, taken to the extreme by Paul Feyerabend, is that the arguments and justifications cannot take place exclusively in the technical vocabulary of one paradigm. Scientific vocabularies are grounded in our ordinary language, even when they extend it; and the competition of theories cannot but invoke the language of perception, consequences, simplicity, and usefulness as advocates defend and attack each other. As we saw in chapter 1, the particular reasons offered in support of a given position may not be compelling in differing contexts, but this is to be explained by changing beliefs about society, morality, and the world that themselves admit of reasons and arguments. As Kuhn has frequently insisted, his is a battle against an ahistorical, simple-minded, and stultifying positivism, not some subversive tunneling against reason in the cause of irrationalism. (See Kuhn 1980.) If being rational means giving reasons and attempting to justify actions, then both religion and science are reasonable enterprises. Is revolution?

The answer, I've been arguing, is yes, but. Yes it is, but only if it is consonant with justice. Can revolution be just? Yes, it can, but only if actions are grounded in practical reason. Can actions be grounded in practical reason? Yes, but only if we are capable of distinguishing real from apparent goods. And so it goes. There may be no way to ensure that an argument be brought to a successful end to which everyone agrees, but that is a far cry from saying that the call for justification is out of place in revolution, religion, or any genuinely human enterprise. The argument from scientific change is no more successful than that from historical relativism in isolating the revolutionary from the claims of justice.

But have I banished revolution from the moral horizon by making it impossible to meet the demands of justice? In attempting to bring revolution under the umbrella of the just war tradition, I have substantially increased the demands that tradition makes on the just revolutionary. At the same time, I have indicated that we neither have reason to think that we can act reasonably in despite of justice nor to suspend the claims of justice when we encounter conflict over the interpretation of evil. Combined, these arguments might suggest that just revolution, although a theoretical possibility, cannot in practice hope to satisfy the criteria of justice. Such a conclusion would lead to condemning all future, present, and probably past revolutions, and this is surely too strong. So it remains for me to sketch, at the very least, what might count as a plausibly just revolution and how we might come to recognize it.

In Thomas Pynchon's *V.*, with its nightmare collage of decadence, waste, and empty conspiracy, the colonial remnants of German Southwest Africa reflect on their lost empire, where they represented life and death. In an epiphany that descends on a certain Fleische while clubbing to death a black prisoner,

things seemed all at once to fall into a pattern: a great cosmic fluttering in the blank, bright sky and each grain of sand, each cactus spine, each feather of the circling vulture above them and invisible molecule of heated air seemed to shift imperceptibly so that this black and he, and he and every other black he would henceforth have to kill slid into alignment, assumed a set symmetry, a dancelike poise. It finally meant something different: different from the recruiting poster, the mural in the church and the natives already extermi-nated.... It had only to do with the destroyer and the destroyed, and the act which united them, and it had never been that way before. (Pynchon 1963:245)

With his knack for detail and twisted juxtaposition, Pynchon captures a frame of mind in which genocidal mass murder becomes not simply a way of life but a vocation, a commitment to cosmic forces dedicated to eradicating not just human beings but every vestige of human feeling. This section of Pynchon's novel is set in 1922, after German South-West Africa had come under South African administration, as a result of the first World War. At the time, the Bondels, a native tribe, were in revolt in protest of a tax on their dogs, necessary helpers in their cattle-herding. The character in question looks back to 1904, when the territory was still under German rule, at the time of the Herero uprising. Of the Herero, Oliver and Atmore write that they

rose against the German settlers who had been infiltrating into their land. Two-thirds of the Herero were exterminated in the course of the German countermeasures. The Herero country was declared the property of the state,

and the survivors were forbidden to keep cattle, since they no longer possessed any land on which to graze them. (1967:153)

Of the Bondel uprising:

A police force was sent against them and their village was bombed. The police
commented: "The effects of the lesson taught in this short campaign will have
an indelible impression not only on the minds of those who resorted to the use
of arms in defiance of lawful authority, but on other native tribes in this territory as well." (1967:199–200)

Pynchon carefully distinguishes Herero from Bondel throughout. In
the context of the novel the clear implication is that superficial
changes of government do not reflect any substantive difference in
the European willingness to exploit and exterminate the native population in the name of civilization and lawful authority. But my purpose
here is not to pursue Pynchon's vision of European lassitude, slouch-
ing toward holocaust. Instead, I want to focus on the vision of South
Africa that suggested itself to a critical observer, without a direct link
to the struggle against the government, at the time Nelson Mandela
became commander in chief of *Umkhonto we Sizwe*, the military arm of
the African National Congress.

Would Pynchon's depraved colonialists have seemed altogether foreign to a black South African of the late 1950s and early 1960s?
Hardly. The year of Nelson Mandela's birth, 1918, saw the founding
of the Afrikaner Broederbond, which soon became a secret organization dedicated to promoting the Afrikaner vision of a Christian nation
carrying out a divinely appointed mission. Leonard Thompson claims
that since 1948, the year apartheid was officially instituted, "all South
African prime ministers and nearly all cabinet ministers have been
Broeders; so have nearly all the heads of the Afrikaans universities
and churches, and of the great state corporations" (Thompson
1985:46). This is a very worrisome state of affairs. As Thompson describes it, the Afrikaner Broederbond is committed to working system-
atically for the good of a particular group as opposed to the good of
other groups within the society. This goes beyond advocating a fair
share for a special interest to claiming merit derived from a source
outside participation in the institutions of the community as a whole.
Insofar as someone adheres to the goals of the Broederbond, he is at
odds with the common good. Justification for pursuing those goals re-

quires some extra-communal account of his status. That committed broeders pulled the levers of government provided the wherewithal to create that justification and put it into action. From their positions of power, it became possible to promulgate a "political mythology," to use Thompson's term, the principal points of which come out in a 1954 letter of Prime Minister Malan to an American clergyman who had written to express his concern about the justice of apartheid. "The difference in colour," Malan writes, "is merely the physical manifestation of the contrast between two irreconcilable ways of life, between barbarism and civilization, between heathenism and Christianity." The Christianity at issue is that of the Dutch Reformed Church, he claims, which "believes that God in His Wisdom so disposed it that the first White men and women who settled at the foot of the Black continent were profoundly religious people, imbued with a very real zeal to bring the light of the Gospel to the heathen nations of Africa." Given this mission, apartheid is absolutely necessary to the Afrikaner, who believes "that if he is to be true to his primary calling of bringing Christianity to the heathen, he must preserve his racial identity in tact." Since the church views the protection of this ministry as its principal mission, it "opposes social equalitarianism which ignores racial and colour differences between White and Black in everyday life" (Kuper 1957:appendix A, 219–21). In addition to the argument from vocation, Malan adds what Thompson considers a central tenet of the apartheid mythos, claiming that "contrary to popular belief abroad, the Whites and Blacks are practically contemporary settlers in South Africa" (Kuper 1957:appendix A, 224), with an aim to undermining any argument that the Afrikaners were colonial invaders displacing an indigenous population. This, despite the fact that the South African historian De Kiewiet had already called such a claim into question in a widely read *History of South Africa* (De Kiewiet 1941:19–26; cf. also Thompson 1969, 1985).

This argument is not an *ad hoc* response to satisfy a distant clergyman. Malan was the architect of apartheid who, when its initial provisions were legally challenged, had the legislature constitute itself the highest court so as to ensure the continuation of the policy. In response to a letter from the African National Congress, protesting the apartheid system, Malan's personal secretary wrote early in 1952 that "it is self-contradictory to claim as an inherent right of the Bantu, who differ in many ways from the Europeans, that they should be regarded as not different, especially when it is borne in mind that these differences are permanent and not man-made" (Kuper 1957:appendix B, 236), subtly invoking the divine distinction between black and white. He closes with the scarcely veiled threat that should the ANC advocate defiance of the law "the Government will make full use of the machinery at its disposal to quell any disturbances, and, thereafter, deal adequately with those responsible for initiating subversive activities of any nature whatsoever" (1957:appendix B, 238). Both the American clergyman and the African resistence movement Malan addresses from the same ideological perspective. It is a perspective around which South African society became ever more polarized from the 1950s to the present; and government powers, more often than not inspired by the vision that animated the Broederbond, took progressively harsher steps to secure themselves against dissent. So much so that the "total strategy" implemented in the 1960s has led more than one commentator to call South Africa not so much a police state as a "military state." (Cf. S. M. Davis 1987:158–202; Lonsdale 1988:64–76.) It was a strategy designed to protect a minority community against a majority, and to do so with force.

Even if it were not regularly in the news, South Africa would present the best available example of a political order satisfying my first conditions for a just revolution. The question is whether the revolutionary action undertaken by the African National Congress can satisfy the rest. Here it is important to distinguish between the fears and speculations of the white South Africans and foreign commentators and the evidence provided by the policies and actions of the ANC and particularly Nelson Mandela. From among a number of powerful and articulate personalities, it is Mandela who has emerged as the preeminent spokesman and the most consistent and farsighted writer on these issues. But since its inception, the ANC has followed in the tradition of liberal reform movements, regularly issuing requests and petitions. From its beginnings, in 1912, the ANC maintained a commitment to passive resistance along the lines of Gandhi, a commitment it maintained through the 1950s (Holland 1989:38–72; Kuper 1957). Although, with the emergence of the Youth League, the tone of confrontation changed, tactics remained well below the level of revolutionary violence: pamphleting, strikes, boycotts, and passive civil disobedience (Mandela 1986:20–30). Nonetheless, these provoked ever more oppressive legislation, which were met by defiance that remained economic and civil. The *Freedom Charter* of June 1955 remains committed to universal franchise, equal rights, and financial security

(Mandela 1986:50–54). The result was the treason trials of 1957–1961.

This sketch barely does justice to the depredations worked by the apartheid system on the black population of South Africa in its first decade. That there existed a history of injustice prior to the formal implementing of apartheid makes it all the more surprising that only in December of 1961 did Mandela, as founder and commander-in-chief, begin to direct armed insurrection through *Umkhonto we Sizwe*, the Spear of the Nation. In a leaflet disseminated the day of the first actions, the policy is made clear:

Units of Umkhonto we Sizwe today carried out planned attacks against government installations, particularly those connected with the policy of apartheid and race discrimination. . . . The main national liberation organisations in this country have consistently followed a policy of non-violence. They have conducted themselves peaceably at all times, regardless of government attacks and persecutions upon them and despite all government-inspired attempts to provoke them to violence. They have done so because the people prefer peaceful methods of change to achieve their aspirations without the suffering and bitterness of civil war. But the people's patience is not endless. The time comes in the life of any nation when there remain only two choices: submit or fight. (Mandela 1986:122)

This is a textbook statement of last resort, amply backed by the available evidence. The echo of the American Declaration of Independence is surely intended and better justified than in the American case. English depredations on the American colonials were insignificant by comparison to the systematic suppression of black South Africans under apartheid. But this initial policy statement evinces more than last resort. The objects of attack were chosen to minimize civilian casualties and were directly connected to the wicked regime. It is harder to assess reasonable hope of victory, although the level of oppression mounted against nonviolent protest suggests that there is very little to be lost. The Sharpeville massacre of the previous year, at the very least, displays a willingness by the government to undertake indiscriminate killing, and Mandela draws the parallel with Pynchon's Bondels in a speech at Addis Ababa in January of 1962:

Almost every African family remembers a similar massacre of our African brothers in South-West Africa when the South African government assembled aeroplanes, heavy machine-guns, artillery, and rifles, killing a hundred people and mutilating scores of others, merely because the Bondelswart people refused to pay dog tax.

He goes on to recount the numbers killed in 1948, 1954, and 1960, concluding that "naked force and violence is the weapon openly used by the South African government to beat down the struggles of the African people and to suppress their aspirations" (Mandela 1986:125). The epiphany of Pynchon's Fleische turns out to be a very real nightmare for black South Africa, and one borne home with the insistency of blood and bullets.

Half a year later Mandela was caught and tried for his work in *Umkhonto we Sizwe*. At the trial he outlined the steps toward armed response, adding the following prescient note:

Each disturbance pointed clearly to the inevitable growth among Africans of the belief that violence was the only way out—it showed that a government which uses force to maintain its rule teaches the oppressed to use force to oppose it. Already small groups had arisen in the urban areas and were spontaneously making plans for violent forms of political strugle. There now arose a danger that these groups would adopt terrorism against Africans, as well as Whites, if not properly directed. (Mandela 1986:165–66)

In 1964 Mandela went to prison. In the twenty-six years that passed until his recent release, the fears evident in this remark were to be realized with ever-growing terror. The late 1960s and early 1970s were a period of eclipse for the ANC, and the vacuum was filled with groups and movements less committed to restraint. This remained somewhat the case with the resurgence of the ANC after the Soweto riots of June 1976; but, nonetheless, a recent chronicler of the revolution concludes that "following ANC guidelines, rebel missions had resulted in remarkably few civilian casualties," despite the fact that a shaky chain of command "had not been able to prevent a rash of terrorist-style attacks by renegade insurgents" (S. M. Davis 1987:156). That individuals get out of control is tragic, but it does not suffice to condemn a policy that manifests clear and consistent concern for all the conditions of justice I've canvassed in this chapter. Davis concludes that perhaps "the African National Congress is the most quixotic guerilla organization in modern times. Its leadership endorses violence, but with manifest reluctance and an aversion to terrorist tactics" (1987:203). I am inclined to think that the ANC has been the only revolutionary organization in recent memory that has been worthy of support. The chances for a successful transformation of South Africa that have attended the recent release of Mandela increase the hope for success, and the possibility for success should increase the resolve for justice in its fullest sense. Although the future teeters on a razor's edge, unpredictable and fragile as all difficult human undertakings, the history of the ANC, from its beginnings in passive resistence to the sabotage campaign of *Umkhonto*, provides hope that justice can be done, even in revolution.

Notes

1. Jefferson's remarks on classical moral thought are typically disparaging, and I do not want to suggest that he is in any way an advocate for Aristotle. Wills (1971), however, traces the details of Jefferson's political thought to the influence of the Scottish Enlightenment, which MacIntyre sees as grounded in a renewed Aristotelianism only later subverted by Hume (1988:chaps. 12–16). As with Clausewitz, Jefferson's is something of a "default" position, the adherence to practical reasonableness natural to a mature and reflective agent unencumbered by philosophical or political ideology. This is, of course, just what we should expect if the orthodox Aristotelian is correct, for Aristotle claims to do little more than clarify how reasonable individuals would go about planning their lives, given sufficient resources and a congenial social order. Both Jefferson and Clausewitz were lucky enough to benefit from their circumstances and to put their moral and intellectual insights to work bettering them.

2. That talk of "vocation" does not appear in Marx or his later followers, or that it does, is not my principal concern. As with the discussion of Yoder in chapter 2, the intent is to draw out the way that values, virtues, goals, and actions hold together. My interest here is not in the exegesis of Marx, a remarkably contentious activity, but in contrasting a certain way of advocating revolution to my own. Nonetheless, I should be clear on my sources. Many of the useful primary texts are collected in Tucker (1972), to which I have referred for convenience's sake. My reading has also been influenced by Marx's early works, as edited by Struik and O'Malley. In addition to Berlin's introduction (1963), I have benefited from Avineri (1968) and Evans (1975). The problem of justice, however, relates directly to the exchange between Allen Wood and Ziyad Husami, as well as the essay by Allen Buchanan, in Cohen et al. (1980).

3. Walzer doesn't expand on the justification for this, although we may assume that it is related to the possibility of autonomous states necessary for the international political order. I would need to provide a more substantial account for the Aristotelian, which is beyond the scope of this chapter. But briefly I would say that the burden of justification falls, as I argued in chapter 5, on the state that would be coercive. The measure of victory in conventional

war is the ability to check aggression with military force. Assassination, however, is directed not against the military force that is the instrument of aggression but against the rulers. It is an attack on sovereignty and this needs to be justified in ways rather different from those provided by the just war criteria. It is worth saying, while I'm on the subject, that this applies to more than assassination. Questions of reparation aside, once aggression has been curtailed and the likelihood of its being renewed minimized, the aggrieved states do not have the authority to legislate for the losers. To say that a new constitution or change in borders is necessary to prevent future aggression is either an act of wishful thinking or, more likely, an excuse for going beyond just redress to benefiting unfairly from victory. The applications to recent history are not difficult to see. The Treaty of Versailles, the American occupation of Japan, and the Israeli occupations subsequent to the Six Day and Yom Kippur wars are but the first examples that come to mind.

4. The restriction to the leaders is necessary because there may well be individuals in the revolutionary forces, as in conventional forces, whose intent is malicious. But that does not pose a problem for the corporate enterprise unless such individuals engage in acts contrary to *ius in bello*. If they do, and if they are not sought out and punished, questions would be raised about the intent of the leaders. But otherwise, this is private malice.

5. I say "suggested by" because Gunnemann seems to me to back away from the more radical suggestions of his first chapter by the time he reaches his conclusion, where he acknowledges that "the ideal of a continuous realm of discourse between the religious and the political then assumes a continuity of tasks, vocabulary, and values before and after the revolution" (1979:256). Here, he seems to read Kuhn in a much less relativist way and along the pragmatic, historical lines I suggest. My interest lies not in following Gunnemann's elaboration of the Christian vision in the revolutionary scene, so I won't pursue the details of his larger argument. But to the extent that he falls back on the nonrelativist reading of Kuhn, his objections to the vocabulary of the just war tradition lose their bite.

7.

Epilogue: The Limits of Justice

Here is a true challenge: to show, in some other way, why it makes sense to adhere, whatever the consequences, to the stringent precept against killing the innocent. (Finnis et al. 1987:370)

So Finnis and his coauthors introduce their sketch of the theological foundations underlying their rejection of nuclear deterrence. But, unable to ground my own moral realism in the belief that "death in this world will be birth into another life" (1987:371), I needed to see whether and how it might be possible to sustain the claims of justice against the pressure of consequences without an appeal to transcendent warrants. The result I have called "orthodox Aristotelianism," in part to have a handy way of distinguishing my argument from others, but in the main to acknowledge my debt to Aristotle's account of the nature of ethics, virtue, and the rational organization of political life. Many problems in the exegesis of Aristotle's ethics I have not found occasion to address, although I think I have been faithful throughout to his central insight, that virtue and happiness are natural concomitants and that rational political action cannot be inconsistent with these goods. Contrasting this Aristotelianism with other approaches in moral and political theory involved both a methodological and epistemic component, though the two are closely related. Methodologically, ethics does not lend itself to fruitful theorizing along the lines of the natural sciences. In the first place, ethics is no more in need of foundations than is mathematics. As Wittgenstein sniped, medieval calculations were not somehow suspect for not having access to *Principia Mathematica*, nor are those of the contemporary shopper. (See Wittgenstein 1983.) Moreover, specialist or technical information only rarely enters into our practical deliberations, and then at the margins of judgment. Normally, any mature agent is in possession of all he needs to make a reasonably informed judgment. Ethical reflection is about how we live and the plans we make for ourselves and with others. A wholesale revision of such plans would in itself be a matter of consequence in a different way from even the most monumental scientific revolution.

This indifference to theory, however, does not involve "subjectivism" or "relativism" of any serious sort. The Aristotelian can and should claim that beliefs about justice and goodness are as capable of being justified and true as those about squirrels and supernovas, though how we learn their truth and justify them to others may be distinctive. But a pluralism about how we learn things is hardly objectionable if we consider the many different activities that make up the life of a community. As in the sciences, a responsible realism goes hand in hand with admitting our own fallibility. Admitting that we make mistakes, however, points to a distinction found in any community sufficiently complex to involve a division of labor, hence, any community recognizably human: making an error is not cheating. The habit of fairness in social interaction requires neither a conscious choice nor a grounding in transcendental duty; like truth-telling in language, it is essential to a recognizable human practice or institution.

Fairness as a presupposition of a stable human community serves as a baseline for critical judgments in action. With that in mind, it is possible to acknowledge both the appeal of pacifism and its inadequacy. It is a prereflective temptation because most of us would hardly dare take the responsibility for someone else's life. We are not sure enough that we can be fair in weighing competing claims, and the idea of killing repels most of us in just the same way that his own acts horrify Oedipus. We need to overcome this revulsion if we are to enter into the relations that make up a mature life. Work, marriage, and parenthood, to mention just the most obvious examples, all require that we take responsibility for others, that we risk coming up against our limitations and the need to foresake some goods in favor of others. Yoder sees this, and his is a genuinely worthy pacifism, even to the nonbeliever who must in all honesty remain outside.

For those who recognize no calling, the unqualified refusal to respond with force can only appear tragic. This doesn't mean, however, that any sort of response may be tolerated. In discussing the traditional just war criteria, two considerations emerged as central. The criteria are singly necessary and only collectively sufficient for conducting a war fairly. Because of the greater gravity of the enterprise, failing to fulfill the demands of the criteria is not simply cheating, it is injustice in the extreme. Weakness under pressure may mitigate our expressions of disapproval, but if we are to avoid wickedness we must be firm and faithful to those virtues that define our community and the place we hope to achieve in it.

Failure to be faithful to the theological virtues was, I argued, the principal defect of the Catholic bishops on deterrence. They were successful, if only barely, in finding a place for a limited deterrence in the contemporary political order, but this seemed too much of a concession to fear and an unwarranted concern for the doubtless fleeting political makeup of the present. The tradition teeters on the brink of formalism, employing its methods to excuse conscience rather than clarify it. If all available deterrent strategies involve a threat to non-combatants, the Aristotelian makes common cause with the older Catholic argument represented by Anscombe, Markus, Finnis et al. To threaten noncombatants is to take hostages and is no different from terrorism, whatever the cause. To say, as Walzer does, that "we are hostages who lead normal lives" (1977:271) misses the point altogether. The gambler who threatens my wife in order to protect a bet acts viciously, even if she never notices a thing. It is simply irrelevant that "we can be threatened without being held captive." What matters is the justice of the threat, and as long as it remains directed against nonparticipants it is wicked. Ramsey, for all the ins and outs of his arguments on deterrence, felt this more acutely than Walzer or the Catholic bishops and articulated a position of unparalleled integrity, although it did not command the assent of the many.

The theoretical interest of deterrence, however, lies in its ability to strain the limits of virtue. Faced with the prospect of large-scale destruction, Walzer slides into consequentialist calculations. The traditional adherent to justice recognizes that there is an end to all things human and places what hope he has in God, or in the resilience of humans as a kind. This latter path attracts the Aristotelian, who is mindful of the fragility of virtue and seeks therefore to build it up. As Clausewitz understood, but we need to be reminded, war in particular puts tremendous strains on the character of the entire community and cannot be made rational without a solid foundation in virtue among the soldiers, their commanders, and the political leaders for whom they provide the instrument of war.

The metaphor of "warcraft" I chose in order to bring out both the ways in which virtue is a skill and the way that virtue in action cannot be divorced from the character of the community and the ability of an individual to function within it. The notion of a craft had the subordinate purpose of opening up the question of embedded communities and conflicting responsibilities. In even a small city or state, most people belong to several different types of group, some of which constitute societies within societies. Extended families, religious affiliations, the various professions all have standards of performance and achievement based on histories and traditions that only partially overlap. When the political order becomes large, it encompasses distinctive groups that may have very little binding them together. Allegiance may only extend to the state in the abstract, and then only to the degree that it provides genuine goods for those embedded communities to which I do feel a responsibility. There is, in short, no general obligation to defend the state; and when a positive obligation does obtain, it may compete unsuccessfully against others. If it is to enlist the allegiance of its citizenry, the state should present itself to as many as possible as a genuine friend, and this means seeking the common good in the broadest sense. Even having done that, we should not lose sight of the ongoing evolution of political relations and the comparatively fleeting lives of political systems. There are more than a few families whose histories go on, although the lands they have passed through have witnessed the birth and death of many regimes. When providing for the community's defense, the demands we make on each other should be tempered by our knowledge of the fragility of all human enterprises. It is tempting to think that any society that feels it must resort to conscription has already forfeited its just claims on the citizenry. Better to retain the integrity of conscience and run the risk of meeting our fate just a little bit sooner.

We may even find ourselves impelled toward an active role in destroying the political order. When government becomes oppressive and rule, tyrannical, it is just and proper to rise up against it. But revolution in accord with justice makes more stringent demands than mere defensive war. When we go to war with ourselves, we put in jeopardy not merely the enemy noncombatants but also our friends. We commit ourselves in large part to ripping up the fabric of our own lives; and whereas in starting a revolution we are mostly aware of the unexceptable aspects of life, civil war threatens everything, the good and the bad alike.

From deterrence to revolution, war can be just only when grounded in the virtues working together. In one way or another, the alternatives forsake or overstep the bounds of justice. But there are costs. A caricature of Platonic and Kantian approaches to ethics would portray them as hoping to make acts of virtue so obviously reasonable that no one would choose otherwise. Such a picture does capture something of the impetus behind moral "theorists" who would at least like to render judgments as well grounded as those of medicine or biology. But such a hope is not only false, it fails to recognize the relation of training to perception. Reading even the best reconstruction of our intuitions about fairness, say *A Theory of Justice*, is no substitute for education into a tradition of craft, responsibility, and pride. Young people, as Aristotle repeatedly remarks, are neither happy nor suitable students of ethics, because they are still apprentice members of the community, "and boys who are called happy are being congratulated by reason of the hopes we have for them" (*Ethics*:1100a). We look forward in imagining how our children will live out their lives, and this is not unreasonable so long as we impart to them the bases for making and acting upon their own judicious schemes for living well. Only training, discipline, and not a little luck will enable them to be truly happy. Reading philosophy won't *make* someone good, it can only clarify how a person of practical reason deliberates about actions.

Perhaps it is no big loss to be disuaded of misplaced philosophical expectations, but that is the least of the hopes the Aristotelian thinks we should give up. There is a persistent inclination, common to revolutionaries and liberals both, to believe that if only we could shake off our inherited prejudices and the torpor brought on by a legacy of injustice, special privilege, and the oppressive allocation of power, we might at least approximate the condition of our mythic parents. Retaking the garden clearly motivates the visionary rhetoric of Marxism, but it is visible as well, without the apocalyptic trappings, in Rawls's "original position." If only, we're invited to think, political leaders and their constituents were persuaded to shape policy as if from the original position, we could bring forth a degree of harmony and social justice previously unseen. For all of the criticism directed against Rawls's position, I'm not sure there is an *argument* against this hope beyond its being an exercise in wishful thinking. (Cf. Aristotle *Ethics*:1111b–13a.) At the same time, our best attempts at working out the fantasy always seem to find a serpent lurking somewhere. I'm thinking as I write this of Ursula LeGuin's *The Dispossessed*, but to each his own utopia. Any serious reader, if he lives long enough, will be persuaded by a good writer at every point on the literary pendulum, from the defiant individualism of Ayn Rand's *Fountainhead* to the manic vision of cultural disintegration in *Gravity's Rainbow*. But the authors who appeal over time and across cultures, the great ones like Sappho, Horace, Basho, and Shakespeare, tend to cluster in the center, between the extremes of redemption and despair where most of our experience takes place. They deal with the precariousness of our joys and disappointments, and what redemption there is takes place, as it must, offstage. This is more than a commentary on the canon of world literature. One of the striking similarities between Aristotle and John Howard Yoder is their unwaivering insistence on the gulf between the human and the divine. The "human" simply *is* the arena of uncertain and conflicting judgments, where we juggle multiple plans and goals, thwarting and being thwarted by others. We think to do *a*, then are caught up by *b*, begin on *c*, then put it aside for the moment. There is no *human* end to this; conflict and tragedy will always be mingled with our loves, and great literature shows us the truth of this. Yoder, of course, believes these tragedies will be redeemed, but not on our initiative.

Just as individuals are born into a web of relationships, some supportive and others conflictive, so communities are as well. Individuals and society alike inherit the consequences of acts that cannot now be undone, and the history between then and now may make restitution impossible. In a scene lifted, no doubt in homage, from Conrad's *Heart of Darkness*, Philip Marlowe tells a lie. Having recovered Lola Barsaly's pearls, he discovers almost accidentally that they are fakes, and he ensures that she will never learn the truth. Buying a poorer imitation set, he tells Lola that the extortionist "gypped you. . . . He sold the real ones, I guess, and made you up a string of ringers, with your clasp" (Chandler 1972:240). Later, looking out over the Pacific, Marlowe considers her originals:

When I had them all loose in my left hand I held them like that for a while and thought. There wasn't really anything to think about. I was sure. "To the memory of Stan Phillips," I said aloud, "Just another four-flusher." I flipped her pearls out into the water one by one at the floating seagulls. They made little splashes and the seagulls rose off the water and swooped at the splashes. (Chandler 1972:244)

The tradition of Hammett and Chandler in the American detective story is a better check of our moral pulse than most of the more academic, "serious" writing of the last half-century, if for no other reason than the need of the popular writer to capture and command an audience. For Chandler, at least, the detective story was an attempt to confront the forces that eat away at society from within and portray them as they were.[1] His characterization of the detective as having "a sense of character, or he would not know his job,...a lively sense of the grotesque, a disgust for sham, and a contempt for pettiness" (1972a:20–21) displays a wonderfully Aristotelian sense of life well before questions of character came to interest most philosophers. The dilemma of Marlowe in *Red Wind* is typical. We normally consider a lie contemptible, and even a compassionate deception such as Marlowe's may seem unworthy. Still, there are occasions when proclaiming the truth, or even risking its discovery, smacks too much of puritanism and self-important disdain for others. Marlowe's namesake loathes the "flavour of mortality" that attaches to a lie, though he tells one anyway when the truth "would have been too dark—too dark altogether" (Conrad 1942:77). Chandler's detective, by virtue of his profession, lives day-to-day with this mortality; and even if he does his best, there are some wrongs and sadnesses that can never be made right, but only gotten over. Like the fragility of virtue, this is endemic to individuals and communities this side of heaven. When restitution is impossible, as in the case of Lola, we fall back on whatever strategies present themselves. This is as true, and even more difficult, at the level of politics. When it is no longer possible to see justice done, it may sometimes be best to accept the fact and move on.

I need to be careful here. Appeasing the wicked is both foolish and wrong. Making concessions or colluding with tyrants may postpone confrontation, but more often than not the clash is more bloody when it comes. Not only that, but appeasement subverts the practice of virtue within the community and without. It deforms us and allows the tyrant to continue down his own twisted path. Walzer's bottom-line consequentialism, however, allows us too much leeway in excusing injustice. Granted that he insists we may "violate the rules of war only when we are face-to-face not merely with defeat but with a defeat likely to bring disaster to a political community" (1977:268), but this concession to consequences begins a decline down a familiar slippery slope. However circumscribed the conditions of supreme necessity, Walzer's misplaced concern for the continuity of nations slides all too easily into the "readiness to murder" that he ruefully condones in his discussion of deterrence (1977:283). Such a readiness should be appalling to conscience. Justice can't countenance the exceptions argued by Walzer without ultimately risking its integrity. The fragility of virtue, as Thucydides recognized, can tolerate external threats much better than corrosion from within.

Thinking back to Thucydides' account of the Melians, we should be struck by the moral transparency of the situation, the fact that only cowardice could keep us from admiting that it would be better to be a Melian, reaffirming "fair play and just dealing," than an Athenian, emissary of a society that has come to believe, "as far as right and wrong are concerned," that "there is no difference between the two, that those who still preserve their independence do so because they are strong" (1954:402–3). For the just war tradition and for those in general who prize character and virtue over mere physical continuity, the wicked and the base constitute an absolute barrier to action. Better to surrender than win unfairly. Surrender at least preserves justice in myself and my compatriots, not to mention the possibility of working from within to restore what has been lost. But if preserving our integrity requires fighting on, better to die in the cause of justice and fair play than win like an Athenian. As best we can, after all, we judge lives as a whole, by their character and accomplishments rather than their length. That Odysseus finds the shade of Achilles longing for even a pitiful existence is not surprising; there is no glory to be gained in Hades. But the whining of the dead makes no one immortal, and Sarpedon better captures what mortals can achieve when he urges on Glaukos in the *Iliad*: "Seeing that the spirits of death stand close about us in their thousands, no man can turn aside nor escape them, let us go on and win glory for ourselves, or yield it to others" (Homer 1951: Book ll, 326–28). Knowing that we have to die, whose lot would we choose, that of Walzer's heroic German or his ex-comrades, living on with the knowledge of having killed him? The evanescent quality of life, individual or corporate, makes memory our ultimate legatee. Even anonymous soldiers, like those of Melos, live better and longer in our memory for the justice of their deeds.

But Marlowe's deception is not a concession to injustice. It is, rather, an acknowledgment of those *lacrimae rerum* that attach to all things of this world. It comes, as inadequate as it is, *after* we have done all the justice we can. Hearkening back to Aristotle for one last time, Marlowe's concern for Lola Barsaly reflects the decency that inclines the good person to prefer fairness over what legal justice might allow. Even though she saved his life, Marlowe has no "obligation" here and to think so misconstrues the act. Nothing anyone can do can erase the loss of her love, the fact that Stan Phillips deceived her, or the indignities visited upon her by her adulterous husband. These are past helping; and as much as Marlowe wants to see Lola happy, he can't make her story other than it is. He can only help her get on with the rest of her life.

When extended to the realm of politics, Marlowe's problem is that of any society large enough to have embedded communities that have been the victims of past injustice. Palestine, Northern Ireland, and South Africa are but the most visible instances at present. Blacks and Native Americans have a history of victimization coterminous with the history of the United States. The iniquities visited on women are legion. Even if we could secure an end to present injustices, it would be impossible to make restitution for all these groups have suffered. They are caught, as are we all, in that web of commitments and institutions that has grown, like language, from countless sources in unpredictable ways. Plains that once supported millions of buffalo are given over to cities and agriculture. Israelites displaced Canaanites and were subsequently overrun by Syrians, Persians, Greeks, Romans, and so on until the Ottoman Empire fell and the mandate passed to Britain and France. If apartheid ends tomorrow, its repercussions will be felt for generations. And so it goes.

Conflicts have their history, but they also have a future. If they become institutionalized, as in Israel and South Africa, it is hard to see how injustice can be avoided. The argument of chapter 5 might incline us to think that the conflicts in distant nations are their business, something to be made our own only if we have a vested interest. In terms of responsibility, there is something right about this, but once again Marlowe's predicament should remind us how limited such an analysis would be. Some of our friends are Jews and blacks, even if we are not, and it's hard to imagine being so detached that we don't care about other countries and their peoples. Whether we think that much about it or not, we want everything to turn out right for Israel and South Africa, for the Palestinians and the Native Americans. If we don't, there is something wrong with us. But as private citizens we can't make it happen and as public servants we're not much better off.

At least one moral to be drawn from Chandler's Marlowe is that faced with this sadness there's nothing to be gained by invoking some contemporary ideology. Sacrificing the poor and disenfranchised on the alter of democracy is at least as revolting as murdering intellectuals and professionals in a "cultural revolution." Seen in the glass of history, each is wretched beyond tolerating. At least acknowledging the fleeting and contingent qualities of life allows us the small comfort of knowing that nothing will last all that long. But that's little help for the poor people ground down by vicious regimes and their indifferent heirs. I wish I could offer some redemptive hope, but I can't: neither philosophy nor good intentions are likely to save the world or anyone in it. But that doesn't mean there is no point in working out our ideas. Particularly in thinking about war and society, a philosopher should remember Wittgenstein's loathing of cant and exculpatory, self-righteous posturing. "What is the use," he wrote to Malcolm, "of studying philosophy if all that it does for you is to enable you to talk with some plausibility about some abstruse questions of logic, etc. & if it does not improve your thinking about the important questions of everyday life?" (Monk 1990:424).

Notes

1. Chandler's reflections on the genre, particularly the title essay to his 1972a, with its amalgam of artistic and moral outrage at the Agatha Christie style of detective story, indicate how intent he was on giving crime and its victims their full moral weight. On the genre as a whole, Steven Marcus's introduction to Hammett (1974) is useful as is Herbert Ruhm's to his 1977 collection.

References

With the exception of literary works to which I have merely alluded, I have attempted to provide complete references for all my sources. In the process of editing, titles may have been left even though the original citation has been excised.

Achebe, Chinua
1959   *Things Fall Apart*. New York: Fawcett Crest Books.
Ackrill, J. R.
1973   *Aristotle's Ethics*. New York: Humanities Press.
Adams, Robert M.
1987   *The Virtue of Faith and Other Essays in Philosophical Theology*. Oxford: Oxford University Press.
Anderson, Martin, ed.
1976   *Conscription: A Select and Annotated Bibliography*. Stanford: Hoover Institution Press.
Anscombe, G. E. M.
1958   "Modern Moral Philosophy." *Philosophy* 33:1–19.
Aquinas, St. Thomas
S.Theo. *Summa Theologica*. Translated by the Fathers of the Dominican Province of England, 1911. Reprinted in five vol. Westminster, Maryland: Christian Classics.
Aristophanes
1973   *Clouds*. Translated by Alan H. Sommerstein. Harmondsworth: Penguin Books.
Aristotle
Ethics   *Nicomachean Ethics*. Translated by W. D. Ross. Rev. ed. Edited by J. L. Ackrill and J. O. Urmson. Oxford: Oxford University Press, 1980. (See also Ackrill 1973 and Irwin 1985)
Met.   *Metaphysics, Books ., ;, E*. Translated by Cristopher Kirwan. Oxford: Oxford University Press, 1971.
Poet.   *Poetics*. Translated by Ingram Bywater. In *The Rhetoric and Poetics of Aristotle*, edited by Friedrich Solmsen. New York: Modern Library, 1954.
Pol.   *Politics*. Translated by Ernest Barker. Oxford: Oxford University Press, 1946.

Rhet.   *Rhetoric*. Translated by Rhys Roberts. In *The Rhetoric and Poetics of Aristotle*, edited by Friedrich Solmsen. New York: Modern Library, 1954.

Augustine of Hippo, St.

C.Dei   *City of God*. Translated by Marcus Dods. Edinburgh: T. & T. Clark, 1872. (See also Oates 1948)

Avineri, Schlomo

1968   *The Social and Political Thought of Karl Marx*. Cambridge: Cambridge University Press.

Barker, Ernest, ed.

1947   *Social Contract: Essays by Locke, Hume and Rousseau*. Oxford: Oxford University Press.

Beitz, Charles R., M. Cohen, T. M. Scanlon, and A. J. Simmons, eds.

1985   *International Ethics: A Philosophy and Public Affairs Reader*. Princeton: Princeton University Press.

Bellah, Robert N., ed.

1985   *Habits of the Heart: Individualism and Commitment in American Life*. Berkeley: University of California Press.

Berlin, Isaiah

1963   *Karl Marx*. 3d ed. Oxford: Oxford University Press.

Bowman, William, Roger Little, and G. Thomas Sicilia, eds.

1986   *The All-Volunteer Force after a Decade: Retrospect and Prospect*. McLean, Virginia: Pergamon-Brassey's International Defense Publishers.

Brooke, Christopher

1989   *The Medieval Idea of Marriage*. Oxford: Oxford University Press.

Cavell, Stanley

1969   *Must We Mean What We Say?* New York: Scribners.

1979   *The Claim of Reason*. New York: Oxford University Press.

Chandler, Raymond

1972   *Trouble is My Business*. New York: Ballantine Books.

1972a   *The Simple Art of Murder*. New York: Ballantine Books.

Childress, James

1982   *Moral Responsibility in Conflict: Essays on Nonviolence, War and Conscience*. Baton Rouge, Louisiana: Louisiana State University Press.

Clark, J. Desmond

1959   *The Prehistory of Southern Africa*. Harmondsworth: Penguin Books.

Clausewitz, Carl Von

1976   *On War*. Edited and translated by Michael Howard and Peter Paret. Princeton: Princeton University Press.

Cohen, Eliot A.

1985   *Citizens and Soldiers: The Dilemmas of Military Service*. Ithaca: Cornell University Press.

Cohen, Marshall, Thomas Nagel, and Thomas Scanlon, eds.

1980   *Marx, Justice, and History: A Philosophy and Public Affairs Reader*. Princeton: Princeton University Press.

Conrad, Joseph
1942   *A Conrad Argosy*. Introduction by Wm. McFee. New York: Double-
        day, Doran & Co.
Contamine, Philip
1984   *War in the Middle Ages*. Oxford: Basil Blackwell.
Cooper, John M.
1980   "Aristotle on Friendship." Reprinted in Amelie Rorty (1980).
Cuomo, Mario
1984   "Religious Belief and Public Morality: A Catholic Governor's Per-
        spective." *Notre Dame Journal of Law, Ethics and Public Policy*
        1/1:13–31.
Curran, Charles E.
1988   *Tensions in Moral Theology*. Notre Dame: University of Notre Dame
        Press.
Daniels, Norman, ed.
1989   *Reading Rawls: Critical Studies on Rawls "A Theory of Justice."* Stan-
        ford: Stanford University Press.
Davidson, Donald
1984   *Inquiries into Truth and Interpretation*. Oxford: Oxford University
        Press.
Davis, G. Scott
1983   "Ethical Properties and Divine Commands." *Journal of Religious
        Ethics* 11/2:280–300.
1986   "The Structure and Function of the Virtues in Augustine's Moral
        Theology." *Acts of the International Congress on Augustinian Studies*,
        Rome, 1987, vol. 3:9–18.
1987   "Warcraft and the Fragility of Virtue." *Soundings* 70/3–4
        (Fall/Winter): 475–94.
1991   "Et fac quod vis: The Role of Augustine in the Development of
        Ramsey's Ethics." *Journal of Religious Ethics*, 19/2:31–69.
Davis, Stephen M.
1987   *Apartheid's Rebels: Inside South Africa's Hidden War*. New Haven: Yale
        University Press.
De Kiewiet, Cornelius W.
1941   *A History of South Africa*. Oxford: Oxford University Press.
De Vitoria, Francisco
1944   *De Indiis et de Iure Belli Relectiones*. Translated by J. P. Bate.
        Reprinted in part in Arthur F. Holmes (1975).
Dodds, E. R.
1973   *The Ancient Concept of Progress and other Essays on Greek Literature and
        Belief*. Oxford: Oxford University Press.
Douglas, Mary
1966   *Purity and Danger*. London: Routledge and Kegan Paul.
Dubois, Abbé J. A.
1906   *Hindu Manners, Customs and Ceremonies*. 3d ed. Edited and trans-
        lated by H. K. Beauchamp. Oxford: Oxford University Press.

Duby, Georges
1985   *William Marshal, the Flower of Chivalry*. Translated by Richard Howard. New York: Pantheon Books.
Dunn, John
1972   *Modern Revolutions: An Introduction to the Analysis of a Political Phenomenon*. Cambridge: Cambridge University Press.
1980   *Political Obligation in Its Historical Context*. Cambridge: Cambridge University Press.
1985   *Rethinking Modern Political Theory*. Cambridge: Cambridge University Press.
d'Entreves, A. P.
1951   *Natural Law, An Introduction to Legal Philosophy*. London: Hutchison University Library.
Evans, Michael
1975   *Karl Marx*. London: George Allen & Unwin.
Fadiman, Jeffrey A.
1982   *An Oral History of Tribal Warfare: The Meru of Mt. Kenya*. Athens, Ohio: University of Ohio Press.
Feyerabend, Paul
1975   *Against Method*. London: New Left Books.
Finnis, John
1980   *Natural Law and Natural Rights*. Oxford: Oxford University Press.
1983   *Fundamentals of Ethics*. Washington, D.C.: Georgetown University Press.
Finnis, John, Joseph Boyle, and Germain Grisez
1987   *Nuclear Deterrence, Morality and Realism*. Oxford: Oxford University Press.
Ford, John C.
1944   "The Morality of Obliteration Bombing." Reprinted in Richard A. Wasserstrom (1970).
Frankena, W. K.
1975   "Conversations with Carney and Hauerwas." *Journal of Religious Ethics* 3/1:45–62.
Fussell, Paul
1975   *The Great War and Modern Memory*. Oxford: Oxford University Press.
Gallie, W. B.
1978   *Philosophers of Peace and War: Kant, Clausewitz, Marx, Engels and Tolstoy*. Cambridge, Cambridge University Press.
Gass, William H.
1971   "The Case of the Obliging Stranger." In his *Fiction and the Figures of Life*. Boston: Nonpareil Books.
Geach, Peter
1969   *God and the Soul*. New York: Schocken Books.
Gilby, Thomas, ed.
1966   *Principles of Morality: Summa Theologiae 1a2ae, 18–21*. London: Eyre and Spottiswoode.

Gombrich, E. H.
1963 *Meditations on a Hobby Horse and Other Essays on the Theory of Art*. London: Phaidon Press.
Gould, Stephen Jay
1989 *Wonderful Life: The Burgess Shale and the Nature of History*. New York: W. W. Norton.
Griaule, Marcel
1965 *Conversations with Ogotemmeli: An Introduction to Dogon Religious Ideas*. Oxford: Oxford University Press.
Gunnemann, Jon
1979 *The Moral Meaning of Revolution*. New Haven: Yale University Press.
Gustafson, James M.
1978 *Protestant and Roman Catholic Ethics*. Chicago: University of Chicago Press.
1981 *Ethics from a Theocentric Perspective*. Vol. 1, *Theology and Ethics*. Chicago: University of Chicago Press.
Hale, J. R.
1985 *War and Society in Renaissance Europe, 1450–1620*. Baltimore: Johns Hopkins University Press.
Hammett, Dashiell
1974 *The Continental Op*. Edited and introduction by Steven Marcus. New York: Vintage Books.
Hampshire, Stuart
1971 *Freedom of Mind and Other Essays*. Princeton: Princeton University Press.
1989 *Innocence and Experience*. Cambridge, Mass.: Harvard University Press.
Hanson, Victor Davis
1989 *The Western Way of War: Infantry Battle in Classical Greece*. New York: Knopf.
Hauerwas, Stanley
1974 *Vision and Virtue*. Notre Dame: University of Notre Dame Press.
1981 *A Community of Character: Toward a Constructive Christian Social Ethic*. Notre Dame: University of Notre Dame Press.
1983 *The Peaceable Kingdom*. Notre Dame: University of Notre Dame Press.
1985 *Against the Nations: War and Survival in a Liberal Society*. San Francisco: Winston/Seabury.
1990 "Happiness, the Life of Virtue and Friendship: Theological Reflections on Aristotelian Themes." *Asbury Theological Journal* 45/1:13–31.
Hauerwas, Stanley, and Alasdair MacIntyre, eds.
1983 *Revisions*. Notre Dame: University of Notre Dame Press.
Hittinger, Russell
1987 *A Critique of the New Natural Law Theory*. Notre Dame: University of Notre Dame Press.

Hobbes, Thomas
1960   *Leviathan or the Matter, Forme and Power of a Commonwealth Ec-clestiasticall and Civil.* Edited by Michael Oakeshott. Oxford: Basil Blackwell.
Holland, Heidi
1989   *The Struggle: A History of the African National Congress.* New York: George Braziller.
Holmes, Arthur F., ed.
1975   *War and Christian Ethics.* Grand Rapids, Michigan: Baker Book House.
Homer
1951   *Iliad.* Translated by Richmond Lattimore. Chicago: University of Chicago Press.
1965   *Odyssey.* Translated by Richmond Lattimore. New York: Harper & Row.
Howard, Michael
1971   *Studies in War and Peace.* New York: Viking Press.
1976   *War in European History.* Oxford: Oxford University Press.
Irwin, Terence
1985   *Aristotle's Nicomachean Ethics, Translated with Introduction, Notes and Glossary.* Indianapolis: Hackett Publishing.
1988   *Aristotle's First Principles.* Oxford: Oxford University Press.
Jacobs, Jane
1961   *The Death and Life of Cities.* New York: Random House.
James, William
1896   *"The Will to Believe" and Other Essays in Popular Philosophy.* New York: Longman, Green & Company.
Jefferson, Thomas
1944   *The Life and Selected Writings of Thomas Jefferson.* Edited by Adrienne Koch and William Peden. New York: Modern Library.
Johnson, James T.
1975   *Ideology, Reason, and the Limitation of War: Religious and Secular Concepts, 1200–1740.* Princeton: Princeton University Press.
1981   *Just War Tradition and the Restraint of War: A Moral and Historical Inquiry.* Princeton: Princeton University Press.
1984   *Can Modern War Be Just?* New Haven: Yale University Press.
1990   "Michael Walzer and Religious Ethics." *Religious Studies Review* 16/3:201–3.
Keegan, John
1976   *The Face of Battle: A Study of Agincourt, Waterloo and the Somme.* London: Penguin Books.
1987   *The Mask of Command.* London: Penguin Books.
Kennan, George F.
1983   *The Nuclear Delusion: Soviet-American Relations in the Atomic Age.* Expanded ed. New York: Pantheon Books.

Kenny, Anthony, ed.
1969   *Aquinas: A Collection of Critical Essays*. Garden City, New York: Doubleday Anchor.
Kuhn, Thomas
1980   *The Essential Tension*. Chicago: University of Chicago Press.
Kuper, Leo
1957   *Passive Resistance in South Africa*. New Haven: Yale University Press.
Lee, Richard Borshay
1979   *The !Kung San: Men, Women, and Work in a Foraging Society*. Cambridge: Cambridge University Press.
Lehrer, Keith
1974   *Knowledge*. Oxford: Oxford University Press.
Lenin, V. I.
1932   *State and Revolution*. New York: International Publishers.
Lonsdale, John, ed.
1988   *South Africa in Question*. Portsmouth, New Hampshire: Heinemann Educational Books.
McCormick, Richard A.
1984   *Notes on Moral Theology, 1981 through 1984*. Washington, D.C.: University Press of America.
McCormick, Richard, and Paul Ramsey, eds.
1978   *Doing Evil to Achieve Good*. Chicago: Loyola University Press.
McInerny, Ralph
1982   *Ethica Thomistica*. Washington, D.C.: Catholic University of America Press.
MacIntyre, Alasdair
1981   *After Virtue*. Notre Dame: University of Notre Dame Press.
1984   "Postscript" to *After Virtue*. 2d ed. Notre Dame: University of Notre Dame Press.
1988   *Whose Justice? Which Rationality?* Notre Dame: University of Notre Dame Press.
Mandela, Nelson
1986   *The Struggle Is My Life*. New York: Pathfinder Press.
Marx, Karl
1969   *Critique of Hegel's "Philosophy of Right."* Edited by Joseph O'Malley. Cambridge: Cambridge University Press.
1971   *Economic and Philosophical Manuscripts of 1844*. Edited by Dirk Struik. New York: International Press.
Meilaender, Gilbert
1981   *Friendship: A Study in Theological Ethics*. Notre Dame: Notre Dame University Press.
1990   "A View from Somewhere: The Political Thought of Michael Walzer." *Religious Studies Review* 16/3:197–201.
Monk, Ray
1990   *Ludwig Wittgenstien: The Duty of Genius*. New York: The Free Press.

Narveson, Jan
1965   "Pacifism: A Philosophical Analysis." Reprinted in Richard A. Was-
        serstrom (1970).
National Conference of Catholic Bishops
1983   *The Challenge of Peace: God's Promise and Our Response*. Washington,
        D.C.: United States Catholic Conference.
Nussbaum, Martha
1986   *The Fragility of Goodness: Luck and Ethics in Greek Tragedy and Philoso-
        phy*. Cambridge: Cambridge University Press.
Oates, Whitney, ed.
1948   *The Basic Writings of Saint Augustine*. 2 vols. New York: Random
        House.
O'Donovan, Oliver
1980   *The Problem of Self-Love in Augustine*. New Haven: Yale University
        Press.
Ogletree, Thomas W.
1983   *The Use of the Bible in Christian Ethics*. Philadelphia: Fortress Press.
Oliver, Roland, and Anthony Atmore
1969   *Africa since 1800*. Cambridge: Cambridge University Press.
Origen of Alexandria
1953   *Contra Celsum*. Edited and translated by Henry Chadwick. Cam-
        bridge: Cambridge University Press.
Outka, Gene
1972   *Agape: An Ethical Analysis*. New Haven: Yale University Press.
Paret, Peter
1985   *Clausewitz and the State: The Man, His Theories, and His Times*. Rev.
        ed. Princeton: Princeton University Press.
———, ed.
1986   *Makers of Modern Strategy, from Machiavelli to the Nuclear Age*. Prin-
        ceton: Princeton University Press.
Putnam, Hilary
1981   *Reason, Explanation and History*. Cambridge: Cambridge University
        Press.
Pynchon, Thomas
1963   *V.* New York: Bantam Books.
1973   *Gravity's Rainbow*. New York: Viking Books.
Ramsey, Paul
1961   *War and the Christian Conscience: How Shall Modern War Be Conducted
        Justly?* Durham, North Carolina: Duke University Press.
1968   *The Just War: Force and Political Responsibility*. New York: Scribner.
Ramsey, Paul, and Stanley Hauerwas
1988   *Speak Up for Just War or Pacifism, with an Epilogue by Stanley
        Hauerwas*. University Park, Penn.: Pennsylvania State University
        Press.
Rawls, John
1971   *A Theory of Justice*. Cambridge, Mass.: Harvard University Press.

Raz, Joseph, ed.
1978   *Practical Reasoning*. Oxford: Oxford University Press.
Reed, John
1977   *Ten Days That Shook the World*. Introduction by A. J. P. Taylor. Harmondsworth: Penguin Books.
Rifaat, Alifa
1983   *Distant View of a Minaret and Other Stories*. Translated by D. Johnson-Davies. London: Heinemann Educational Books.
Rorty, Amelie, ed.
1980   *Essays on Aristotle's Ethics*. Berkeley: University of California Press.
Ruhm, Herbert, ed.
1977   *The Hard-Boiled Dectective*. New York: Vintage Books.
Russell, Frederick H.
1975   *The Just War in the Middle Ages*. Cambridge: Cambridge University Press.
Sandel, Michael J.
1982   *Liberalism and the Limits of Justice*. Cambridge: Cambridge University Press.
Sheils, W. J., ed.
1983   *Studies in Church History*. Vol. 20: *The Church and War*. Oxford: Basil Blackwell.
Simmons, A. John
1979   *Moral Principles and Political Obligations*. Princeton: Princeton University Press.
Skinner, Quentin
1978   *The Foundations of Modern Political Thought*. 2 vol. Cambridge: Cambridge University Press.
Southern, R. W.
1970   *Western Society and the Church in the Middle Ages*. Harmondsworth: Penguin Books.
Sophocles
O.Col   *Oedipus at Colonus*. Translated by Robert Fitzgerald. Chicago: University of Chicago Press, 1941.
Oed.   *Oedipus the King*. Translated by David Grene. Chicago: University of Chicago Press, 1942.
Stein, Walter, ed.
1961   *Nuclear Weapons and Christian Conscience*. London: Merlin Press.
Stout, Jeffrey
1988   *Ethics after Babel: The Languages of Morals and Their Discontents*. Boston: Beacon Press.
Sullivan, William
1983   *Reconstructing Public Philosophy*. Berkeley and Los Angeles: University of California Press.
Sun Tzu
1963   *The Art of War*. Translated by Samuel B. Griffith. Oxford: Oxford University Press.

Suppe, Frederik, ed.
1977   *The Structure of Scientific Theories*. 2d ed. Urbana: University of Illinois Press.
Thompson, Leonard
1985   *The Political Mythology of Apartheid*. New Haven: Yale University Press.
———, ed.
1969   *African Societies in Southern Africa: Historical Studies*. Berkeley: University of California Press.
Thomson, Judith J.
1971   "A Defense of Abortion." *Philosophy and Public Affairs* 1/1:47–66.
Thucydides
1954   *History of the Peloponnesian War*. Translated by Rex Warner. Harmondsworth: Penguin Books.
Tucker, Robert C., ed.
1972   *The Marx-Engels Reader*. New York: W. W. Norton.
Veyne, Paul, ed.
1987   *A History of the Private Life*. Vol 1: *From Pagan Rome to Byzantium*. Translated by Arthur Goldhammer. Cambridge, Mass: Harvard University Press.
Walzer, Michael
1970   *Obligations: Essays on Disobedience, War, and Citizenship*. New York: Simon & Schuster.
1977   *Just and Unjust Wars: A Moral Argument with Historical Illustrations*. New York: Basic Books.
1990   "A Particularism of My Own." *Religious Studies Review* 16/3:193–7.
Wasserstrom, Richard A., ed.
1970   *War and Morality*. Belmont, California: Wadsworth Publishing.
Watson, James B.
1980   *The Double Helix*. Edited by Gunther Stent. New York: Norton Critical Editions.
Whitmore, Todd, ed.
1989   *Ethics in the Nuclear Age: Strategy, Religious Studies and the Churches*. Dallas, Texas: Southern Methodist University Press.
Williams, Bernard
1985   *Ethics and the Limits of Philosophy*. Cambridge, Mass.: Harvard University Press.
Wills, Garry
1978   *Inventing America: Jefferson's Declaration of Independence*. New York: Vintage Books.
Wittgenstein, Ludwig
1958   *Philosophical Investigations*. Translated by Elizabeth Anscombe. 3d ed. Oxford: Basil Blackwell.
1983   *Remarks on the Foundations of Mathematics*. Rev. ed. Edited by G. H. von Wright and Rush Rhees. Translated by Elizabeth Anscombe. Cambridge, Mass.: MIT Press.

Wolterstorff, Nicholas
1976   *Reason within the bounds of Religion.* Grand Rapids, Michigan: Eerdman's Books.

Yearley, Lee
1990   "Recent Work on Virtue." *Religious Studies Review* 16/1:1–9.

Yoder, John Howard
1971   *Nevertheless: The Varieties and Shortcomings of Religious Pacifism.* Scottdale, Penn.: Herald Press.

1972   *The Politics of Jesus.* Grand Rapids, Michigan: Eerdmann's Books.

1977   *The Original Revolution: Essays on Christian Pacifism.* Scottdale, Penn.: Herald Press.

1984   *When War is Unjust.* Minneapolis, Minn.: Augsburg Publishing House.

1984a   *The Priestly Kingdom: Social Ethics as Gospel.* Notre Dame: University of Notre Dame Press.

Index